THE PEOPLE OF GLASGOW
1725 - 1775

The People of
GLASGOW
1725 - 1775

By
David Dobson

CLEARFIELD

Copyright © 2012
by David Dobson
All Rights Reserved

Printed for Clearfield Company by
Genealogical Publishing Company
Baltimore, Maryland
2012

ISBN 978-0-8063-5574-0

Made in the United States of America

INTRODUCTION

The political union of Scotland and England in 1707 had significant benefits for Glasgow. Formerly its foreign trade was relatively small scale but the opening up of the English home and colonial markets caused a major expansion of Glasgow's overseas trade and consequently stimulated the development of industry in and around Glasgow. Much of the surpluses generated by the sugar and tobacco trades were invested in manufacturing industries the output of which was largely exported. By 1740 Glasgow merchants dominated the Virginia tobacco trade, their factors settled around the Chesapeake distributing goods exported from Scotland and shipping tobacco back to Glasgow much of which was sold in markets from Scandinavia to France. By the late eighteenth century Glasgow had become a major international entrepot.

The importance of sugar and tobacco and other colonial products to the economy of Glasgow led to merchant companies settling personnel in the colonies along the American eastern seaboard and in the West Indies. Many of these men were from Glasgow and its neighborhood. The colonies also attracted individual farmers, physicians, tutors, and other professional workers. Within Glasgow, as in other Scottish burghs, the economy and society was dominated by the burgesses. Only the burgesses could operate businesses or elect the town council. Acquiring burgess-ship was a prerequisite for economic or social success. The right of burgess-ship was held by a minority of the citizens and only by men, some had it through inheritance, some by marrying the daughter of a burgess, others by having served an apprenticeship within the burgh, and a few bought into the system. Town councils would also attract skilled craftsmen to settle in the town by admitting them as burgesses, and sometimes burgess-ship would be bestowed as an honor. Burgesses came in two categories – merchant burgesses who formed merchant guilds, and trades burgesses who formed craft guilds. The majority of people appearing in urban records of the period tend to be burgesses as is reflected in this compilation.

David Dobson

Dundee, Scotland, 2011

The People of Glasgow, 1725-1775

GLOSSARY

Bailie	=	burgh magistrate
Brother german	=	full-blooded brother
Causier	=	road maker
Chapman	=	pedlar
Changekeeper	=	innkeeper
Comm.	=	commissariat
Cordiner	=	shoemaker
Deacon	=	chief official of a craft or trade
Dean of Guild	=	head of the merchants
Dyster	=	dyer
Ferrier	=	farrier
Flesher	=	butcher
Hammerman	=	smith
Horse-setter	=	horse-hirer
Journeyman	=	qualified tradesman
Maltman	=	brewer
Mealman	=	oatmeal vendor
Messenger	=	court official
Milne	=	mill
Portioner	=	joint proprietor
Procurator fiscal	=	public prosecutor
Provost	=	mayor
Relict	=	widow
Sewster	=	sewer
Sister german	=	full blooded sister
Stamp-master	=	quality controller
Tack	=	lease
Wright	=	wood or metal worker
Writer	=	lawyer

The People of Glasgow, 1725-1775

SOURCES

AA	=	Ayrshire Archives
AJ	=	Aberdeen Journal, series
ANY	=	Biographical Register of the St Andrew's Society of New York
CalHOpp	=	Calendar of Home Office Papers, [London, 1878]
Car	=	Caribbeanna, series
CG	=	Cordiners of Glasgow, 1550-1975, [Glasgow, 1977]
CLRO	=	City of London Record Office
CRG	=	Colonial Records of Georgia
EMA	=	List of Emigrant Ministers to America, [London, 1904]
ERG	=	Extracts from Records of Glasgow, [Glasgow, 1909-11]
F	=	Fasti Ecclesiae Scoticanae, [Edinburgh, 1915]
GA	=	Glasgow Archives
GBR	=	Burgesses & Guild Brethren of Glasgow
GM	=	Glasgow Mercury, series
IBG	=	Incorporation of Baxters of Glasgow, [Glasgow, 1931]
LC	=	Calendar of the Laing Charters, [Edinburgh, 1899]
HHG	=	History of the Hammermen of Glasgow, [Paisley, 1912]
ImmNE	=	Immigrants to New England, [Salem, 1931]
MAGU	=	Matriculation Albums of Glasgow University
MCG	=	Chronicles of the Maltman Craft in Glasgow, 1605-1879, [Glasgow, 1895]
MSA	=	Maryland State Archives
MWI	=	Monumental Inscriptions of the West Indies, [London, 1927]
NA	=	National Archives, London
NNQ	=	Northern Notes and Queries, series
NRS	=	National Records of Scotland
OGW	=	Old Glasgow Weavers, [Glasgow, 1905]
P	=	Prisoners of the '45, [Edinburgh, 1929]
PCC	=	Prerogative Court of Canterbury
SCHM	=	South Carolina Historical Magazine, series
SCS	=	Scottish Charitable Society of Boston

SHR	=	Scottish Historical Review, series
SM	=	Scots Magazine, series
SFG	=	History of the Skinners, Furriers, and Glovers of Glasgow. [Glasgow, 1937]
UNC	=	University of North Carolina
VaGaz	=	Virginia Gazette, series
VSA	=	Virginia State Archives
WMQ	=	William and Mary Quarterly Review, series

Glasgow, 1764

THE PEOPLE OF GLASGOW
1725 - 1775

The People of Glasgow, 1725-1775

ADAM, ANDREW, a cordiner burgess, 1770. [CG][GBR]
ADAM, JOHN, the elder, a merchant, husband of Marion Bowie, a burgess and guilds-brother of Glasgow in 1718, [GBR]; testament, 1735 & 1747, Comm. Glasgow.[NRS]
ADAM, JOHN, a merchant in Glasgow, 1756. [NRS.AC7.48.930]
ADAM, JOHN, a mason in Glasgow, 1759. [ERG.VI.554]
ADAM, JOHN and MARGARET, children of the late Andrew Adam a maltman, testament, 1751, Comm. Glasgow. [NRS]
ADDISON, JOHN, born 1748, a clergyman from Glasgow, emigrated to New York in 1774. [NA.T47.12]
AIKEN, JOHN, eldest son of John Aiken a maltman, . a freeman maltman, 1742. [MCG.140]
AIKEN, JOHN, former apprentice to Matthew Wilson a maltman, a freeman maltman, 1745. [MCG.140]
AIKEN, WILLIAM, master weaver of the Incorporation of Weavers, 1725. [OGW#108]
AINSLIE, JOHN, minister of the Scots Kirk in Rotterdam, a burgess and guilds-brother of Glasgow, 1725. [GBR]
AINSLIE, ROBERT, a baxter, testaments, 1768/1769, Comm. Glasgow. [NRS]
AIRD, MARY, relict of John Gray a minister in Glasgow, testament, 1739, Comm. Glasgow. [NRS]
AITCHISON, SAMUEL, a merchant from Glasgow, settled at Northampton, Virginia, by 1773. [GA.T76/6.3]
AITCHISON, THOMAS, younger son of Mathew Aitchison a merchant, a burgess and guildsbrother of Glasgow in 1757; a merchant from Glasgow, settled in Virginia before 1764. [NRS.CS16.1.120; CS17.1.1/97] [VaGaz.4.4.1766][GBR][NA.AO12.54.273]
AITCHISON, WALTER, of Ruchsulloch, a resident of Glasgow, testaments, 1731 & 1743, Comm. Glasgow. [NRS]
AITKEN, PETER, a tobacco spinner in Glasgow, testament, 1742, Comm. Glasgow. [NRS]
AITKEN, WALTER, a wright, second son of the late William Aitken a merchant, a burgess and guilds-brother of Glasgow in 1746, [GBR], testament, 1762, Comm. Glasgow. [NRS]

The People of Glasgow, 1725-1775

AITKEN, WILLIAM, of Orchard, a merchant in Glasgow, testament, 1727, Comm. Glasgow. [NRS]

AITKIN, JAMES, son of James Aitken a cordiner deceased, a cordiner, a burgess and guilds-brother of Glasgow, 1759. [CG][GBR]

AITKIN, JOHN, a cordiner, eldest son of the late John Aitkin a maltman, and former apprentice to John Aitkin a cordiner, a burgess and guilds-brother of Glasgow in 1731. [CG][GBR]

AITKINHEAD, JANET, spouse to John Reid a shipmaster in Glasgow, testament, 1738, Comm. Glasgow. [NRS]

AITON, ANDREW, in Glasgow, 1753. [NRS.E326.1.172]

ALEXANDER, AGNES, daughter of Robert Alexander a merchant and bailie of Glasgow, spouse of John Blair a merchant there, sasines, 1730, etc. [NRS.RS.Lanark.xiv.288; xvi.341]

ALEXANDER, DAVID, a shipmaster in Glasgow, son of James Alexander a sailor in Irvine, 1756; [NRS.S/H]; testament, 1758, Comm. Glasgow. [NRS]

ALEXANDER, DAVID, from Glasgow, died in Maryland before 1757, probate 1757, PCC.

ALEXANDER, DAVID, a shipmaster in Glasgow, and James Alexander in the parish of Barr, sometime resident of Glasgow, testaments, 1766, Comm. Glasgow. [NRS]

ALEXANDER, ELIZABETH, relict of Archibald Gray late Deacon of the Cordiners in Glasgow, testament, 1754, Comm. Glasgow. [NRS]

ALEXANDER, JAMES, a candle-maker in Glasgow, testament, 1726, Comm. Glasgow. [NRS]

ALEXANDER, JANET, daughter of Robert Alexander a merchant and bailie of Glasgow, sasine, 1730. [NRS.RS.Lanark.xiv.288]

ALEXANDER, JOHN, a cordiner, eldest son of the late Robert Alexander a cordiner, a burgess and guilds-brother of Glasgow in 1729. [CG][GBR]

ALEXANDER, MATTHEW, a comb maker in Glasgow, 1770. [ERG.VII.311]

ALEXANDER, ROBERT, a merchant and late baillie of Glasgow, testament, 1734, Comm. Glasgow. [NRS]

ALEXANDER, WILLIAM, a baxter, eldest son of William Alexander a baxter, was admitted to the Baxter Incorporation, and as a burgess and guilds-brother of Glasgow in 1737, [IBG.109][GBR]; testament, 1749, Comm. Glasgow. [NRS]

ALEXANDER, WILLIAM, in Glasgow, 1753. [NRS.E326.1.172]

The People of Glasgow, 1725-1775

ALEXANDER, WILLIAM, from Glasgow, in Boston, 1759. [SCS]

ALGIE, JAMES, a baxter, former apprentice to John Auchencloss a baxter, a burgess and guilds-brother of Glasgow in 1718, [GBR], late Deacon of the Baxters in Glasgow, testament, 1741, Comm. Glasgow. [NRS]

ALGIE, JAMES, a baxter, eldest son of James Algie a baxter, was admitted to the Baxter Incorporation, 1754; a burgess and guilds-brother of Glasgow, 1754. [IBG.109][GBR]

ALISON, JOHN, a merchant from Glasgow, settled in Virginia before 1748. [NRS.CS16.1.80]

ALISON, JOHN, a merchant in Glasgow, a burgess of Irvine in 1766. [AA]

ALISON, WILLIAM, son of John Alison and his spouse Mary Maxwell in Glasgow, a surgeon who settled in Virginia by 1748, died in Port Royal, Virginia, 1768. [NRS.CS16.1.80; B10.15.7345; S/H 1770]

ALLAN, GEORGE, head miller at the wheat mills at Partick in the barony of Glasgow, testament, 1727, Comm. Glasgow. [NRS]

ALLAN, GEORGE, a maltman in Glasgow, testaments, 1735/1740, Comm. Glasgow. [NRS]

ALLAN, JAMES, born 1709, from Glasgow, to Pennsylvania, 1728. [CLRO/AIA]

ALLAN, RICHARD, eldest son of Richard Allan a merchant, a burgess and guildsbrother of Glasgow, 1752; a merchant in Glasgow, a sasine, 1753. [GBR][NRS.E326.1.172; RS.Lanark.xvi.298]

ALLAN, ROBERT, late Deacon of the Cordiners of Glasgow, testament, 1729, Comm. Glasgow. [NRS]

ALLAN, ROBERT, son of Robert Allan, admitted at the Baxter Incorporation, 1732.[IBG.109]

ALLAN, ROBERT, a miller at the wheat mills of Partick in the barony of Glasgow, testament, 1741, Comm. Glasgow. [NRS]

ALLAN, THOMAS, a hammerman, 1728. [HHG.293]

ALLASON, DAVID, born 1736 in Glasgow, to America 1760, a storekeeper in Rappahannock and Winchester, Virginia. [GA][VMHB.1931]

ALLASON, JEAN, relict of James Dunlop a tobacconist in Glasgow, testament, 1746, Comm. Glasgow. [NRS]

ALLASON, JOHN, a tanner in Glasgow, testament, 1735, Comm. Glasgow. [NRS]

ALLASON, JOHN, son of Zacharias Allason, was admitted to the Baxter Incorporation, 1747. [IBG.109]

The People of Glasgow, 1725-1775

ALLASON, JOHN, late Deacon of the Fleshers in Glasgow, testament, 1768, Comm. Glasgow. [NRS]

ALLASON, JOHN, son of John Allason in Glasgow, settled in Virginia before 1772. [NRS.CS16.1.151]

ALLASON, ROBERT, born in Glasgow 1721, son of Zachariah Allason and his wife Janet Grahame, a merchant, settled in Virginia, 1761. [GA]

ALLASON, ROBERT, a baxter, son of Zacharias Allason, was admitted to the Baxter Incorporation, 1738. [IBG.109]

ALLASON, ROBERT, a baxter, former apprentice to William Cowan, was admitted to the Baxter Incorporation, 1746. [IBG.109]

ALLASON, ROBERT, a merchant in Glasgow, 1770. [ERG.VII.311]

ALLASON, THOMAS, a flesher, eldest son of John Allason a flesher, a burgess and guilds-brother of Glasgow in 1752 and to the Skinners Craft, 1753. [SFG.267][GBR]

ALLASON, THOMAS, in Glasgow, 1753. [NRS.E326.1.172]; younger son of the late Thomas Allason a merchant, a burgess and guilds-brother of Glasgow, 1762, [GBR]; a merchant tailor in Glasgow, testament, 1769, Comm. Glasgow. [NRS]

ALLASON, THOMAS, a merchant in Glasgow, testament, 1775, Comm. Glasgow. [NRS]

ALLASON, WILLIAM, son of Zachariah Allason and his wife Isabel Hall in Glasgow, emigrated in 1737, settled in Falmouth, Virginia. [GA][VMHB.85.45]

ALLASON, WILLIAM, son of Zacharias Allason, was admitted to the Baxter Incorporation, 1747. [IBG.109]

ALLASON, WILLIAM, born 1712 in Glasgow, son of John Allason and his wife Mary Maxwell, a surgeon, settled in Port Royal, Virginia, died 1768. [NRS.B10.15.7345; S/H 1770]

ALSTON, JOHN, a merchant in Glasgow, sasines, 1753, etc.; a burgess and guilds-brother of Glasgow in 1768. [NRS.E326.1.172; RS.Lanark.xv.138; CS16.1.161/168/281; CS17.1.2; AC7.55; NRAS.332F/980]; 1771. [LC#3233] [NA.AO12.37.161][GBR]

ANDERSON, ALEXANDER, a baxter, former apprentice to John Charity, was admitted to the Baxter Incorporation, and as a burgess and guilds-brother of Glasgow, 1762, 1763. [GBR][IBG.109]; testament, 1766, Comm. Glasgow. [NRS]

The People of Glasgow, 1725-1775

ANDERSON, ANDREW, a merchant from Glasgow, settled in Virginia before 1747. [NRS.CS16.1.79]

ANDERSON, ARCHIBALD, a merchant in Glasgow, testament, 1731, Comm. Glasgow. [NRS]

ANDERSON, ARCHIBALD, son of Archibald Anderson a cordiner, a cordiner ca.1745. [CG]

ANDERSON, CHRISTAIN, relict of John Gibson a merchant bailie of Glasgow, and daughter of John Anderson of Dowhill late Provost of Glasgow, 1725. [ERG.V. 206]

ANDERSON, HUGH, a weaver in Glasgow, a deed, 1750, [NRS.RD2.167.164]; testament, 1754, Comm. Glasgow. [NRS]

ANDERSON, JAMES, a merchant in Glasgow, heir to his father George Anderson a merchant there who died in 1728. [NRS.SH.1751]

ANDERSON, JAMES, a baxter, former apprentice to James Yuil, was admitted to the Baxter Incorporation, 1748. [IBG.109]

ANDERSON, JAMES, a merchant in Glasgow, deeds, 1750, sasines, 1720s. [NRS.RD4.176/1.406; RD4.176/2.221/315][NRS.RS Lanark, xiii.449; 1753. [NRS.E326.1.172]

ANDERSON, JAMES, a merchant from Glasgow, settled in Brokesbank, Rappahannock, Virginia, before 1772. [NRS.RD3.231.708]

ANDERSON, JOHN, born 1671 in Edinburgh, minister of Ramshorn, Glasgow, from 1718 until 1721, testament, 1745, Comm. Glasgow. [NRS][F.3.438]

ANDERSON, JOHN, a hammerman, 1726. [HHG.293]

ANDERSON, JOHN, a cordiner burgess, 1730. [CG]

ANDERSON, JOHN, a merchant from Glasgow, emigrated to Jamaica before 1748. [NRS.SC36.63.2]

ANDERSON, JOHN, a merchant in Glasgow, 1750, [NRS.RD2.167.15]; 1753. [NRS.E326.1.172]

ANDERSON, JOHN, from Glasgow, in Boston, 1759. [SCS]

ANDERSON, MARGARET, daughter of the deceased John Anderson a writer in Glasgow, 1725. [ERG.V.206]

ANDERSON, MARGARET, in Glasgow, 1753. [NRS.E326.1.172]

ANDERSON, ROBERT, a cordiner burgess, 1726, son of William Anderson a cordiner. [CG]

The People of Glasgow, 1725-1775

ANDERSON, ROBERT, a merchant in Glasgow, testament, 1729, Comm. Glasgow. [NRS]

ANDERSON, THOMAS, a cordiner burgess 1734, son of Archibald Anderson a cordiner deceased. [CG]

ANDERSON, WILLIAM, the younger, a merchant in Glasgow, testament, 1726, Comm. Glasgow. [NRS]

ANDERSON, WILLIAM, Professor of Church History in the University of Glasgow, husband of Janet Cross, sasine, 1730. [NRS.RS.Lanark.xiv.168]

ANDERSON, WILLIAM, a merchant in Glasgow, testament, 1743, Comm. Glasgow. [NRS]

ANDERSON, WILLIAM, a merchant in Glasgow, testament, 1750, Comm. Glasgow. [NRS]

ANDERSON, WILLIAM, junior, a maltman in Glasgow, testament, 1751, Comm. Glasgow. [NRS]

ANDERSON, WILLIAM, an inn-keeper in Glasgow, testaments, 1751 & 1761, Comm. Glasgow. [NRS]

ANDERSON, WILLIAM, heir to his father William Anderson Professor of Church History in Glasgow, who died 1751. [NRS.SH.1752]

ANDERSON, WILLIAM, in Glasgow, 1753. [NRS.E326.1.172]

ANDERSON, WILLIAM, a tanner in Glasgow, a deed, 1750, sasine, 1764, [NRS.RD3.210.378; RS.Lanark.xvii.449]; testament, 1768, Comm. Glasgow. [NRS]

ANDERSON, WILLIAM, a wright in Glasgow, 1759. [ERG.VI.540]

ANDERSON, WILLIAM, in Glasgow, a bond, 1774. [NRS.RD2.217/1.214]

ANDERSON, Mrs, in Glasgow, 1753. [NRS.E326.1.172]

ANDREW, DAVID, husband of Jane Tarbett, a cordiner burgess of Glasgow in 1770. [CG][GBR]

ANGELLY, ROBERT, a baxter, former apprentice to James Edmond, was admitted to the Baxter Incorporation, 1747. [IBG.109]

ANGUS, JOHN, maltman, husband of Lillias Anderson, a burgess and guilds-brother of Glasgow in 1770, [GBR]; a deed, 1771. [NRS.RD218.92]

ANGUS, JOSEPH, a merchant from Glasgow, settled in St Kitts by 1761. [NRS.B10.12.2]

ANGUS, MARGARET, widow of John Buchanan a maltman in Bell's Wynd, Glasgow, testament, 1750, Comm. Glasgow. [NRS]

The People of Glasgow, 1725-1775

ANGUS, MARION, relict of James Kilpatrick a flesher in Glasgow, testament, 1772, Comm. Glasgow. [NRS]

ARBUCKLE, EUPHEMIA, in Glasgow, 1753. [NRS.E326.1.172]

ARMOUR, ANDREW, in Glasgow, 1753. [NRS.E326.1.172]

ARMOUR, JOHN, a tailor and bailie of Glasgow, 1725; sasine, 1727. [NRS.RS.Lanark.xiii.557] [ERG.V.243]

ARMOUR, JOHN, a merchant in Glasgow, 1727. [NRS.AC7.36.328]

ARRALL, WILLIAM, a hammerman, 1732. [HHG.294]

ARROLL, ARCHIBALD, a cordiner burgess 1771, son in law of William Fleming a cordiner. [CG]

ARTHUR, WILLIAM, a merchant in Glasgow, testament, 1726, Comm. Glasgow. [NRS]

AUCHENCLOSS, JOHN, son of John Auchencloss, was admitted to the Baxter Incorporation, 1743. [IBG.109]

AUCHENCLOSS, JOHN, eldest son of Robert Auchencloss, a burgess and guilds-brother of Glasgow in 1763; a merchant in Glasgow, 1766. [GBR][NRS.CS16.1.126]

AUCHENCLOSS, ROBERT, a cooper in Glasgow, 1759. [ERG.VI.542]

AUCHENCLOSS, THOMAS, from Glasgow, in Boston, 1769. [SCS]; a merchant in Portsmouth, New Hampshire, pre 1776, settled in Halifax, Nova Scotia, by 1777. [NA.AO13.96.1-5]

AULD, JANET, relict of James Stewart a merchant in Glasgow, testament, 1734, Comm. Glasgow. [NRS]

AULD, JOHN, a cordiner burgess of Glasgow in 1767. [CG][GBR]

AULD, JOHN, a shoemaker burgess of Glasgow in 1771, son of John Auld a shoemaker. [CG][GBR]

AULD, WILLIAM, a baxter, son in law of William Duncan a baxter, was admitted to the Baxter Incorporation, and as a burgess and guilds-brother of Glasgow in 1776. [IBG.109][GBR]

AULDCORN, ELIZABETH, sometime spouse of James Lamond a tanner in Glasgow, testament, 1772, Comm. Glasgow. [NRS]

AULDCORN, ROBERT, a skinner, eldest son of the late Patrick Auldcorn a skinner, was admitted to the Skinners Craft, also as a burgess and guilds-brother of Glasgow in 1760. [SFG.267][GBR]

AYTON, ANDREW, a merchant in Glasgow, a deed, 1750. [NRS.RD3.585]

The People of Glasgow, 1725-1775

AYTON, JAMES, a tailor in Glasgow, testament, 1774, Comm. Glasgow. [NRS]

BAILLIE, ALEXANDER, a merchant in Glasgow, [NRS.AC9.1056; AC7.34.433], a letter 1734, [NRAS.NRAS.3273/98]; testament, 1735, Comm. Glasgow. [NRS]

BAILLIE, ROBERT, a merchant in Glasgow, 1773; younger son of Alexander Baillie a merchant, a burgess and guildsbrother of Glasgow in 1776. [NRS.CS16.1.154][GBR]

BAILLIE, WILLIAM, a cow-feeder in Glasgow, testament, 1746, Comm. Glasgow. [NRS]

BAIN, ALEXANDER, a flax-dresser in Glasgow, testament, 1751, Comm. Glasgow. [NRS]

BAIN, ARCHIBALD, a cordiner burgess of Glasgow in 1775, son in law of John Dobbie a maltman. [CG][GBR]

BAIRD, GEORGE, a merchant in Glasgow, heir to his father Thomas Baird of Hole a merchant in Glasgow, in 1753; a burgess and guilds-brother of Glasgow in 1754. [NRS.SH.1753][GBR]

BAIRD, JAMES, a merchant in Glasgow, testament, 1727, Comm. Glasgow. [NRS]

BAIRD, JAMES, a workman in Glasgow, testament, 1746, Comm. Glasgow. [NRS]

BAIRD, JAMES, senior, in Glasgow, 1753. [NRS.E326.1.172]

BAIRD, JAMES, junior, in Glasgow, 1753. [NRS.E326.1.172]

BAIRD, JAMES, a shipmaster in Glasgow, later a merchant in Virginia by 1764. [NRS.CS16.1.120; CS17.1.1][GA][NRS.NRAS.0623/3]

BAIRD, JAMES, in Glasgow, a transportee contractor, 1770. [CalHOpp.445] [NRS.E504.4.5]

BAIRD, JAMES, in Glasgow, a commission, 1775. [NRS.RD3.234,378]

BAIRD, JOHN, a merchant from Glasgow, in Jamaica before 1730, [NRS.AC7.35.485]; testament, 1737, Comm. Glasgow. [NRS]

BAIRD, JOHN, of Craigtoun, a merchant, testament, 1746, Comm. Glasgow. [NRS]

BAIRD, JOHN, a merchant in Glasgow, eldest son of James Baird a merchant, a burgess and guilds-brother of Glasgow in 1755; testament, 1763, Comm. Glasgow. [NRS][GBR]

BAIRD, JANET, relict of John Scott a mill-wright in Glasgow, testament, 1726, Comm. Glasgow. [NRS]

The People of Glasgow, 1725-1775

BAIRD, JOHN, a merchant in Glasgow, trading with Grenada, 1764. [GA.T-MJ]

BAIRD, PETER, son of John Baird, a merchant from Glasgow who settled in Petersburg, Virginia, before 1740. [VSA.DB2.387]

BAIRD, ROBERT, a cordiner burgess 1732, former apprentice to Enoch Waddell a cordiner. [CG]

BAIRD, THOMAS, of Holl, a merchant in Glasgow, testament, 1737, Comm. Glasgow. [NRS]

BAIRD, WILLIAM, a merchant in Glasgow, heir to his father Rev. Robert Baird in Dunlop, 1759. [NRS.SH.1759]

BAIRD, Mrs, in Glasgow, 1753. [NRS.E326.1.172]

BALD, ADAM, a merchant, testament, 1737, Comm. Glasgow. [NRS]

BALD, WILLIAM, born 1745, a wright from Glasgow, emigrated to New York in 1775. [NA.T47/12]

BALFOUR, JOHN, a merchant from Glasgow, settled at Black River, Jamaica, testament, 1750, Comm. Edinburgh. [NRS]

BALFOUR, WILLIAM, a weaver, husband of Bethia Barbour, a burgess and guilds-brother of Glasgow in 1750. [GBR]

BALLANTYNE, JOHN, a shoemaker in Glasgow, his wife Helen Naismith, and children Henrietta, John, and Margaret, a sasine, 1763. [NRS.RS.Lanark.xvii.397]

BALLANTYNE, MARGARET, relict of John Hamilton a minister in Glasgow, testament, 1750, Comm. Glasgow. [NRS]

BALLINIE, JAMES, a cordiner burgess 1739, former apprentice to Thomas Ballantyne. [CG]

BALLINIE, JAMES, the younger, a cordiner burgess of Glasgow in 1754, second son of James Ballinie a cordiner. [CG][GBR]

BALLINNIE, JOHN, a tobacco spinner in Glasgow, testament, 1731, Comm. Glasgow. [NRS]

BALLINIE, JOHN, a cordiner burgess 1749, former apprentice to John Ballinie a cordiner. [CG]

BALLINNIE, PETER, a fencing master in Glasgow, 1725, later in Edinburgh, thereafter in Glasgow, testament, 1744, Comm. Glasgow. [NRS] [ERG.V.236]

BALLINIE, WILLIAM, a baxter, former apprentice to Robert Ballinie, was admitted to the Baxter Incorporation, 1730. [IBG.111]

BALLOCH, JOHN, jr, a weaver in Glasgow, testament, 1760, Comm. Glasgow. [NRS]

BALMANNO, JOHN, a painter in Glasgow, 1763. [ERG.VII.116]

BANNATYNE, FRANCIS, a merchant from Glasgow, settled in New Providence, the Bahamas, probate 1760 the Bahamas

BANNATYNE, or BOGLE, ISOBEL, wife of Niel Bannatyne a merchant in Glasgow, heir to her brother Robert Bogle a merchant there. [NRS.SH.1755]

BANNATYNE, JOHN, a cordiner burgess 1736, son of James Bannatyne the Deacon of the Cordiners. [CG]

BANNATYNE, JOHN, a cordiner burgess of Glasgow in 1759. [CG][GBR]

BANNATYNE, NEIL, a bailie of Glasgow, died 4 March 1767. [ERG.VII.241]

BARBOUR, ROBERT, in Glasgow, 1753. [NRS.E326.1.172]; a weaver and late baillie of Glasgow, testament, 1768, Comm. Glasgow. [NRS]

BARCLAY, JAMES, a chapman in Glasgow, testament, 1763, Comm. Glasgow. [NRS]

BARCLAY, JOHN, a skinner, youngest son of James Barclay, was admitted to the Skinners Craft, 1753. [SFG.267]

BARCLAY, ROBERT, of Capplerigg, a writer in Glasgow, a deed, 1750, [NRS.RD2.168.100]; 1753. [NRS.E326.1.172]; a sasine, 1773. [NRS.RS.Lanark.xx.177]

BARCLAY, THOMAS, a cordiner burgess 1744. [CG]

BAREY, JAMES, from Glasgow, in Boston, 1729. [SCS]

BARNS, ELIZABETH, relict of Thomas Kennedy MD in Glasgow, testament, 1729, Comm. Glasgow. [NRS]

BARNS, JOHN, a merchant in Glasgow, 1744, trading in Virginia after 1757. [NRS.E504.28.2; B10.15.7036]

BARR, JANET, relict of James Forsyth a cooper in Glasgow, testament, 1739, Comm. Glasgow. [NRS]

BARR, JOHN, son in law of James Clark a maltman, a freeman maltman, 1753. [MCG.133]

BARR, JOHN, second son of John Barr a maltman, a freeman maltman, 1771. [MCG.133]

BARR, THOMAS, in Glasgow, 1753. [NRS.E326.1.172]

The People of Glasgow, 1725-1775

BARRIE, JAMES, a baxter, former apprentice to James Muirhead a baxter, was admitted to the Baxter Incorporation, also as a burgess and guilds-brother of Glasgow in 1725. [IBG.111][GBR]

BARRIE, JAMES, a merchant, husband of Janet Dickson, a burgess and guilds-brother of Glasgow in 1738, [GBR], to Charleston, South Carolina, by 1745. [NRS.B10.15.7105]

BARRIE, JOHN, a baxter, former apprentice to the late Thomas Yuil a baxter, was admitted to the Baxter Incorporation, also as a burgess and guilds-brother of Glasgow in 1739. [IBG.111][GBR]

BARRIE, JOHN, a book-seller in Glasgow, testament, 1760, Comm. Glasgow. [NRS]

BARRIE, ROBERT, a cordiner burgess of Glasgow in 1760, former apprentice of Alexander Short a cordiner. [CG][GBR]

BARRON, ALEXANDER, a baxter, eldest son of the late John Barron a baxter, was admitted to the Baxter Incorporation, and as a burgess and guilds-brother of Glasgow in 1736. [IBG.111][GBR]

BARROWFIELD, Lady, in Glasgow, 1753. [NRS.E326.1.172]

BARRY, JAMES, a land surveyor in Glasgow, 1759. [ERG.VI.554]

BARRY, JOHN, a merchant in Glasgow, a deed, 1750. [NRS.RD4.176/2.22]

BARRY, JOHN, a baxter, eldest son of John Barry a baxter, was admitted to the Baxter Incorporation, and as a burgess and guilds-brother of Glasgow in 1763. [IBG.111][GBR]

BARRY, ROBERT, a merchant, husband of Anna Dickson, a burgess and guilds-brother of Glasgow in 1738, [GBR]; in Glasgow, 1744. [NRS.AC7.46.185; E504.15.2]

BARTON, BENJAMIN, in Glasgow, bonds, 1775. [NRS.RD2.217/2.866; RD4.217.768/784]

BARTON, HENRY, a cordiner burgess of Glasgow in 1759, eldest son of Henry Barton a merchant. [CG][GBR]

BAXTER, AGNES and JANET, heirs to their father Joseph Baxter a corkcutter in Glasgow, 1755. [NRS.SH.1755]

BAXTER, DANIEL, a book-seller, eldest son of the late David Baxter a book-binder, a burgess and guilds-brother of Glasgow in 1747, [GBR], in Glasgow 1753. [NRS.E326.1.172]

BAXTER, JOHN, a cork-cutter in Glasgow, a deed, 1749. [NRS.RD2.167.73]

The People of Glasgow, 1725-1775

BAXTER, JOSEPH, a maltman, son in law of Walter Buchanan a maltman, a burgess and guilds-brother of Glasgow in 1741, [GBR]; a cork-cutter in Glasgow, and his spouse Grissell Buchanan, testaments, 1754, Comm. Glasgow. [NRS.RS.Lanark.xiv.458]

BAXTER, THOMAS, a maltman, eldest son of the late John Baxter a tailor, a burgess and guilds-brother of Glasgow in 1720, [GBR], testament, 1732, Comm. Glasgow. [NRS]

BAXTER, WILLIAM, a merchant in Glasgow, testament, 1739, Comm. Glasgow. [NRS]

BAYN, JOHN, a sheep-stealer from Glasgow, was banished to the colonies in 1752. [AJ.248]

BEATTIE, GEORGE, a clerk in the Customs House of Glasgow, testament, 1733, Comm. Glasgow. [NRS]

BELL, ALEXANDER, a merchant from Glasgow, to America, settled in West Florida before 1777. [NA.CO5.613.414]

BELL, DAVID, a merchant and planter from Glasgow, settled in Virginia before 1745. [NRS.B10.15.5959/60]

BELL, JANET, relict of John Henderson of Barrachy, a resident of Glasgow, testament, 1731, Comm. Glasgow. [NRS]

BELL, JOHN, from Glasgow, died in Jamaica, 1773, testament, 1773, Comm. Edinburgh. [NRS]

BELL, MALCOLM, a merchant, a burgess and guilds-brother of Glasgow in 1729, [GBR], testament, 1753, Comm. Glasgow. [NRS]

BELL, MARGARET, daughter of the late Patrick Bell of Cowcaddens, a merchant and baillie of Glasgow, testament, 1731, Comm. Glasgow. [NRS]

BELL, PATRICK, of Cowcaddens, a merchant in Glasgow, sasines, 1729, etc, [NRS.RS.Lanark.xiv.413, etc]; 1753. [NRS.E326.1.172]

BELL, RICHARD, a merchant, husband of Margaret Miller, a burgess and guilds-brother of Glasgow in 1717, [GBR] and portioner of Anderstoun in the barony parish of Glasgow, testament, 1739, Comm. Glasgow. [NRS]

BELL, RICHARD, a merchant in Glasgow, only child of the late Richard Bell, a merchant in Glasgow and portioner of Anderstoun, and his spouse Margaret Miller, testament, 1748, Comm. Glasgow. [NRS]

The People of Glasgow, 1725-1775

BELL, ROBERT, born 1732 in Glasgow, a printer and publisher, emigrated to America in 1766, possibly in Boston 1770, died in Richmond, Virginia, 1784. [SOS.67][SCS]

BELL, WILLIAM, born 1745, a farmer from Glasgow, emigrated to New York in 1774. [NA.T47.12]

BERRIE, ANDREW, a tobacconist in Glasgow, testament, 1733, Comm. Glasgow. [NRS]

BERRIE, JAMES, a merchant in Glasgow, testament, 1736, Comm. Glasgow. [NRS]

BERRIE, JAMES, a baxter, son of James Berrie, was admitted to the Baxter Incorporation, 1748. [IBG.111]

BERRIE, JAMES, a merchant in Glasgow, a deed, 1750. [NRS.RD4.176/2.427]

BERRIE, JOHN, a baxter, son of James Berrie, was admitted to the Baxter Incorporation, 1750. [IBG.111]

BERRIE, ROBERT, a merchant in Glasgow, 1750, [NRS.RD4.176/2.427]; 1753. [NRS.E326.1.172] ; testaments, 1764/1768, Comm. Glasgow. [NRS]

BERRIE, WILLIAM, the younger, a merchant in Glasgow, testament, 17 July 1725, Comm. Glasgow. [NRS]

BEVERIDGE, ANDREW, son in law of Andrew Duncan, was admitted to the Baxter Incorporation, also as a burgess and guildsbrother of Glasgow in 1768. [IBG.111][GBR]; a baxter in Glasgow, testament, 1771, Comm. Glasgow. [NRS]

BIGGAR, WILLIAM, from Glasgow, in Boston, 1748. [SCS]

BIGGART, ANDREW, a tailor, eldest son of the late John Biggart a maltman, and husband of Katherine Wilson, a burgess of Glasgow in 1676, [GBR]; testament, 1731, Comm. Glasgow. [NRS]

BIGGART, ANDREW, the younger, second son of Andrew Biggart the elder a tailor, a burgess and guilds-brother of Glasgow in 1706, [GBR]; late Deacon of the Tailors of Glasgow, testament, 1733, Comm. Glasgow. [NRS]

BIGGART, BERNARD, a servant to Lord Pollock, a burgess and guilds-brother of Glasgow in 1726, [GBR]; a merchant in Glasgow, and his spouse Margaret Rankine, testaments, 1747, Comm. Glasgow. [NRS]

BILSLAND, WILLIAM, a cow-feeder in Glasgow, testament, 1759, Comm. Glasgow. [NRS]

BISHOP, JOHN, son of James Bishop a weaver in Calton of Glasgow, heir to his uncle Walter Bryce a merchant in Glasgow, 1752. [NRS.SH.1752]

The People of Glasgow, 1725-1775

BISKET, DAVID, a tailor in Glasgow, testament, 1730, Comm. Glasgow. [NRS]

BLACK, ARCHIBALD, a merchant in Glasgow, a deed, 1750. [NRS.RD2.167.435]

BLACK, ARCHIBALD, a cordiner burgess and guilds-brother of Glasgow in 1773, son in law of Alexander Gillies a cordiner. [CG][GBR]

BLACK, ARCHIBALD, a tailor, third son of Gavin Black a merchant, a burgess and guilds-brother of in 1744, [GBR]; in Glasgow, 1775. [ERG.VII.450]

BLACK, DAVID, a merchant from Glasgow, husband of Janet Greenlaw, settled in Boston before 1775. [Glasgow OPR]

BLACK, GAVIN, a merchant, second son of the late Gavin Black a merchant, a burgess and guilds-brother of Glasgow in 1738, [GBR];1750, a deed, [NRS.RD2.168.9]; 1753. [NRS.E326.1.172]

BLACK, GEORGE, a merchant, a burgess and guilds-brother of Glasgow in 1740, [GBR], heir to his father Hugh Black a merchant there, 1753. [NRS.SH.1753]

BLACK, HUGH, a merchant in Glasgow, testament, 1736, Comm. Glasgow. [NRS]

BLACK, JAMES, a cordiner, former apprentice to Patrick Maxwell a cordiner, a burgess and guilds-brother of Glasgow in 1747. [CG][GBR]

BLACK, JOHN, a merchant in Glasgow, testament, 1772, Comm. Glasgow. [NRS]

BLACK, WILLIAM, a Supervisor of Excise in Glasgow, testament, 1748, Comm. Glasgow. [NRS]

BLACK, Mrs, in Glasgow, 1753. [NRS.E326.1.172]

BLACKBURN, ANDREW, eldest son of John Blackburn a merchant and guilds-brother of Glasgow, a merchant and guilds-brother of Glasgow in 1741 [GBR], was granted land in Georgia, 1751. [NA.CO5.669][GA.B10.15.6183]

BLACKBURN, JOHN, a merchant, eldest son of the late William Blackburn a merchant, a burgess and guilds-brother of Glasgow in 1715, testaments, 1737/1739, Comm. Glasgow. [NRS]

BLACKBURN, JOHN, a merchant from Glasgow, settled in Norfolk, Virginia, before 1752. [NRS.B10.15.6183]

BLACKSTOCK, JOHN, in Glasgow, 1753. [NRS.E326.1.172]; Collector of HM Excise in Glasgow, testament, 1766, Comm. Glasgow. [NRS]

BLACKSTOCK, THOMAS, a distiller in Glasgow, heir to his father Robert Blackstock in the lands of Caerlaverock, 1755. [NRS.SH.1755]

BLACKWOOD, JAMES, a thief from Glasgow, transported to the colonies in 1753. [SM.15.437]

BLACKWOOD, JOHN, a hammerman in Glasgow, testament, 1731, Comm. Glasgow. [NRS]

BLACKWOOD, ROBERT, a flesher in Glasgow, testament, 1738, Comm. Glasgow. [NRS]

BLACKWOOD, WALTER, a brewer in Glasgow, testament, 1773, Comm. Glasgow. [NRS]

BLACKWOOD, ..., a cordiner burgess, 1772. [CG]

BLAIR, ANN, in Glasgow, a deed, 1752. [NRS.RD4.218.1052]

BLAIR, DAVID, of Adamtoun, HM Customs Collector resident in Glasgow, testament, 1754, Comm. Glasgow. [NRS]

BLAIR, GEORGE, former apprentice to John Auchencloss, was admitted to the Baxter Incorporation, 1747. [IBG.111]

BLAIR, JAMES, a merchant in Glasgow, 1727. [NRS.AC7.36.328]

BLAIR, JAMES, a cordiner burgess of Glasgow in 1751, eldest son of Bryce Blair a cordiner. [CG][GBR]

BLAIR, JEAN, relict of Patrick Bryce a maltman in Glasgow, testament, 1726, Comm. Glasgow. [NRS]

BLAIR, JOHN, tenant in Easter Craigs in the Barony parish of Glasgow, testament, 1741, Comm. Glasgow. [NRS]

BLAIR, JOHN, in Glasgow, 1753; only son of the late James Blair a weaver, a burgess and guildsbrother of Glasgow in 1762; a merchant in Glasgow, 1764. [NRS.E326.1.172; CS16.1.120/122] [GBR]

BLAIR, JOHN, a baxter, eldest son of George Blair a baxter, was admitted to the Baxter Incorporation, and as a burgess and guilds-brother of Glasgow in 1772. [IBG.111][GBR]

BLAIR, KATHERINE, daughter of the late John Blair a tanner in Glasgow, and late spouse to Andrew Duncan a baxter in Glasgow, testament, 1745, Comm. Glasgow. [NRS]

BLAIR, MARION, a resident of Glasgow, and daughter of William Blair a maltman there, testament, 1735, Comm. Glasgow. [NRS]

BLAIR, THOMAS, from Glasgow, settled in Virginia, died 1739, probate 1740 Accomack County, Virginia.

BLAIR, WALTER, the elder, a merchant and bailie of Glasgow, testament, 1742, Comm. Glasgow. [NRS]

The People of Glasgow, 1725-1775

BLANE, JOHN, a merchant from Glasgow, in Jamaica pre 1730. [NRS.AC7.35.485]

BLYTH, JAMES, a merchant in Glasgow, testament, 1747, Comm. Glasgow. [NRS]

BOGLE, ANDREW, a maltman in Glasgow, testament, 1750, Comm. Glasgow. [NRS]

BOGLE, ARCHIBALD, heir to his mother Agnes Stewart widow of Robert Bogle jr. a merchant in Glasgow, 1751. [NRS.SH.1751]

BOGLE, BEATRIX, daughter of George Bogle a merchant in Glasgow, heir to her brother Robert Bogle a merchant there, 1755. [NRS.SH.1755]

BOGLE, GEORGE, in Glasgow, 1753. [NRS.E326.1.172]; a merchant and former Dean of Guild of Glasgow, testament, 1755, Comm. Glasgow. [NRS]

BOGLE, ISOBEL, third daughter of the late James Bogle a merchant in Glasgow, testament, 1728, Comm. Glasgow. [NRS]

BOGLE, ISOBEL, wife of James Wardrop a merchant in Glasgow, heir to her father John Bogle of Bogleshall a Writer to the Signet; also heir to her brother William Bogle of Bogleshole, 1758. [NRS.SH.1756/1758]

BOGLE, JAMES, master weaver of the Incorporation of Weavers, 1725. [OGW#108]

BOGLE, JAMES, a merchant in Glasgow, heir to his father George Bogle a merchant there, 1755; a burgess and guilds-brother of Glasgow in 1756. [NRS.SH.1755][GBR]

BOGLE, JAMES, president of the Red Dye Society of Glasgow, 1759. [ERG.VI.547]

BOGLE, MARGARET, relict of Andrew Armour a merchant in Glasgow, a bond, 1747. [NRS.RD2.167.303]

BOGLE, MATHEW, a merchant in Glasgow, in Virginia 1729-1736, owner of the President of Glasgow, 1750; testament, 1767, Comm. Glasgow. [NRS.AC9.1746]

BOGLE, PATRICK, a merchant in Glasgow, testament, 1737, Comm. Glasgow. [NRS]

BOGLE, PATRICK, of Hamilton's Farm, a merchant in Glasgow, testament, 1764, Comm. Glasgow. [NRS]

BOGLE, ROBERT, the elder, a merchant in Glasgow, testaments, 1734/1736/1740, Comm. Glasgow. [NRS]

The People of Glasgow, 1725-1775

BOGLE, ROBERT, a merchant in Glasgow, trading with Grenada, 1764. [GA.T-MJ]

BOGLE, THOMAS, from Glasgow, in Boston, 1747. [SCS]

BOGLE, THOMAS, a skipper in Glasgow, 1750. [NRS.AC9.1746/1764]

BOGLE, WILLIAM, in Glasgow, 1753; master of the Red Dye Society of Glasgow, 1759. [NRS.E326.1.172] [ERG.VI.547]

BOGLE, Mrs, in Glasgow, 1753. [NRS.E326.1.172]

BONTINE, NICOL, a merchant in Glasgow, testament, 1740, Comm. Glasgow. [NRS]

BORLAND, JOHN, in Glasgow, 1753. [NRS.E326.1.172]

BOWEN, JAMES, in Glasgow, 1753. [NRS.E326.1.172]

BOWER, JOHN, a tailor from Glasgow, transported as a Jacobite in 1747, landed at Port North Potomac, Maryland. [NA.T1.328][P.2.44]

BOWIE, JOHN, a merchant in Glasgow, his spouse Marion Gow, and their son Thomas Bowie, testament, 1734, Comm. Glasgow. [NRS]

BOWIE, JOHN, in Glasgow, 1753. [NRS.E326.1.172]

BOWIE, WILLIAM, a maltman and former town officer of Glasgow, testament, 1751, Comm. Glasgow. [NRS]

BOWMAN, ANDREW, a merchant in Glasgow, testament, 1764, Comm. Glasgow. [NRS]

BOWMAN, ARCHIBALD, formerly a merchant in New York, died in Glasgow, 1790, testament 1790, Comm. Glasgow. [NRS.CC9.7.74]

BOWMAN, JAMES, in Glasgow, 1753. [NRS.E326.1.172]

BOWMAN, JOHN, a merchant in Glasgow, 1726. [NRS.AC9.1056; AC7.34.433-451]

BOWMAN, JOHN, a merchant in Glasgow, 1759. [ERG.VI.546]

BOWMAN, JOHN, a merchant from Glasgow, to Charleston, South Carolina, by 1769. Charleston County Misc. Records#172]; son of Provost Bowman of Glasgow, settled in East Florida, 1769. [NRS.NRAS.771, bundle 295]; land grant in Christchurch, Georgia, 1772, [Georgia grant book I.678]; in Savanna, 1774. [NRS.GD77.167/168; CS16.1.122]

BOWMAN, MARGARET, relict of William Cunninghame a merchant in Glasgow, testament, 1732, Comm. Glasgow. [NRS]

BOWMAN, SAMUEL, from Glasgow, in Boston, 1738. [SCS]

The People of Glasgow, 1725-1775

BOWS, ALLAN, a cordiner burgess 1737, former apprentice to Patrick Wotherspoon a cordiner. [CG]

BOYD, ANN, a resident of Glasgow and spouse of Alexander Brown a surgeon in Jamaica, testament, 1749, Comm. Glasgow. [NRS]

BOYD, CHRISTIAN, relict of Peter Gemmill a merchant in Glasgow, testament, 1729, Comm. Glasgow. [NRS]

BOYD, HUGH, born 1746, son of Robert Boyd and his wife Janet Grindlay, a pickpocket from Glasgow, transported to the colonies in 1766. [NRS.HCR.I.98]

BOYD, JOHN, a sailor in Glasgow, master of the Hunter, testament, 1733, Comm. Glasgow. [NRS]

BOYD, MARION, a resident of Glasgow and relict of Thomas Roberton a surgeon in Edinburgh, testaments, 1741/1742/1744, Comm. Glasgow. [NRS]

BOYD, MARY, heir to her father John Boyd a surgeon in Glasgow, also to her mother Elizabeth Robertson his wife. [NRS.SH.1750]

BOYD, ROBERT, a merchant in Glasgow, 1725. [ERG.V.211]

BOYD, ROBERT, born 1748, son of Robert Boyd and his wife Janet Grindlay, a pickpocket from Glasgow, transported to the colonies in 1766. [NRS.HCR.I.98]

BOYD, ROBERT, a merchant in Glasgow, heir to his father Robert Boyd a merchant there, 1750. [NRS.SH.1750]

BOYLE, JAMES, late Deacon of the Weavers in Glasgow, testaments, 1735/1736, Comm. Glasgow. [NRS]

BOYLE, PETER, a weaver in Glasgow, testament, 1743, Comm. Glasgow. [NRS]

BRAIDIE, WILLIAM, a merchant in Glasgow, testament, 1745, Comm. Glasgow. [NRS]

BRAIDWOOD, ALEXANDER, a cordiner burgess 1726, son of Alexander Braidwood a cordiner. [CG]

BRAIDWOOD, ALEXANDER, a cordiner in Glasgow, testament, 1746, Comm. Glasgow. [NRS]

BRASH, JOHN, a baxter, eldest son of John Brash a merchant, former apprentice to (1) Hugh Purdon, (2)John Riddell, was admitted to the Baxter Incorporation, and as a burgess and guilds-brother of Glasgow in 1772. [IBG.111][GBR]

BREDIE, WILLIAM, in Glasgow, 1753. [NRS.E326.1.172]

BRICE, NINIAN, from Glasgow, in Boston, 1731. [SCS]

The People of Glasgow, 1725-1775

BRISBANE, JOHN, MD, in Glasgow, heir to his father Thomas Brisbane MD, 1750. [NRS.SH.1750]

BRISBANE, PATRICK, the younger, a weaver in Glasgow, testaments, 1749/1756, Comm. Glasgow. [NRS]

BRISBANE, ROBERT, born 1707, third son of William Brisbane and his wife Catherine Patterson in Glasgow, a physician educated at Glasgow University, emigrated to South Carolina, 1733, died 1781. [SCHM.14.123]

BRISBANE, ROBINA, daughter of the late Mathew Brisbane a physician in Glasgow and late spouse to Charles Morthland the Professor of Oriental Languages in the University of Glasgow, testament, 1738, Comm. Glasgow. [NRS]

BRISBANE, WALTER, in Glasgow, 1753. [NRS.E326.1.172]

BRISBANE, WILLIAM, born 1710, fourth son of William Brisbane and his wife Catherine Patterson in Glasgow, a surgeon educated at Glasgow University, settled in South Carolina in 1732, a planter on the Ashley River, died 1771. [SCHM.14.125]

BROADFOOT, ALEXANDER, schoolmaster of Glasgow Grammar School, 1775. [ERG.VII.445]

BROCK, JAMES, a stocking maker, husband of Margaret Neill, was admitted to the Skinners Craft, and as a burgess and guilds-brother of Glasgow in 1760. [SFG.268][GBR]

BROCK, WALTER, in Glasgow, 1753. [NRS.E326.1.172]

BROCK, WALTER, born 1746, a grocer and husband of Janet Stewart, a burgess and guilds-brother of Glasgow in 1771; a merchant from Glasgow, to New York in 1775. [NA.T47.12][GBR]

BROTHERSTON, JEAN, a resident of Glasgow, testament, 1775, Comm. Glasgow. [NRS]

BROWN, or MILNE, Mrs AGNES, a widow resident in Glasgow, testament, 1733, Comm. Glasgow. [NRS]

BROWN, ALEXANDER, a mealman in Glasgow, testament, 1740, Comm. Glasgow. [NRS]

BROWN, ALEXANDER, a surgeon in Glasgow, settled in Jamaica by 1749, returned to Glasgow [NRS.RS8.3423]; husband of Ann Boyd in Glasgow, testament, 1749, Comm. Glasgow. [NRS]

The People of Glasgow, 1725-1775

BROWN, ALEXANDER, a merchant in Glasgow, heir to his father John Brown a merchant and late Provost of Glasgow, 1757; a burgess and guilds-brother of Glasgow in 1757. [NRS.SH.1757][GBR]

BROWN, ALEXANDER, a cordiner burgess and guilds-brother of Glasgow in 1769, son of Alexander Brown a cordiner. [CG][GBR]

BROWN, DAVID, a shoemaker 1771. [CG]

BROWN, GEORGE, a merchant in Glasgow, a burgess of Irvine, 1767, [AA]; 1768. [NRS.CS16.1.133]

BROWN, HUGH, from Glasgow, in Boston, 1746. [SCS]

BROWN, JAMES, a carter in Glasgow, testament, 1757, Comm. Glasgow. [NRS]

BROWN, JAMES, a merchant in Glasgow, a deed, 1750; in Bladensburg, Maryland, by 1770. [NRS.RD3.210.517][NA.AO12.9.59]

BROWN, JAMES, a cordiner burgess of Glasgow in 1769, younger son of Alexander Brown a cordiner. [CG][GBR]

BROWN, JAMES, a carter and a horse-thief from Glasgow, transported to the colonies in 1774. [NRS.RH2.4.255][CalHOpp.1774.847]

BROWN, JOHN, a shipmaster in Glasgow, 1736. [NRS.S/H]

BROWN, JOHN, from Glasgow, in Boston, 1738. [SCS]

BROWN, JOHN, merchant in Glasgow, 1741. [GA.D-TC13/603s]

BROWN, JOHN, a baxter, son of John Brown, was admitted to the Baxter Incorporation, 1747. [IBG.111]

BROWN, JOHN, in Glasgow, 1753. [NRS.E326.1.172]

BROWN, JOHN, a merchant and late Provost of Glasgow, testament, 1757/1773, Comm. Glasgow. [NRS]

BROWN, JOHN, a baxter, son in law to Robert Allan, was admitted to the Baxter Incorporation, and as a burgess and guilds-brother of Glasgow in 1764. [IBG.111][GBR]

BROWN, JOHN, a book-seller in Glasgow, testament, 1766, Comm. Glasgow. [NRS]

BROWN, JOHN, a thread-maker in Glasgow, testament, 1775, Comm. Glasgow. [NRS]

BROWN, PETER, a flesher in Glasgow, testament, 1750, Comm. Glasgow. [NRS]

BROWN, PETER, a flesher, eldest son of Peter Brown a flesher deceased, a burgess and guilds-brother of Glasgow in 1763. [GBR]

The People of Glasgow, 1725-1775

BROWN, PETER, born 1752, a barber from Glasgow, to New York in 1775. [NA.T47.12]

BROWN, ROBINA, relict of William Mitchell of Blairgoats a merchant in Glasgow, testament, 1743, Comm. Glasgow. [NRS]

BROWN, THOMAS, a merchant from Glasgow, settled in King and Queen County, Virginia, 1770. [NRS.RD2.233.108; CS17.1.2/145; CS17.1.1]

BROWN, WILLIAM, a merchant in Glasgow, deeds, 1750. [NRS.TD2.168.219/224]

BROWN, WILLIAM, senior, in Glasgow, 1753. [NRS.E326.1.172]; a merchant in Glasgow, testament, 1768, Comm. Glasgow. [NRS]

BROWN, WILLIAM, a merchant, eldest son of William Brown, was admitted to the Skinners Craft, 1762. [SFG.268][NRS.CS16.1.95]

BROWN, WILLIAM, from Glasgow, in Boston, 1763. [SCS]

BROWN, WILLIAM, brother of Alexander Brown of Quarter a merchant in Glasgow, a merchant and planter from Glasgow, settled in St Kitts and Tobago, died 1767. [NRS.B10.15.7493]

BROWSTER, JAMES, a weaver, former apprentice to Matthew McAulay a weaver, a burgess and guildsbrother of Glasgow in 1752; a deed, 1768. [GBR][NRS.RD2.217/1.130]

BRYCE, ARCHIBALD, a factor from Glasgow, settled in Richmond, Virginia, before 1776. [NRS.B10.12.4; AC7.58]

BRYCE, JOHN, a hammerman, 1728. [HHG.293]

BRYCE, JOHN, a writer in Glasgow, testament, 1732, Comm. Glasgow. [NRS]

BRYCE, JOHN, a janitor at the College of Glasgow, testament, 1772, Comm. Glasgow. [NRS]

BRYCE, ROBERT, a baxter in Glasgow, testaments, 1751/1753, Comm. Glasgow. [NRS]

BRYCE, ROBERT, a weaver in Glasgow, testament, 1761, Comm. Glasgow. [NRS]

BRYCE, WILLIAM, a merchant in Glasgow, [NRS.AC7.43.4]; testament, 1749, Comm. Glasgow. [NRS]

BRYCE, WILLIAM, a tenant in Lochburn, barony parish of Glasgow, testament, 1752, Comm. Glasgow. [NRS]

BRYDEN, THOMAS, in Glasgow, 1753. [NRS.E326.1.172]

The People of Glasgow, 1725-1775

BRYSON, DAVID, a coppersmith, youngest son of Hugh Bryson, was admitted to the Skinners Craft, also as a burgess and guilds-brother in 1753. [SFG.267][GBR]

BRYSON, HUGH, a skinner, eldest son of Hugh Bryson a skinner, a burgess and guilds-brother of Glasgow in 1752, testament, 1770, Comm. Glasgow. [NRS][GBR]

BRYSON, THOMAS, a maltman in Glasgow, testament, 1755, Comm. Glasgow. [NRS]

BRYSON, WILLIAM, late Deacon of the Incorporation of Weavers, 1725. [OGW#108]

BRYSON, WILLIAM, a baxter, former apprentice to Thomas Scott, was admitted to the Baxter Incorporation, also as a burgess and guilds-brother of Glasgow in 1739. [IBG.111][GBR]

BRYSON, WILLIAM, a weaver, former apprentice to John McIndoe a weaver, a burgess and guilds-brother of Glasgow in 1746, [GBR], testament, 1757, Comm. Glasgow. [NRS]

BUCHANAN, ALEXANDER, a baxter, eldest son of George Buchanan a baxter, was admitted to the Baxter Incorporation, also as a burgess and guilds-brother of Glasgow in 1742. [IBG.111][GBR]

BUCHANAN, ANDREW, a merchant, second son of George Buchanan a maltman, a burgess and guilds-brother of Glasgow in 1716, [GBR], in Glasgow, 1726. [NRS.AC7.24.710; AC9.6398]

BUCHANAN, ANDREW, junior, a tailor, a burgess and guilds-brother of Glasgow in 1733, [GBR], a merchant tailor in Glasgow, testaments, 1741/1744, Comm. Glasgow. [NRS]

BUCHANAN, ANDREW, in Glasgow, 1753. [NRS.E326.1.172]; a merchant tailor in Glasgow, testament, 1754, Comm. Glasgow. [NRS]

BUCHANAN, ANDREW, a baxter, former apprentice to Moses Provan a baxter, was admitted to the Baxter Incorporation, and as a burgess and guilds-brother of Glasgow in 1764. [IBG.111][GBR]

BUCHANAN, ARCHIBALD, son of Archibald Buchanan of Drumhead and his wife Janet Buchanan, a merchant from Glasgow, to America by 1757, settled as a factor at Silverbank, Prince Edward County, Virginia. [NRS.RS10.9.84; CC9.16.53]

The People of Glasgow, 1725-1775

BUCHANAN, COLIN, a hammerman, second son of Patrick Buchanan a gunsmith, a burgess and guilds-brother of Glasgow in 1750, [GBR], testaments, 1767/1768, Comm. Glasgow. [NRS]

BUCHANAN, DOUGAL, of Craigievern, a merchant in Glasgow, testament, 1774, Comm. Glasgow. [NRS]

BUCHANAN, DUGALD, in Glasgow, 1753. [NRS.E326.1.172]

BUCHANAN, DUNCAN, born 1756, from Glasgow, to Jamaica in 1774. [NA.T47.12]

BUCHANAN, GEORGE, an inn-keeper in Glasgow, testament, 1732, Comm. Glasgow. [NRS]

BUCHANAN, GEORGE, a maltman in Glasgow, testament, 1740, Comm. Glasgow. [NRS]

BUCHANAN, GEORGE, a vintner in Glasgow, testament, 1749, Comm. Glasgow. [NRS]

BUCHANAN, GEORGE, in Glasgow, 1753. [NRS.E326.1.172]

BUCHANAN, GEORGE, the youngest, a merchant in Glasgow, testament, 1766, Comm. Glasgow. [NRS.AC7.47.32]

BUCHANAN, GEORGE, a merchant from Glasgow, settled in Bladensburg, Maryland, and in Virginia before 1773. [NRS.CS16.1.154][NA.AO12.9.1]

BUCHANAN, GEORGE, senior, a maltman in Glasgow, testaments, 1774/1775, Comm. Glasgow. [NRS]

BUCHANAN, GILBERT, of Bankell, a merchant and late Dean of Guild in Glasgow, testaments, 1731/1737, Comm. Glasgow. [NRS]

BUCHANAN, GILBERT, late merchant in Glasgow, testaments, 1733/1735, Comm. Glasgow. [NRS]

BUCHANAN, GILBERT, a merchant, eldest son of William Buchanan merchant in Glasgow and his wife Janet Colquhoun, a burgess and guilds-brother of Glasgow in 1731, [GBR], testament, 1738, Comm. Glasgow. [NRS]

BUCHANAN, GRISSELL, relict of Joseph Baxter a cork-cutter in Glasgow, testament, 1773, Comm. Glasgow. [NRS]

BUCHANAN, HENRY, born 1751, a wright from Glasgow, to Salem, New England, in 1775. [NA.T47.12]

BUCHANAN, JAMES, from Glasgow, in Boston, 1729. [SCS]

BUCHANAN, JAMES, of Ballochruen, a merchant in Glasgow, testament, 1760, Comm. Glasgow. [NRS]

The People of Glasgow, 1725-1775

BUCHANAN, JAMES, Professor of Oriental Languages in the University of Glasgow, testament, 1762, Comm. Glasgow. [NRS]

BUCHANAN, JAMES, in Glasgow, 1753. [NRS.E326.1.172]; a freeman maltman, 1759, [MCG.136]; a vintner in Glasgow, testament, 1764, Comm. Glasgow. [NRS]

BUCHANAN, JAMES, a baxter, son of James Buchanan a baxter, was admitted to the Baxter Incorporation, and as a burgess and guilds-brother of Glasgow in 1769. [IBG.111][GBR]

BUCHANAN, JAMES, only son of James Buchanan a maltman, a freeman maltman, 1771. [MCG.136]

BUCHANAN, JEAN, born 1738, from Glasgow, to Salem, New England, in 1775. [NA.T47.12]

BUCHANAN, JOHN, a merchant in Glasgow, [NRS.AC7.34.697; AC40.137]; testament, 1731, Comm. Glasgow. [NRS]

BUCHANAN, JOHN, a baxter, eldest son of the late John Buchanan a baxter, was admitted to the Baxter Incorporation, also as a burgess and guilds-brother of Glasgow in1733. [IBG.111][GBR]

BUCHANAN, JOHN, senior, a merchant in Glasgow, testament, 1752, Comm. Glasgow. [NRS]

BUCHANAN, JOHN, in Glasgow, 1753. [NRS.E326.1.172]

BUCHANAN, JOHN, in Glasgow, deeds, 1763/1773, [NRS.RD2.218.34; RD2.217/1.386; CS16.1.157]

BUCHANAN, MARGARET, relict of John Murray a merchant in Glasgow, testament, 1726, Comm. Glasgow. [NRS]

BUCHANAN, MARGARET, born 1740, from Glasgow, to New York in 1775. [NA.T47.12]

BUCHANAN, MOSES, of Ballochneck, a writer in Glasgow, testaments, 1747, Comm. Glasgow. [NRS]

BUCHANAN, MUNGO, a merchant in Glasgow, husband of Jean Buchanan, a burgess and guilds-brother of Glasgow in 1751, testament, 1772, Comm. Glasgow. [NRS][GBR]

BUCHANAN, NEIL, a merchant in Glasgow, 1773. [NRS.CS16.1.154]

BUCHANAN, PATRICK, a merchant in Glasgow, testament, 1732, Comm. Glasgow. [NRS]

The People of Glasgow, 1725-1775

BUCHANAN, ROBERT, a writer in Glasgow, testament, 1759, Comm. Glasgow. [NRS]

BUCHANAN, ROBERT, in Glasgow, 1753. [NRS.E326.1.172]

BUCHANAN, ROBERT, a merchant from Glasgow, settled in Annapolis, Maryland, before 1760. [ANY.I.262][NA.AO12.6.239]

BUCHANAN, THOMAS, a shipmaster in Glasgow, testament, 1739, Comm. Glasgow. [NRS]

BUCHANAN, THOMAS, a surgeon, former apprentice to Robert Graham of Gartmore a surgeon, a burgess and guilds-brother of Glasgow in 1718, [GBR], in Glasgow, 1725; testament, 1761, Comm. Glasgow. [NRS] [ERG.V.245]

BUCHANAN, WALTER, a writer, husband of Janet Lecky, a burgess and guilds-brother of Glasgow in 1719, [GBR], testaments, 1734/1742, Comm. Glasgow. [NRS]

BUCHANAN, WALTER, in Glasgow, son of the late William Buchanan of Ballat, testaments, 1742/1751, Comm. Glasgow. [NRS]

BUCHANAN, WALTER, a maltman in Glasgow, testament, 1759, Comm. Glasgow. [NRS]

BUCHANAN, WILLIAM, of Bankell, resident of Glasgow, eldest son of the late Gilbert Buchanan of Bankell, testament, 1733, Comm. Glasgow. [NRS]

BUCHANAN, WILLIAM, son of John Buchanan junior a merchant in Glasgow, a planter in Granville County, South Carolina, by 1737, probate 1758, South Carolina.

BUCHANAN, WILLIAM, a baxter, former apprentice to William Ballinie a baxter, was admitted to the Baxter Incorporation, also as a burgess and guilds-brother of Glasgow in 1748. [IBG.111][GBR]

BUCHANAN, WILLIAM, from Glasgow, settled in Petersburg, Virginia, before 1776. [NA.AO13.4.195]

BULLOCH, JAMES, born 1701 in Glasgow, to Charleston, South Carolina, in 1728, died 1780. [SHR.I.416]

BURNET, DAVID, an Excise officer in Glasgow, testament, 1731, Comm. Glasgow. [NRS]

BURNS, ELIZABETH, in Glasgow, testament, 1726, Comm. Glasgow. [NRS]

BURNS, JOHN, in Glasgow, 1753. [NRS.E326.1.172]

BURNS, JOHN, of the Coffee House in Glasgow, 1753. [NRS.E326.1.172]

The People of Glasgow, 1725-1775

BURNS, THOMAS, a merchant in Glasgow, testament, 1732, Comm. Glasgow. [NRS]

BURNSIDE, ANDREW, a saddler, former apprentice to John Greg a hammerman, a hammerman, also a burgess of Glasgow in 1729. [HHG.293][GBR]

BURNSIDE, PATRICK, a baxter, second son of the late Patrick Burnside a tailor, a burgess and guilds-brother of Glasgow in 1756, and as former apprentice to Gabriel Lochhead a baxter, was admitted to the Baxter Incorporation in 1766. [GBR] [IBG.111]

BURT, CHARLES, born 1748, a wright from Glasgow, to New York in 1774. [NA.T47.12]

BURTON, MARGARET, spouse of John Walker a skinner in Glasgow, testament, 1769, Comm. Glasgow. [NRS]

BUTCHER, EUPHAN, spouse of Robert Foulis a printer in Glasgow, testament, 1775, Comm. Glasgow. [NRS]

BUTTER, WILLIAM, a wright, husband of Margaret Hamilton, a burgess and guilds-brother of Glasgow in 1741, [GBR], testament, 1768, Comm. Glasgow. [NRS]

CALDER, EUPHAN, relict of Walter Stirling a merchant and former bailie of Glasgow, testament, 1762, Comm. Glasgow. [NRS]

CALDER, JOHN, a watch and clockmaker, former apprentice to John Jaffrey a hammerman in Glasgow, a burgess and guilds-brother of Glasgow in 1775, a hammerman in 1775. [HHG.294][GBR]

CALDER, THOMAS, of Shirva, a merchant in Glasgow, testaments, 1734/1735/1741, Comm. Glasgow. [NRS]

CALDERHEAD, THOMAS, a merchant from Glasgow, settled in Norfolk, Virginia, before 1775. [NA.AO13.2.355; AO12.54.147]

CALDERHEAD, WILLIAM, a merchant from Glasgow, settled in Norfolk, Virginia, testament, 1788 Comm. Edinburgh. [NRS.CC8.8.127] [NA.AO13.2.355]

CALDWELL, WILLIAM, a wright, husband of Sarah Winning, a burgess and guilds-brother of Glasgow in 1758, testament, 1774, Comm. Glasgow. [NRS][GBR]

CALHOUN, BETTY, in Trongate, Glasgow, letters, 1770. [NRS.NRAS.396/301]

CAMERON, ARCHIBALD, in Glasgow, 1753. [NRS.E326.1.172]

The People of Glasgow, 1725-1775

CAMERON, ELIZABETH, in Glasgow, daughter of Rev. William Cameron and his wife Mary Wauchop in Greenock, testaments, 1736/1737, Comm. Glasgow. [NRS]

CAMERON, JOHN, of Carntyne, a merchant in Glasgow, testament, 1754, Comm. Glasgow. [NRS]

CAMPBELL, ALEXANDER, from Glasgow, husband of Ann Arthur, emigrated before 1757, settled in Falmouth, Prince George County, Maryland, [NRS.RD3.224.480][Prince William County Deeds, R154]

CAMPBELL, ALEXANDER, in Glasgow, 1753. [NRS.E326.1.172]

CAMPBELL, ALEXANDER, in Glasgow, a deed, 1768. [NRS.RD4.207/1.32]

CAMPBELL, ALEXANDER, of Lecquarry, born 1711, a merchant in Glasgow, died 12 April 1771, his spouse Ann Campbell, born 1731, died 10 September 1786. [Ramshorn MI, Glasgow]

CAMPBELL, ANDREW, a merchant from Glasgow, settled in Jamaica before 1744. [NRS.RD2.169.74]

CAMPBELL, Captain ARCHIBALD, of Inveraw, resident in Glasgow, testament, 1761, Comm. Glasgow. [NRS]

CAMPBELL, ARCHIBALD, former apprentice to John Craig, was admitted to the Baxter Incorporation, 1772. [IBG.114]

CAMPBELL, ARCHIBALD, a horse-setter in Glasgow, testament, 1775, Comm. Glasgow. [NRS]

CAMPBELL, COLIN, a factor from Glasgow, settled in Virginia by 1775, a Loyalist who moved to Penobscot, New Brunswick, in 1786. [NA.AO13.22.403]

CAMPBELL, DANIEL, a merchant from Glasgow, settled in Falmouth, King George County, Virginia, before 1770. [Prince William County, Va., deeds R154]

CAMPBELL, DUNCAN, a merchant in Glasgow, testament, 1729, Comm. Glasgow. [NRS]

CAMPBELL, ELIZABETH, in Glasgow, daughter of the late John Campbell of Succoth, testament, 1741, Comm. Glasgow. [NRS]

CAMPBELL, GEORGE, a sailor in Glasgow, testament, 1732, Comm. Glasgow. [NRS]

CAMPBELL, GEORGE, minister of Glasgow High Church, testament, 1757, Comm. Glasgow. [NRS]

CAMPBELL, HEW, a merchant from Glasgow, settled in Jamaica before 1744. [NRS.RD2.169.74]

CAMPBELL, JAMES, a merchant in Glasgow, testament, 1745, Comm. Glasgow. [NRS]

CAMPBELL, JAMES, a barber and wig-maker in Glasgow, testament, 1755, Comm. Glasgow. [NRS]

CAMPBELL, JAMES, of Kames, Cowal, formerly a merchant in Glasgow, sometime in Hanover, Jamaica, died 1758, testament, 1761, Comm. of the Isles. [NRS]

CAMPBELL, JANET, relict of George Houston a merchant in Glasgow, testament, 1726, Comm. Glasgow. [NRS]

CAMPBELL, JOHN, eldest son of John Campbell a merchant, a hammerman, also as a burgess and guilds-brother of Glasgow in 1728. [HHG.293][GBR]

CAMPBELL, JOHN, a maltman in Glasgow, testament, 1735, Comm. Glasgow. [NRS]

CAMPBELL, JOHN, a dyer in Glasgow, testament, 1738, Comm. Glasgow. [NRS]

CAMPBELL, JOHN, a weaver in Glasgow, testament, 1750, Comm. Glasgow. [NRS]

CAMPBELL, JOHN, in Glasgow, 1753. [NRS.E326.1.172]

CAMPBELL, JOHN, a merchant from Glasgow, to Virginia in 1760, settled in Occoquan and Bladensburg, Virginia. [GA]

CAMPBELL, JOHN, a merchant in Glasgow, a deed, 1770. [NRS.RD2.207.156; CS16.1.143]

CAMPBELL, LACHLAN, a merchant from Glasgow, to America in 1764, settled in Fredericksburg, Virginia, a Loyalist in 1776. [NA.AO13.28.81, etc]

CAMPBELL, PETER, born 1755, a merchant from Glasgow, to Jamaica 1775. [NA.T47.12]

CAMPBELL, ROBERT, a merchant from Glasgow, settled in Jamaica before 1744. [NRS.RD2.169.74]

CAMPBELL, ZACHARIAH, born 1740, second son of the late James Campbell a merchant in Glasgow, a merchant, to America by 1763, settled in Vienna, Maryland, and Fredericksburg, Virginia. [NRS.B10.15.6863]

CAMPBELL, Mrs, in Glasgow, 1753. [NRS.E326.1.172]

CARENS, JOHN, from Glasgow, an indentured servant in Philadelphia, 1772. [Records of Indentures in Philadelphia]

CARLILE, ALEXANDER, from Glasgow, in Boston 1744. [SCS]

The People of Glasgow, 1725-1775

CARLYLE, ALEXANDER, a bookseller in Glasgow, testament, 1752, Comm. Glasgow. [NRS]

CARLYLE, ANDREW, a merchant, husband of Mary Waills, a burgess and guilds-brother of Glasgow in 1726, [GBR], testament, 1740, Comm. Glasgow. [NRS]

CARLYLE, GEORGE, a merchant in Glasgow, testament, 1769, Comm. Glasgow. [NRS]

CARLYLE, JAMES, a merchant, a burgess and guilds-brother of Glasgow in 1710, [GBR], testaments, 1729/1730, Comm. Glasgow. [NRS]

CARLYLE, JAMES, a merchant in Glasgow, testaments, 1760/1762, Comm. Glasgow. [NRS]

CARLYLE, JOHN, son of Alexander Carlyle, a merchant from Glasgow, settled in Virginia before 1748. [NRS.SC36.63.1]

CARLYLE, JOHN, in Glasgow, 1753. [NRS.E326.1.172]

CARLYLE, WILLIAM, gaoler of Glasgow, 1725. [ERG.V.244]

CARLYLE, WILLIAM, the elder, a merchant in Glasgow, testament, 1728, Comm. Glasgow. [NRS]

CARLYLE, WILLIAM, a merchant in Glasgow, testaments, 1731/1735, Comm. Glasgow. [NRS]

CARLYLE, WILLIAM, a merchant in Glasgow, testament, 1768, Comm. Glasgow. [NRS]

CARMICHAEL, ALEXANDER, a merchant, eldest son of Gershom Carlyle a Regent of the College of Glasgow, a burgess and guilds-brother of Glasgow in 1724, [GBR], there in 1753. [NRS.E326.1.172]

CARMICHAEL, GEORGE, a merchant, husband of Margaret Craig, a burgess and guilds-brother of Glasgow in 1738, [GBR], a merchant and bailie of Glasgow, testament, 1772, Comm. Glasgow. [NRS.CS16.1.99/192]

CARMICHAEL, GERSHOME, Professor of Philosophy at Glasgow University, a burgess and guilds-brother of Glasgow in 1708, [GBR], testaments, 1730/1736, Comm. Glasgow. [NRS]

CARMICHAEL, GERSHOME, master of the Red Dye Society in Glasgow, 1759. [ERG.VI.547]

CARMICHAEL, JAMES, a merchant, a burgess and guilds-brother of Glasgow in 1746, [GBR], settled in Jamaica by 1750. [NRS.B10.15.7166]

CARMICHAEL, JOHN, a weaver, former apprentice of James Neilson a weaver, a burgess and guilds-brother of Glasgow in 1738, [GBR], testament, 1744, Comm. Glasgow. [NRS]

CARMICHAEL, JOHN, a merchant in Glasgow, testament, 1772, Comm. Glasgow. [NRS]

CARMICHAEL, MARY, relict of John Hardie a tobacco spinner in Glasgow, testament, 1743, Comm. Glasgow. [NRS]

CARMICHAEL, WILLIAM, a merchant from Glasgow, settled in Jamaica by 1750. [NRS.B10.15.7166]

CARNEGIE, PATRICK, from Glasgow, in Boston, 1750. [SCS]

CARRICK, JAMES, from Glasgow, in Boston, 1747. [SCS]

CARRUITH, JANET, a mason in Glasgow, testament, 1729, Comm. Glasgow. [NRS]

CARRUITH, SAMUEL, a mason in Glasgow, 1725. [ERG.V.236]

CARSE, RICHARD, in Glasgow, testament, 1729, Comm. Glasgow. [NRS]

CARSS, JOHN, son in law of William Meiklom a maltman, a freeman maltman, 1748. [MCG.132]

CARSTAIRS, SARAH, relict of William Dunlop the Principal of Glasgow College, testament, 1734, Comm. Glasgow. [NRS]

CATHCART, ANDREW, a merchant, eldest son of the late Andrew Cathcart a merchant, a burgess and guilds-brother of Glasgow in 1727, [GBR], a merchant in Glasgow trading with New England and Maryland, 1739-1741, dead before 1741. [NRS.AC9.1476]; testament, 1740, Comm. Glasgow. [NRS]; his wife Helen Wardrop, wife of Robert Wardrop a merchant in Glasgow, testament, 1767, Comm. Glasgow. [NRS]

CATHCART, HUGH, a merchant, second son of the late Andrew Cathcart a merchant, a burgess and guilds-brother of Glasgow in 1735, [GBR], testaments, 1743/1744, Comm. Glasgow. [NRS]

CATHCART, HUGH, born 1706, son of Andrew Cathcart and his wife Janet Nisbet, a merchant from Glasgow, settled in Kingston, Jamaica, dead by 1772. [GA]

CATHCART, WILLIAM, born 1732, son of Hugh Cathcart and his wife Helen Woodrop, a merchant from Glasgow, emigrated before 1768, settled in Kingston, Jamaica. [NRS.SC36.63.12.51]

CAUTION, DAVID, a wright and carver, a burgess of Glasgow in 1742,

The People of Glasgow, 1725-1775

[GBR], an architect in Glasgow by 1767. [ERG.VII.244]
CAVERHILL, THOMAS, a merchant in Glasgow, testament, 1767, Comm. Glasgow. [NRS]
CHALMERS, DONALD, a merchant from Glasgow, settled in Virginia by 1765. [NRS.CS16.1.125]
CHALMERS, JAMES, a merchant in Jamaica by 1765, brother of John Chalmers a merchant in Glasgow, and Donald Chalmers a merchant in Virginia. [NRS.CS16.1.125/13]
CHALMERS, JOHN, a merchant in Glasgow, testament, 1765, Comm. Glasgow. [NRS]
CHALMERS, JOHN, born 1750, a laborer from Partick, Glasgow, to New York in 1775. [NA.T47.12]
CHALMERS, JOHN, eldest son of Alexander Chalmers a hammerman, a hammerman, also as a burgess and guilds-brother of Glasgow in 1725. [HHG.293][GBR]
CHAPMAN, JOHN, a writer, eldest son of the late Robert Chapman, a burgess and guilds-brother of Glasgow in 1733, [GBR], testaments, 1745/1746, Comm. Glasgow. [NRS]
CHAPMAN, ROBERT, a chapman in Glasgow and Procurator Fiscal of Glasgow, testament, 1774, Comm. Glasgow. [NRS]
CHARITY, JAMES, from Glasgow, in Boston, 1762, [SCS]; a merchant in Massachusetts, before 1765. [NRS.SC36.63.8.168]
CHARITY, JOHN, a baxter, former apprentice to Robert Ballinie a baxter, was admitted to the Baxter Incorporation, also as a burgess and guilds-brother of Glasgow in 1730. [IBG.111][GBR]
CHARITY, MARY, in Glasgow, daughter of James Charity portioner of Balgrochan, testament, 1731, Comm. Glasgow. [NRS]
CHARTERS, JOHN, a merchant, a burgess and guilds-brother of Glasgow in 1708, [GBR], testament, 1725, Comm. Glasgow. [NRS]
CHIESLY, SAMUEL, a merchant, former apprentice of Thomas Wallace a merchant, a burgess and guilds-brother of Glasgow in 1735, [GBR], testament, 1774, Comm. Glasgow. [NRS]
CHESTER, HENRY, a pin-maker, husband of Christine King, a burgess and guilds-brother of Glasgow in 1707, [GBR], testaments, 1735/1739, Comm. Glasgow. [NRS]

The People of Glasgow, 1725-1775

CHRYSTIE, HENRY, the elder, a merchant, a guilds-brother of Glasgow in 1688, [GBR], testament, 1728, Comm. Glasgow. [NRS]

CHRISTIE, JOHN, born 1754, a wright from Glasgow, to New York in 1775. [NA.T47.12]

CHRISTIE, ROBERT, merchant who transported two women from the Correction House to Virginia, 1727. [ERG.V.289]

CHRISTIE, WILLIAM, in Glasgow, 1753. [NRS.E326.1.172]

CLARK, ADAM, a maltman, husband of Margaret Paterson, a burgess and guilds-brother of Glasgow in 1718, [GBR], testament, 1737, Comm. Glasgow. [NRS]

CLARK, JAMES, a merchant in Glasgow, testaments, 1738/1741, Comm. Glasgow. [NRS]

CLARK, JAMES, a merchant from Glasgow, settled in Virginia before 1754. [NRS.B10.15.6653]

CLARK, JAMES, in Glasgow, 1753. [NRS.E326.1.172]; a merchant tailor in Glasgow, testaments, 1772/1777, Comm. Glasgow. [NRS]

CLARK, JOHN, a merchant in Glasgow, testament, 1743, Comm. Glasgow. [NRS]

CLARK, JOHN, a merchant in Glasgow, testament, 1746, Comm. Glasgow. [NRS]

CLARK, JOHN, in Glasgow, 1753. [NRS.E326.1.172]

CLARK, JOHN, a divinity student at Glasgow University, eldest son of the late John Clark a merchant, library keeper of Glasgow, 1759. [ERG.VI.555]

CLARK, JOHN, a merchant in Glasgow, testament, 1767, Comm. Glasgow. [NRS]

CLARK, JOHN, a merchant tailor in Glasgow, testament, 1761, Comm. Glasgow. [NRS]

CLARK, MATHEW, a weaver and foreman in Provost Aiton's factory, a burgess and guilds-brother of Glasgow in 1740, [GBR], in Glasgow 1753. [NRS.E326.1.172]

CLARK, PATRICK, a merchant, husband of Agnes Smith, a burgess and guilds-brother of Glasgow in 1735, [GBR], testament, 1770, Comm. Glasgow. [NRS]

CLARK, Dr WILLIAM, in Glasgow, 1753. [NRS.E326.1.172]

CLARK, WILLIAM, from Glasgow, in Boston, 1753. [SCS]

CLARK, WILLIAM, a shipmaster in Glasgow, master of the snow Elliot of Glasgow, testament, 1763, Comm. Glasgow. [NRS]

CLARK, WILLIAM, born 1754, a shoemaker from Glasgow, to New York in 1774. [NA.T47.12]

CLARKSON, JEAN, a shopkeeper in Glasgow, testament, 1745, Comm. Glasgow. [NRS]

CLARKSON, MARGARET and JEAN, in Glasgow, daughters of Robert Clarkson, a notary in Coldingham, and his wife Margaret Fogo, testament, 1762, Comm. Glasgow. [NRS]

CLARKSON, MARY, in Glasgow, 1753. [NRS.E326.1.172]

CLAYTOUN, THOMAS, a stucco-man in Glasgow, 1759; a deed, 1766. [NRS.RD2.207.11] [ERG.VI.540]

CLEGHORN, JOHN, a merchant in Glasgow, testament, 1726, Comm. Glasgow. [NRS]

CLELAND, JAMES, a merchant in Glasgow, testament, 1742, Comm. Glasgow. [NRS]

CLELLAND, JAMES, heir to his father James Clelland a maltster in Glasgow. [NRS.SH.1750]

CLENDINNING, JOHN, a hair merchant in Glasgow, testament, 1767, Comm. Glasgow. [NRS]

CLINDINNING, THOMAS, from Glasgow, settled in Baltimore, Maryland, probate 1762 Baltimore. [MSA.Will.31/570]

CLYDESDALE, JAMES, a tailor in Glasgow, a burgess and guilds-brother of Glasgow in 1714, [GBR], testament, 1751, Comm. Glasgow. [NRS]

CLYDESDALE, WILLIAM, in Gartcraig, barony parish of Glasgow, testament, 1743, Comm. Glasgow. [NRS]

CLYDESDALE, WILLIAM, a mealman in Glasgow, testament, 1759, Comm. Glasgow. [NRS]

COATS, ARCHIBALD, in Glasgow, 1753. [NRS.E326.1.172]; a merchant in Glasgow, 1768. [Ramshorn MI, Glasgow][NRS.CS16.1.134]

COATS, JOHN, a hammerman, son of Thomas Coats a maltman, and servant of Robert Craig a hammerman, a burgess and guilds-brother of Glasgow in 1742, [GBR], a smith, hammerman, and comb maker in Glasgow, testaments, 1751/1752, Comm. Glasgow. [NRS]

COATS, JOHN, a merchant, eldest son of Archibald Coats a merchant, burgess and guilds-brother of Glasgow in 1743, [GBR], there around 1750. [NRS.CS16.1.85]

COATS, WILLIAM, a merchant in Glasgow, 1769. [NRS.CS16.1.134]

The People of Glasgow, 1725-1775

COCHRANE, ANDREW, a merchant in Glasgow, 1753; 1764. [NRS.E326.1.172; CS16.1.117/120/122]; a deed, 1767. [NRS.RD3.229/1.176]; 1775. [ERG.VII.442]

COCHRAN, DAVID, merchant who transported women from the Correction House to Virginia, 1727. [ERG.V.289]

COCHRANE, DAVID, born 1739, son of David Cochrane a merchant burgess and his wife Helen Hamilton, a merchant from Glasgow, settled in Richmond, Virginia, before 1766. [NRS.CS16.1.125; RD3.242.127]

COCHRANE, JOHN, Master of Work in Glasgow, 1759. [ERG.VI.540]

COCHRANE, THOMAS, master weaver of the Incorporation of Weavers, 1725. [OGW#108]

COCHRANE, THOMAS, a merchant traveller, son of John Cochrane in Dalbeth, barony parish of Glasgow, testament, 1743, Comm. Glasgow. [NRS]

COCKEAN, ALEXANDER, a vintner in Glasgow, a burgess and guilds-brother of Glasgow in 1741, [GBR], there in 1753. [NRS.E326.1.172]

COLHOUN, JAMES, merchant in Glasgow, 1728. [NRS.CS96.3814]

COLQUHOUN, AGNES, relict of John Melvill a surgeon in Glasgow, testament, 1770, Comm. Glasgow. [NRS]

COLQUHOUN, JAMES, son of the late James Colquhoun, the elder, of Langloan, a merchant in Glasgow, testament, 1730, Comm. Glasgow. [NRS.AC9.6415]

COLQUHOUN, JAMES, of Langloan, master of a pipe works in Glasgow, son of the late Reverend James Colquhoun in Penningham, testament, 1731, Comm. Glasgow. [NRS]

COLQUHOUN, JAMES, from Glasgow, in Boston, 1759. [SCS]

COLQUHOUN, JOHN, a merchant in Glasgow, 1730. [NRS.AC9/6415]

COLQUHOUN, LAWRENCE, a merchant, second son of Andrew Colquhoun of Garscaddan, a burgess and guilds-brother of Glasgow in 1734, [GBR], there in 1753. [NRS.E326.1.172; B10.15.6183]

COLQUHOUN, Mrs MARGARET, daughter of the late Sir John Colquhoun, in Glasgow, testament, 1725, Comm. Glasgow. [NRS]

COLQUHOUN, ROBERT, a merchant, second son of the late Alexander Colquhoun a merchant, a burgess and guilds-brother of Glasgow in 1731, [GBR], heir to his cousin James Colquhoun a merchant there, [NRS.SH.1752]; testament, 1755, Comm. Glasgow. [NRS]

COLQUHOUN, ROBERT, a writer in Glasgow, testament, 1758, Comm. Glasgow. [NRS]

The People of Glasgow, 1725-1775

COLQUHOUN, WILLIAM, a merchant in Glasgow, testaments, 1726/1728, Comm. Glasgow. [NRS]

COLQUHOUN, WILLIAM, in Glasgow, 1753. [NRS.E326.1.172]

COLQUHOUN, WILLIAM, a sailor in Glasgow, son of Robert Colquhoun a merchant in Glasgow, 1765. [NRS.S/H]

CONNEL, ARTHUR, a merchant, third son of Rev. Matthew Connel in Kilbryde, . a burgess and guilds-brother of Glasgow in 1740, [GBR] there in 1753. [NRS.E326.1.172]

CONNEL, JAMES, in Glasgow, a bond, 1766. [NRS.RD3.234.744]

CORBET, JAMES, a merchant in Glasgow, testament, 1737, Comm. Glasgow. [NRS]

CORBET, JAMES, a merchant, eldest son of the late James Corbet a merchant, a burgess and guilds-brother of Glasgow in 1727, [GBR], testament, 1754, Comm. Glasgow. [NRS]

CORBET, JAMES, heir to his father James Corbet a merchant in Glasgow who died in 1754. [NRS.SH.1756]

CORBET, JOHN, a merchant in Glasgow, testaments, 1774, Comm. Glasgow. [NRS]

CORBETT, WILLIAM, son of James Corbett a merchant burgess of Glasgow, a merchant from Glasgow, settled in Boston by 1756, died 1768. [SCS][NRS.B10.15.7137/7234]

COULT, ALEXANDER, a merchant in Glasgow, testaments, 1767/1768, Comm. Glasgow. [NRS]

COULTER, ALEXANDER, a cabinetmaker from Glasgow, settled in Chestertown, Kent County, Maryland, died 1742, probate 1742 Maryland

COULTER, HUGH, born 1717 son of Michael Coulter and his spouse Janet Cumming, a merchant from Glasgow, possibly in Boston 1747, settled in Maryland, died 1763, testament, 1766, Comm. Edinburgh. [NRS.CC8.8.120][SCS]

COULTER, JAMES, a merchant in Glasgow, heir to his father John Coulter a merchant there, 1750. [NRS.SH.1750; AC7.47.32; CS16.1.170/175]

COULTER, JOHN, a merchant and late Provost of Glasgow, testaments, 1748/1749, Comm. Glasgow. [NRS]

COULTER, MARY, in Glasgow, 1753. [NRS.E326.1.172]

The People of Glasgow, 1725-1775

COWAN, ALEXANDER, born 1754, a weaver from Glasgow, to New York in 1774. [NA.T47.12]

COWAN, WILLIAM, a baxter, former apprentice to James Morison a baxter, was admitted to the Baxter Incorporation, and as a burgess and guilds-brother of Glasgow in 1741. [IBG.114][GBR]; a baxter in Glasgow, testament, 1746, Comm. Glasgow. [NRS]

COWLIE, JAMES, a maltman, eldest son of the late Richard Cowlie a tailor, a burgess and guilds-brother of Glasgow in 1731, [GBR], testament, 1747/1750, Comm. Glasgow. [NRS]

COWLIE, JEAN, wife of John Ranken a tailor in Glasgow, heir to her brother James Cowlie a maltster there. [NRS.SH.1753]

COWLIE, JOHN, a soldier and eldest son of the late Richard Cowlie a tailor in Glasgow, heir to his uncle James Cowlie a meal dealer in Glasgow, and to his grandfather Richard Cowlie a tailor and meal dealer in Glasgow, [NRS.SH.1747/1751]; testament, 1743, Comm. Glasgow. [NRS]

COWLIE, JOHN, son of the late John Cowlie sometime tailor in Glasgow afterwards a soldier of the Cameronians and his wife Margaret McKechnie, testament, 1753, Comm. Glasgow. [NRS]

COWLIE, RICHARD, a tailor, eldest son of the late Richard Cowlie a gardener, and former apprentice to John Gibson a tailor, a burgess of Glasgow in 1694, and as a guilds-brother in 1703, [GBR]; in Glasgow, 1725. [ERG.V.222]

CRAIG, GEORGE, a wright in Glasgow, a tack, 1725. [ERG.V.207]

CRAIG, GEORGE, a hammerman in Glasgow, testament, 1739, Comm. Glasgow. [NRS]

CRAIG, JOANNA, heir to her father James Craig a farmer in Glasgow, [NRS.SH.1751]

CRAIG, JOHN, a baxter, former apprentice to John Menzies, was admitted to the Baxter Incorporation, 1753. [IBG.114]

CRAIG, JOHN, a merchant in Glasgow, testament, 1753, Comm. Glasgow. [NRS]

CRAIG, JOHN, a wright in Glasgow, testament, 1735, Comm. Glasgow. [NRS]

CRAIG, JOHN, a wright in Glasgow, testament, 1739, Comm. Glasgow. [NRS]

CRAIG, JOHN, a schoolmaster in Glasgow, testament, 1745, Comm. Glasgow. [NRS]

CRAIG, NINIAN, a town officer of Glasgow, testament, 1740, Comm. Glasgow. [NRS]

CRAIG, ROBERT, a maltman, eldest son of George Craig a hammerman, a hammerman, also a burgess and guilds-brother of Glasgow in1733. [HHG.294][GBR]; testament, 1754, Comm. Glasgow. [NRS]

CRAIG, ROBERT, the elder, a smith and plumber in Glasgow, 1759. [ERG.VI.540]

CRAIG, ROBERT, a baxter, former apprentice to John Craig, was admitted to the Baxter Incorporation, 1761. [IBG.114]

CRAIG, WILLIAM, the elder, a merchant in Glasgow,1730, [NRS.AC7.35.1065]; testament, 1736, Comm. Glasgow. [NRS]

CRAIG, WILLIAM, a merchant in Glasgow, testament, 1743, Comm. Glasgow. [NRS]

CRAIG, WILLIAM, a merchant in Glasgow, heir to his uncle William Stewart a merchant there, [NRS.SH.1750]; 1753. [NRS.E326.1.172]; a merchant in Glasgow, testament, 1756, Comm. Glasgow. [NRS]

CRAIG, WILLIAM, a wright in Glasgow, 1759. [ERG.VI.553]

CRAIG, WILLIAM, born 1709 son of Andrew Craig a merchant in Glasgow, minister at St Andrew's, Glasgow, from 1738 until his death in 1784. [F.3.433]

CRAMOND, JOHN, from Glasgow, settled in Norfolk, Virginia, in 1759, a Loyalist, removed to Jamaica in 1777. [NRS.CS16.1.170][VaGaz.4.4.1766][NA.AO13.28.120]

CRAWFORD, AGNES, in Glasgow, 1753. [NRS.E326.1.172]

CRAWFORD, ALEXANDER, a merchant, fourth son of the late Matthew Crawford a merchant, a burgess and guilds-brother of Glasgow in 1744, [GBR], testament, 1758, Comm. Glasgow. [NRS]

CRAWFORD, ANDREW, a merchant in Glasgow, testament, 1775, Comm. Glasgow. [NRS]

CRAWFORD, ARCHIBALD, late servant to Dr John Johnston a physician in Glasgow, testament, 1746, Comm. Glasgow. [NRS]

CRAWFORD, CATHERINE, spouse of David Stark a carter in Glasgow, testament, 1767, Comm. Glasgow. [NRS]

CRAWFORD, CHARLES, a merchant in Glasgow, testament, 1725, Comm. Glasgow. [NRS]

CRAWFORD, FRANCIS, a wright, eldest son of the late James Crawford a merchant, a burgess and guilds-brother of Glasgow in 1732, [GBR], 1753.

[NRS.E326.1.172]; a wright in Glasgow, 1759; testament, 1766, Comm. Glasgow. [NRS] [ERG.VI.553]

CRAWFORD, HUGH, senior, a writer in Glasgow, testament, 1749, Comm. Glasgow. [NRS]

CRAWFORD, JAMES, from Glasgow, in Boston, 1733. [SCS]

CRAWFORD, JAMES, from Glasgow, in Boston, 1750. [SCS]

CRAWFORD, JANET, daughter of the late Charles Crawford a merchant in Glasgow and his spouse Christian Lees, thereafter widow of James Patrick a merchant in Glasgow, testament, 1775, Comm. Glasgow. [NRS]

CRAWFORD, JOHN, a merchant in Glasgow, testaments, 1760/1766, Comm. Glasgow. [NRS]

CRAWFORD, JOHN, a surgeon in Glasgow, testaments, 1767/1768, Comm. Glasgow. [NRS]

CRAWFORD, MATHEW, eldest son of John Crawford a surgeon in Glasgow, educated at Glasgow University 1762, a deed in 1768, settled at Giffnock Hall, St Elizabeth, Jamaica, by 1787, died in Edinburgh, 1815.
[MAGU][NRS.RD2.243.329; AC7.35.485; RD4.208.23]

CRAWFORD, ROBERT, from Glasgow, in Boston, 1750. [SCS]

CRAWFORD, STEPHEN, a copper-smith in Glasgow, testament, 1733, Comm. Glasgow. [NRS]

CRAWFORD, WILLIAM, senior, a merchant in Glasgow, testament, 1735, Comm. Glasgow. [NRS]

CRAWFORD, WILLIAM, junior, in Glasgow, 1753. [NRS.E326.1.172]; a merchant in Glasgow, testaments, 1759/1766/1772, Comm. Glasgow. [NRS.CS16.1.100]

CRAWFORD, Mrs, in Glasgow, 1753. [NRS.E326.1.172]

CREIGHTON, ALEXANDER, born 1753, a merchant from Glasgow, to Nevis in 1774. [NRS.CE60.1.7]

CRIGHTON, JAMES, a smith burgess in 1775, a hammerman, 1775. [HHG.294]

CROOKSHANKS, JOHN, in Glasgow, 1753. [NRS.E326.1.172]

CROSBIE, GABRIEL, a tailor, a burgess and guilds-brother of Glasgow in 1709, [GBR]; in Glasgow, testament, 1747, Comm. Glasgow. [NRS]

CROSBIE, JAMES, a chapman in Glasgow, testament, 1758, Comm. Glasgow. [NRS]

CROSBIE, JOHN, portioner of Sandiehills, barony parish of Glasgow, testament, 1727, Comm. Glasgow. [NRS]

The People of Glasgow, 1725-1775

CROSBIE, JOHN, a weaver, son of the late Robert Crosbie, and husband of Isobel Tod a weaver, a burgess of Glasgow in 1706, [GBR], testament, 1730, Comm. Glasgow. [NRS]

CROSS, JAMES, a mason in Glasgow, 1725. [ERG.V.220]

CROSS, JAMES, a merchant from Glasgow, settled in Manchester, Prince Edward County, Virginia, before 1776, died in Norfolk, Virginia, 1787. [GA.TD131.13][NRS.S/H.1788; AC7.47.32][VaGaz.25.1.1787]

CROSS, JOHN, a merchant in Glasgow, testament, 1734, Comm. Glasgow. [NRS]

CROSS, JOHN, a merchant in Glasgow, 1750. [NRS.AC9.1746&1764]

CROSS, JOHN, in Glasgow, 1753. [NRS.E326.1.172]

CROSS, JOHN, a merchant in Glasgow, trading with Grenada in 1764; deeds, 1774. [GA.T-MJ][NRS.RD3.234.72; RD4.217.640]]

CROSS, ROBERT, junior, a merchant in Glasgow, testament, 1740, Comm. Glasgow. [NRS]

CROSS, WILLIAM, a tailor in Glasgow, testament, 1734, Comm. Glasgow. [NRS]

CROSS, Mrs, in Glasgow, 1753. [NRS.E326.1.172]

CRUICKSHANK, CHARLES, born 1746, a merchant from Glasgow, to Maryland by 1775. [GA]

CRUICKSHANKS, ELIZABETH, daughter of John Cruickshanks a barber in Glasgow, and spouse of David Black a merchant in Glasgow, testament, 1773, Comm. Glasgow. [NRS]

CRUICKSHANKS, GEORGE, Excise Supervisor in Glasgow, testament, 1759, Comm. Glasgow. [NRS]

CRUICKSHANKS, MARGARET, fifth daughter of the late John Cruickshanks a barber and wigmaker in Glasgow and Cecil Baillie his spouse, testament, 1773, Comm. Glasgow. [NRS]

CULLEN, JAMES, a preacher, a burgess and guilds-brother of Glasgow in 1744, [GBR], testament, 1769, Comm. Glasgow. [NRS]

CULLEN, WILLIAM, a mason in Glasgow, testament, 1743, Comm. Glasgow. [NRS]

CUMMING, CHRISTIAN, relict of Robert Boyd a merchant in Glasgow, testament, 1728, Comm. Glasgow. [NRS]

CUMMING, FRANCIS, a tailor, former apprentice of David Bisket a tailor, a burgess and guilds-brother of Glasgow in 1718, [GBR], a merchant tailor in Glasgow, testament, 1756, Comm. Glasgow. [NRS]

CUMMING, PATRICK, in Glasgow, 1753. [NRS.E326.1.172]

CUMMING, THOMAS, a baxter, former apprentice to Walter Lang, was admitted to the Baxter Incorporation, 1763. [IBG.114]

CUNNINGHAM, ALEXANDER, a merchant in Glasgow, testament, 1773, Comm. Glasgow. [NRS]

CUNNINGHAM, CHARLES, in Glasgow, a deed, 1766. [NRS.RD4.208.745]

CUNNINGHAM, JOHN, from Glasgow, in Boston, 1734. [SCS]

CUNNINGHAM, JOHN, in Glasgow, a bond, 1758. [NRS.RD2.208.823]

CUNNINGHAM, MARGARET, daughter of William Cunningham a merchant in Glasgow, heir to her grandfather John Robison a merchant there. [NRS.SH.1751]

CUNNINGHAM, ROBERT, a writer in Glasgow, testaments, 1732/1734, Comm. Glasgow. [NRS]

CUNNINGHAM, WILLIAM, master weaver of the Incorporation of Weavers, 1725. [OGW#108]

CUNNINGHAM, WILLIAM, a merchant in Glasgow 1726, and Westmoreland, Jamaica, 1744. [NRS.AC9.1098; AC7.35.485; RD2.169.70]

CUNNINGHAM, WILLIAM, born 1727, a merchant from Glasgow, in Boston, 1747. [SCS][NRS.GD247.140; CS16.1.133/174][NA.AO12.56.289]

CUNNINGHAM, WILLIAM, a merchant in Glasgow, a burgess of Irvine, 1762. [AA]

CURRIE, DONALD, a workman in Glasgow, testament, 1737, Comm. Glasgow. [NRS]

CURRIE, GEORGE, a merchant in Glasgow, testaments, 1732/1735/1736/1738, Comm. Glasgow. [NRS.AC9.1085]

CURRIE, JOHN, a merchant in Glasgow, testament, 1748, Comm. Glasgow. [NRS]

CURRIE, WALTER, a sailor in Glasgow, son of George Currie a merchant there, 1749. [NRS.S/H]

CURRIE, WALTER, from Glasgow, in Boston, 1756. [SCS]

CURRIE, WILLIAM, born 1710 in Glasgow, educated at Glasgow University, to America by 1730, a tutor in Virginia, a minister in Delaware and Pennsylvania, died Radnor, Chester Valley, 1803. [AP.159][EMA.23]

CUTHBERTSON, WILLIAM, in Glasgow, 1753. [NRS.E326.1.172]

CUTHBERTSON, WILLIAM, a maltman burgess in 1763, a hammerman, 1775. [HHG.294]

CUTHILL, MATHEW, in Glasgow, a bond, 1761. [NRS.RD4.217.789]

DALMAHOY, ALEXANDER, a hammerman, was admitted to the Skinners Craft, 1753. [SFG.267]

DALMAHOY, JOHN, a saddler, husband of Margaret Speir, a burgess and guilds-brother of Glasgow in 1744, [GBR], a deed, 1749. [NRS.RD4.176/1.78]

DALRYMPLE, DAVID, merchant in Glasgow, 1764. [NRS.CS16.1.120]

DALZIEL, DAVID, a merchant in Glasgow, testament, 1773, Comm. Glasgow. [NRS]

DALZIELL, DAVID, a merchant, husband of Margaret Buchanan a merchant, a burgess and guilds-brother of Glasgow in 1746, [GBR], heir to his father Lieutenant Colonel Thomas Dalziell son of Sir Robert Dalziell of Glenae, 1755.]NRS.SH.1755]

DANZIEL, GEORGE, a merchant , eldest son of George Danziel a wright, a burgess and guilds-brother of Glasgow in 1715, [GBR], testaments, 1740/1743/1747, Comm. Glasgow. [NRS]

DANZIEL, GEORGE, only son of George Danziel, a burgess and guilds-brother of Glasgow, 1757, [GBR]; a merchant in Glasgow, 1763. [ERG.VII.116]; a burgess of Irvine, 1762. [AA]

DAVIDSON, JAMES, master weaver of the Incorporation of Weavers, 1725. [OGW#108]

DAVIDSON, JANET, relict of John Fork minister at Killalan, and thereafter of Thomas Orr writer in Glasgow, testament, 1741, Comm. Glasgow. [NRS]

DAVIDSON, MATTHEW, a hammerman, husband of Agnes Kerr, a hammerman, and as a burgess and guilds-brother of Glasgow in 1732. [HHG.294][GBR]

DEAN, JOHN, a merchant from Glasgow, to America by 1757, settled in Tappahannock, Virginia. [NRS.B10.15.7036]

DEANS, JOHN, a baxter, eldest son of James Deans a currier and son in law of John Hoggan, was admitted to the Baxter Incorporation and as a burgess and guilds-brother of Glasgow in 1773. [IBG.117][GBR]

DEMPSTER, THOMAS, a painter, only son of the late John Dempster a painter, . a burgess and guilds-brother of Glasgow in 1736, [GBR], in Glasgow, 1759. [ERG.VI.549]

The People of Glasgow, 1725-1775

DENNISTOUN, JAMES, a merchant, eldest son of John Dennistoun of Colgrain, . a burgess and guilds-brother of Glasgow in 1743, [GBR], in Glasgow, 1753. [NRS.E326.1.172; AC7.46.185]

DENNISTOUN, RICHARD, son of James Dennistoun, a merchant from Glasgow, settled in Hanover County, Virginia, by 1776, a Loyalist, returned to Glasgow, a burgess and guilds-brother of Glasgow in 1785. [NA.AO13.33.124][GBR]

DICK, ANDREW, a shopkeeper in Glasgow, testaments, 1774, Comm. Glasgow. [NRS]

DICK, JAMES, son of Richard Dick a writer in Lanark, minister at St Andrew's, Glasgow, from 1730 until his death in 1737. [F.3.433]

DICK, JANET, relict of Robert Stark a cordiner in Glasgow, testament, 1727, Comm. Glasgow. [NRS]

DICK, WILLIAM, a painter in Glasgow, testament, 1770, Comm. Glasgow. [NRS]

DICKIE, ..., widow of John Glen a merchant in Glasgow, heir to her father Robert Dickie the Deacon of the Wrights there, in 1752. [NRS.SH.1752]

DICKIE, JEAN, heir to her father Robert Dickie the Deacon of the Wrights in Glasgow, [NRS.SH.1751]; widow of William Millar a merchant in Glasgow, testament, 1763, Comm. Glasgow. [NRS]

DICKIE, ROBERT, a wright in Glasgow, 1725. [ERG.V.232]

DICKIE, ROBERT, a merchant in Glasgow, testament, 1729, Comm. Glasgow. [NRS]

DICKSON, ADAM, a merchant in Glasgow, a burgess and guildsbrother of Glasgow in 1756, testament, 1771, Comm. Glasgow. [GBR] [NRS]

DICKSON, DAVID, born 1754, a laborer from Glasgow, to New York, 1774. [NA.T47.12]

DICKSON, JOHN, a merchant in Glasgow, testaments, 1739/1742, Comm. Glasgow. [NRS]

DICKSON, ROBERT, husband of Elizabeth Harvie, a burgess and guilds-brother of Glasgow in 1754, a merchant in Glasgow, 1770. [GBR] [NRS.CS16.1.138]

DINN, or DUNN, MALCOLM, a tailor, husband of Mary Grieve, a burgess and guilds-brother of Glasgow in 1734, [GBR], testament, 1738, Comm. Glasgow. [NRS]

DINNING, ADAM, land laborer in Sandiehills, barony parish of Glasgow, testament, 1727, Comm. Glasgow. [NRS]

The People of Glasgow, 1725-1775

DINNING, JOHN, sometime in Jermiestoun, thereafter in Riddrie, barony parish of Glasgow, testament, 1760, Comm. Glasgow. [NRS]

DINWIDDIE, JOHN, born 1698, a merchant in Glasgow, late in Hanover, King George County, and Rappahannock, Virginia, died 1726 in Glasgow, testament, 1726, Comm. Glasgow. [NRS]

DINWIDDIE, LAURENCE, a merchant, fourth son of the late Robert Dinwiddie a merchant, a burgess and guilds-brother of Glasgow in 1723, [GBR], testament, 1737, Comm. Glasgow. [NRS]

DOBBIE, ISOBEL, spouse to Mathew Herbertson a merchant in Glasgow, testament, 1726, Comm. Glasgow. [NRS]

DOBBIE, JOHN, a carter in Glasgow, testament, 1737, Comm. Glasgow. [NRS]

DOBBIE, ROBERT, a hammerman, former apprentice to William Mackie a hammerman, a burgess and guilds-brother of Glasgow in 1719, [GBR], Glasgow, testament, 1727, Comm. Glasgow. [NRS]

DOBBIE, THOMAS, son in law of Alexander Leggat, a freeman maltman, 1748. [MCG.134]

DOBSON, ROBERT, in Glasgow, 1753. [NRS.E326.1.172]; a teacher of mathematics in Glasgow, a burgess and guildsbrother of Glasgow, 1754; testament, 1774, Comm. Glasgow. [NRS][GBR]

DODDS, JOHN, a baxter, son in law of James Glen, was admitted to the Baxter Incorporation, and as a burgess and guilds-brother of Glasgow in 1743. [IBG.117][GBR]

DONALD, ALEXANDER, son of James Donald in Glasgow, to Virginia in 1760; partner in the Thistle Distillery, Norfolk, pre 1776. [GA][NA.AO12.74.335]

DONALD, ANN, relict of Henry Glen a tobacco spinner in Glasgow, testament, 1735, Comm. Glasgow. [NRS]

DONALD, JAMES, a merchant, husband of Marion Yuill, a burgess and guilds-brother of Glasgow in 1741, [GBR], a merchant and bailie of Glasgow, testaments, 1760/1761, Comm. Glasgow. [NRS]

DONALD, JANET, second daughter of the late James Donald a merchant and bailie of Glasgow, testament, 1761, Comm. Glasgow. [NRS]

DONALD, JOHN, a merchant in Glasgow, a deed, 1749. [NRS.RD2.167.57]

DONALD, JOHN, a sailor in Glasgow, testament, 1774, Comm. Glasgow. [NRS]

DONALDSON, GRIZELL, spouse to Robert Calder a maltman in Glasgow, testament, 1743, Comm. Glasgow. [NRS]

The People of Glasgow, 1725-1775

DONALDSON, ROBERT, in Glasgow, 1753. [NRS.E326.1.172]; a merchant in Glasgow, son of Matthew Donaldson a merchant, a burgess and guilds-brother in 1764, testament, 1767, Comm. Glasgow. [NRS]

DONALDSON, WILLIAM, a merchant in Glasgow, testament, 1732, Comm. Glasgow. [NRS]

DONALDSON, WILLIAM, a merchant in Glasgow, 1748. [NA.AC11.231]

DOUGALL, ADAM, a merchant in Glasgow, testament, 1762, Comm. Glasgow. [NRS]

DOUGALL, JAMES, a merchant in Glasgow, testament, 1735, Comm. Glasgow. [NRS]

DOUGALL, JAMES, son of James Dougall a merchant in Glasgow, a bond, 1748. [NRS.RD3.210.175]

DOUGALL, JAMES, a merchant in Glasgow, 1773. [NRS.NRAS.1892, bundle 79]

DOUGALL, JOHN, a cordiner in Glasgow, son of John Dougall, a cordiner in Glasgow, and his wife Janet Wilson, testament, 1750, Comm. Glasgow. [NRS]

DOUGALL, MARGARET, in Glasgow, testament, 1744, Comm. Glasgow. [NRS]

DOUGAL, THOMAS, a surgeon in Glasgow, 1725. [ERG.V.245]

DOUGALL, Mrs, in Glasgow, 1753. [NRS.E326.1.172]

DOUGLAS, BARBARA, in Glasgow, spouse of Andrew Spreull a writer in Edinburgh, testaments, 1741/1777, Comm. Glasgow. [NRS]

DOUGLAS, ELIZABETH, relict of James Steven a tailor in Glasgow, testament, 1726, Comm. Glasgow. [NRS]

DOUGLAS, JAMES, born 1722, in Glasgow, 1753. [NRS.E326.1.172]; a merchant in Glasgow, settled in Dumfries, Prince William County, Virginia, died 1766, testament, 1769, Comm. Glasgow. [NRS.CS16.1.165][Frederick County deeds .25/357][VMHB.19.94; 22.273][SM.29.55][MAGU]

DOUGLAS, MARGARET, in Glasgow, a deed, 1762. [NRS.RD3.229/2.493]

DOUGLAS, WILLIAM, a sailor in Glasgow, mate of the Mally of Glasgow, testament, 1741, Comm. Glasgow. [NRS]

DOW, JOHN, a teacher at Glasgow Grammar School, 1767, a burgess and guilds-brother of Glasgow in 1769. [ERG.VII.240][GBR.67]

DOWNIE, JAMES, late a land laborer in Carntyne, thereafter in Sandiehills, last in Glasgow, testament, 1775, Comm. Glasgow. [NRS]

DOWNIE, WILLIAM, husband of Margaret Kinniburgh, a hammerman, also as a burgess of Glasgow in 1729 and 1731. [HHG.294][GBR]

The People of Glasgow, 1725-1775

DREGHORN, ALLAN, of Ruchill, a merchant in Glasgow, deed, 1750, [NRS.RD2.167.419]; testament, 1774, Comm. Glasgow. [NRS]

DREGHORN, JANET, heir to her father James Dreghorn a wright in Glasgow, 1752. [NRS.SH.1752]

DREGHORN, ROBERT, a wright, husband of Margaret Dickie, a burgess and guilds-brother of Glasgow in 1703, [GBR], tacksman of coal in the Muir of Gorbals, 1725. [ERG.V.231/232]

DREW, HENRY, a hammerman, 1731. [HHG.294]

DREW, JAMES, son of John Drew a maltman, a freeman maltman, 1731, [MCG.133]; in Glasgow, testament, 1750, Comm. Glasgow. [NRS]

DREW, JOHN, a merchant in Glasgow, testament, 1772, Comm. Glasgow. [NRS]

DREW, ROBERT, from Glasgow, settled in Maryland before 1776. [NRS.CS16.1.168]

DREW, WILLIAM, eldest son of James Drew a maltman, a freeman maltman, 1776. [MCG.133]

DRUMMOND, ANDREW, a dyer in Glasgow, testament, 1739, Comm. Glasgow. [NRS]

DRUMMOND, ANDREW, former apprentice of Patrick Reid maltman, a freeman maltman, and as a burgess and guilds-brother of Glasgow in 1775. [MCG.133][GBR]

DUFF, JOHN, a wright in Glasgow, heir to his uncle John Dunlop a wright there, 1758. [NRS.SH.1758]; testament, 1747, Comm. Glasgow. [NRS]

DUFF, ROBERT, born 1722, a painter in Glasgow, a Jacobite transported in 1747, landed at Port North Potomac, Maryland. [NA.T1.328][P.2.168]

DUNCAN, ALLAN, younger son of William Duncan a hammerman, a burgess and guildsbrother of Glasgow in 1766, a coppersmith in Glasgow, 1773. [Ramshorn MI, Glasgow][GBR]

DUNCAN, ANDREW, a baxter, former apprentice to James Algie a baxter, was admitted to the Baxter Incorporation, also as a burgess and guilds-brother of Glasgow in 1731. [IBG.117][GBR]

DUNCAN, ANDREW, a baxter, former apprentice to Andrew Duncan a baxter, was admitted to the Baxter Incorporation, 1773. [IBG.117]

DUNCAN, ANDREW, a merchant from Glasgow, settled in Worcester, Massachusetts, by 1768, a Loyalist, died 1787. [NA.AO13.24.72-74] [NRS.CS16.1.161]

DUNCAN, JANET, spouse of Alexander Bruce a mealman in Glasgow, testament, 1751, Comm. Glasgow. [NRS]

DUNCAN, JOHN, a baxter, former apprentice to Andrew Scott a baxter, was admitted to the Baxter Incorporation, and as a burgess and guilds-brother of Glasgow in 1745. [IBG.117][GBR]; in Glasgow, 1753. [NRS.E326.1.172]

DUNCAN, JOHN, a brush manufacturer from Glasgow, in Maryland by 1778. [NRS.CS16.1.173/88]

DUNCAN, PATRICK, a baxter, eldest son of John Duncan a baxter, was admitted to the Baxter Incorporation, and as a burgess and guilds-brother of Glasgow in 1769. [IBG.117][GBR]

DUNCAN, ROBERT, from Glasgow, in Boston, 1758. [SCS]

DUNCAN, SAMUEL, a merchant, husband of Marion Corrie, a burgess and guilds-brother of Glasgow in 1743, [GBR], testaments, 1760/1764, Comm. Glasgow. [NRS]

DUNCAN, WILLIAM, junior, a printer in Glasgow, testament, 1765, Comm. Glasgow. [NRS]

DUNCAN, WILLIAM, in Glasgow, 1753. [NRS.E326.1.172]

DUNCAN, WILLIAM, a baxter, former apprentice to Patrick Whyte, and eldest son of the late William Duncan a merchant, was admitted to the Baxter Incorporation, and as a burgess and guilds-brother of Glasgow in 1765. [IBG.117][GBR]

DUNDAS, WALTER, a merchant, former apprentice to John Stark a merchant, a burgess and guilds-brother of Glasgow in 1728, [GBR], testament, 1743, Comm. Glasgow. [NRS]

DUNLOP, ALEXANDER, Professor of Greek at Glasgow University, testaments, 1747/1750/1751, Comm. Glasgow. [NRS]

DUNLOP, ANN, spouse of John Muir late an Excise officer in Glasgow, testament, 1733, Comm. Glasgow. [NRS]

DUNLOP, ARCHIBALD, a merchant from Glasgow, emigrated in 1762, settled at Cabin Point, James River, Virginia. [GA][NRS.CS.GMB51; AC7.51; CS16.1.134]

DUNLOP, COLIN, a merchant, fourth son of James Dunlop of Garnkirk a merchant, a burgess and guilds-brother of Glasgow in 1741, [GBR], a deed, 1749. [NRS.RD4.176/1.23]; Dean of Guild of Glasgow, 1759. [ERG.VI.546]

DUNLOP, COLIN, a merchant from Glasgow, emigrated to the Chesapeake before 1776. [NA.AO13.28.275; AO13.102.58][NRS.GD1.572.33.1-31]

The People of Glasgow, 1725-1775

DUNLOP, DAVID, was admitted to the Skinners Craft, 1753. [SFG.267]

DUNLOP, ELIZABETH, relict of George Hutcheson a merchant in Glasgow, and their daughter Elizabeth, spouse of James Wotherspoon a merchant in Glasgow, testament, 1748, Comm. Glasgow. [NRS]

DUNLOP, GEORGE, a baxter, eldest son of Robert Dunlop, was admitted to the Baxter Incorporation in 1740, and as a burgess and guilds-brother of Glasgow in 1738. [IBG.117][GBR]

DUNLOP, ISOBEL, relict of Thomas Pollock of Balgray, a resident of Glasgow, testaments, 1733/1735, Comm. Glasgow. [NRS]

DUNLOP, JAMES, a tobacconist and merchant in Glasgow, testament, 1736, Comm. Glasgow. [NRS]

DUNLOP, JAMES, of Househill, Glasgow, testaments, 1738/1739, Comm. Glasgow. [NRS]

DUNLOP, JAMES, a merchant in Glasgow, 1746, 1765, in America 1769-1785. [NRS.E504.28.2; AC7.51; NRAS.0631.4; CS16.1.134/141; GD1.151.1; GD1.850.43][ERG.VII.446]

DUNLOP, JAMES, sometime in Edinburgh thereafter in Glasgow, testament, 1750, Comm. Glasgow. [NRS]

DUNLOP, JAMES, a maltman in Glasgow, testaments, 1751/1757, Comm. Glasgow. [NRS]

DUNLOP, JAMES, son of the late Alexander Dunlop, Professor of Greek at the University of Glasgow, and his second wife Abigail Mure, testament, 1751, Comm. Glasgow. [NRS]

DUNLOP, JAMES, born 1757 son of David Dunlop, a merchant in Glasgow, settled on the James River, Virginia, 1773, a Loyalist, removed to Quebec in 1779. [DCB][NRS.SH.1799]

DUNLOP, JAMES, in Glasgow, 1753. [NRS.E326.1.172]

DUNLOP, JAMES, in Glasgow, a deed, 1775. [NRS.RD4.234.782]

DUNLOP, JOHN, a merchant from Glasgow, settled in Virginia, died before 1751. [NRS.RD4.177.480]

DUNLOP, JOHN, of Garnkirk, a merchant in Glasgow, in Virginia by 1776. [NRS.CS16.1.168]

DUNLOP, ROBERT, a merchant, second son of James Dunlop of Garnkirk, . a burgess and guilds-brother of Glasgow in 1734, [GBR], a deed of factory, 1750. [NRS.RD2.168.10]

The People of Glasgow, 1725-1775

DUNLOP, THOMAS, a merchant in Glasgow, 1769. [NRS.CS16.1.134]
DUNLOP, WILLIAM, Principal of the College of Glasgow, testament, 1734, Comm. Glasgow. [NRS]
DUNLOP, WILLIAM, from Glasgow, in Boston, 1744, 1751. [SCS]
DUNLOP, WILLIAM, in Glasgow, 1753. [NRS.E326.1.172]; a mason in Glasgow, testament, 1772, Comm. Glasgow. [NRS]
DUNMORE, JOHN, born 1763, from Glasgow, to Salem, New England, 1775. [NA.T47.12]
DUNMORE, MARY, born 1748, from Glasgow, to Salem, New England, 1775. [NA.T47.12]
DUNMORE, ROBERT, a merchant, a burgess and guilds-brother of Glasgow in 1743, [GBR], testament, 1744, Comm. Glasgow. [NRS]
DUNN, ALEXANDER, a merchant in Glasgow, testament, 1769, Comm. Glasgow. [NRS]
DUNN, JAMES, a yarn merchant in Glasgow, testaments, 1771/1772, Comm. Glasgow. [NRS]
DUNN, WILLIAM, a baxter, former apprentice to John Duncan, was admitted to the Baxter Incorporation, 1770. [IBG.117]
DUNSMUIR, THOMAS, a merchant, a burgess and guilds-brother of Glasgow in 1735, [GBR], 1753. [NRS.E326.1.172]
DUNWOODIE, JANE, in Glasgow, 1753. [NRS.E326.1.172]
DYKES, JAMES, a cabinet-maker and thief from Glasgow, transported to the colonies in 1774. [AJ.1374]
DYKES, WILLIAM, a merchant, a burgess and guilds-brother of Glasgow in 1724, [GBR], manager of the Correction House, 1725; testament, 1744, Comm. Glasgow. [NRS] [ERG.V.235]
EASSON, JOHN, a writer in Glasgow, testament, 1746, Comm. Glasgow. [NRS]
EASSON, JOHN, procurator fiscal of Glasgow, 1775. [ERG.VII.455]
EASTON, DAVID, a merchant, former apprentice to John Currie merchant, a burgess and guilds-brother of Glasgow in 1751, [GBR]; in Glasgow, 1753. [NRS.E326.1.172]
ECCLES, WILLIAM, sometime carpenter of the Royal Widow of Glasgow, testament, 1761, Comm. Glasgow. [NRS]
EDMOND, JAMES, a baxter, former apprentice to Alexander Balinie and to John Auchincloss baxters, was admitted to the Baxter Incorporation, 1729, also

The People of Glasgow, 1725-1775

as a burgess and guilds-brother of Glasgow in 1729, [GBR]; late Deacon of the Baxters in Glasgow, testament, 1752, Comm. Glasgow. [NRS][IBG#118]

EDMOND, JAMES, a baxter, former apprentice and eldest son of the late James Edmond a baxter, was admitted to the Baxter Incorporation and as a burgess and guilds-brother of Glasgow in 1760. [IBG#118][GBR]

EDMOND, WALTER, a maltman, husband of Janet Craig, a burgess and guilds-brother of Glasgow in 1726, [GBR], testament, 1743, Comm. Glasgow. [NRS]

EDMONDS, ELIZABETH, relict of Rice Johns a tanner in Glasgow, testament, 1755, Comm. Glasgow. [NRS]

EGLINTON, WILLIAM, a rioter in Glasgow, transported to the colonies in 1751. [AJ.172]

ELDER, JOHN, born 1752, a smith from Glasgow, to New York, 1775. [NA.T47.12]

ESPLIN, ELIZABETH, spouse to John Alexander a tailor in Glasgow, testament, 1761, Comm. Glasgow. [NRS]

EWING, DANIEL, a merchant, husband of Katherine Yuill, a burgess and guilds-brother of Glasgow in 1727, [GBR], testaments, 1729/1730/1732, Comm. Glasgow. [NRS]

EWING, DAVID, a wright, eldest son of the late David Ewing a wright, a burgess and guilds-brother of Glasgow in 1742, [GBR], heir to his grandmother Beatrix Gibson wife of William Morton, a pipemaker there, 1758. [NRS.SH.1758]

EWING, JAMES, from Glasgow, in Boston, 1748. [SCS]

EWING, ROBERT, a baxter, former apprentice and eldest son of William Ewing a baxter, was admitted to the Baxter Incorporation and as a burgess and guilds-brother of Glasgow in 1769. [IBG#118][GBR]

EWING, WILLIAM, a baxter, former apprentice to John Paterson a baxter, was admitted to the Baxter Incorporation, and as a burgess and guilds-brother of Glasgow in 1747. [IBG#118][GBR]

FAIRIE, DAVID, Collector of the Red Dye society of Glasgow, 1759. [ERG.VI.547]

FALCONER, GEORGE, third son of Robert Falconer a maltman, a freeman maltman, and as a burgess and guilds-brother of Glasgow in 1743-1744. [MCG.134][GBR]

FALCONER, JAMES, a rioter in Glasgow, transported to Barbados, 1726. [NA.T53.33.293; SP54.16.38/126]

The People of Glasgow, 1725-1775

FALCONER, ROBERT, second son of Walter Falconer a maltman, a freeman maltman, 1732. [MCG.134]

FAULDS, JOHN, former servant to John Orr in Borrowfield, residing in Glasgow, testament, 1738, Comm. Glasgow. [NRS]

FAWSYDE, HEW, a merchant in Glasgow, testament, 1725, Comm. Glasgow. [NRS]

FELL, ROBERT, a merchant, a burgess and guilds-brother of Glasgow in 1717, [GBR], testaments, 1726/1727, Comm. Glasgow. [NRS]

FERGUS, CHRISTIAN, a shopkeeper in Glasgow, testament, 1743, Comm. Glasgow. [NRS]

FERGUS, JAMES, born 1750, a weaver from Glasgow, to New York, 1774. [NA.T47.12]

FERGUS, JANET, relict of James Brysson a workman in Glasgow, and her sister-german Jean Fergus, testament, 1750, Comm. Glasgow. [NRS]

FERGUS, WILLIAM, a baxter, former apprentice to Andrew Menzies a baxter, was admitted to the Baxter Incorporation and as a burgess and guilds-brother of Glasgow in 1775. [IBG#119][GBR]

FERGUSON, FERGUS, in Glasgow, 1753. [NRS.E326.1.172]

FERGUSON, JAMES, a weaver in Glasgow, testament, 1725, Comm. Glasgow. [NRS]

FERGUSON, JANET, in Glasgow, testament, 1742, Comm. Glasgow. [NRS]

FERGUSON, JOHN, a hatter in Glasgow, testament, 1745, Comm. Glasgow. [NRS]

FERGUSON, JOHN, a stay-maker in Glasgow, testaments, 1763/1772, Comm. Glasgow. [NRS]

FERGUSON, MARGARET, relict of Patrick Wilson a cordiner in Glasgow, testaments, 1745/1751, Comm. Glasgow. [NRS]

FERRIER, CATHERINE, wife of George Menzies a manufacturer in Glasgow, heir to her father James Ferrier in Wallacetoun. [NRS.SH.1751]

FERRIER, CHRISTIAN, wife of Robert Gray a baxter in Glasgow, heir to her father James Ferrier in Wallacetoun. [NRS.SH.1751]

FERRIER, JEAN, wife of Robert Mackin a manufacturer in Glasgow, heir to her father James Ferrier in Wallacetoun. [NRS.SH.1751]

FINLAY, COLIN, a shipmaster in Glasgow, testaments, 1729/1735, Comm. Glasgow. [NRS]

The People of Glasgow, 1725-1775

FINLAY, EDWARD, a merchant in Glasgow, testament, 1768, Comm. Glasgow. [NRS]

FINLAY, ELIZABETH, relict of Robert Barr a cordiner in Glasgow, testament, 1743, Comm. Glasgow. [NRS]

FINDLAY, GEORGE, a maltman, son in law of David Tennant a maltman, a freeman maltman and a burgess and guilds-brother of Glasgow in 1772. [MCG.137][GBR]

FINLAY, JOHN, a plasterer in Glasgow, testament, 1725, Comm. Glasgow. [NRS]

FINLAY, JOHN, a merchant in Glasgow, testament, 1738, Comm. Glasgow. [NRS]

FINLAY, JOHN, in Glasgow, 1753. [NRS.E326.1.172]

FINLAY, ROBERT, minister at Ramshorn, Glasgow, from 1756 to 1783. [F.3.439]

FINLAY, ROBERT, son of Reverend Robert Finlay in Glasgow, settled in Maryland before 1772. [NRS.B10.15.7553]

FINLAY, ROBERT, Master of Works in Glasgow, 1775. [ERG.VII.454]

FINDLAY, WILLIAM, master of the Red Dye Society of Glasgow, 1759. [ERG.VI.547]

FINLAYSON, ALEXANDER, a clerk in Glasgow, 1725. [ERG.V.222]

FINLAYSON, ALEXANDER, in Glasgow, 1753. [NRS.E326.1.172]

FISHER, ARCHIBALD, from Glasgow, in Boston, 1758. [SCS]

FISHER, Reverend JAMES, born 1697, died 1775, husband of Jean Erskine, daughter of Reverend Ebenezer Erskine, born 1706, died 1771. [Ramshorn MI, Glasgow]

FISHER, JOHN, in Glasgow, a deed, 1769. [NRS.RD4.207.882]

FLEMING, AGNES, relict of James Fairrie a merchant and bailie of Glasgow, testament, 1726, Comm. Glasgow. [NRS]

FLEMING, CHRISTIAN, spouse of John Eadie a corkcutter in Glasgow, testament, 1768, Comm. Glasgow. [NRS]

FLEMING, JAMES, in Glasgow, 1753. [NRS.E326.1.172]

FLEMING, JEAN, relict of Hugh Crauford a merchant in Glasgow and late spouse of the deceased Thomas Orr a writer there, testament, 1739, Comm. Glasgow. [NRS]

FLEMING, JOHN, a town officer of Glasgow, 1725. [ERG.V.241]

FLEMING, JOHN, a merchant in Glasgow, 1729. [Ramshorn MI, Glasgow]

FLEMING, JOHN, a maltman in Glasgow, 1763. [ERG.VII.116]

FLEMING, JOHN, a baxter, former apprentice to James Yuill a baxter, and eldest son of the late William Fleming a barber, was admitted to the Baxter Incorporation and as a burgess and guilds-brother of Glasgow in 1763. [IBG#119][GBR]

FLEMING, ROBERT, a shop-keeper in Glasgow, testament, 1747, Comm. Glasgow. [NRS]

FLEMING, ROBERT, a weaver, son –in-law of William Jamieson a skinner, was admitted to the Skinners Craft and as a burgess and guilds-brother of Glasgow in 1753. [SFG.267][GBR]

FLEMING, WILLIAM, water bailie of Glasgow, 1725; a coppersmith in Glasgow, deeds, 1750/1754, [NRS.RD2.168.238; RD4.218.777]; 1753. [NRS.E326.1.172] [ERG.V.243; VII.311]

FLEMING, WILLIAM, a wright in Glasgow, 1759. [ERG.VI.540]; a burgess of Irvine, 1762. [AA]

FLEMING, WILLIAM, a baxter, former apprentice to John Ure a baxter, was admitted to the Baxter Incorporation, also as a burgess and guilds-brother of Glasgow in 1769. [IBG#119][GBR]

FLEMING, WILLIAM, born 1758, a weaver from Glasgow, to New York, 1774. [NA.T47.12]

FLEMING, Mrs, in Glasgow, 1753. [NRS.E326.1.172]

FOGO, HENRY, a merchant, husband of Marion Tennant, a burgess and guilds-brother of Glasgow in 1726, [GBR], 1749. [NRS.AC9.1658]

FOGO, JAMES, son of James Fogo, a merchant from Glasgow, settled in Clarendon, Jamaica, by 1771. [NRS.B10.15.7435]

FOGO, JOHN, a writer in Glasgow, testament, 1768, Comm. Glasgow. [NRS]

FOGO, MARGARET, relict of Robert Clarkson feuar at Cowdingstone, late in Glasgow, testament, 1737, Comm. Glasgow. [NRS]

FOGO, MARGARET, relict of Walter Blair of Camoquhile, resident of Glasgow, testament, 1748, Comm. Glasgow. [NRS]

FOGO, MARY, in Glasgow, 1753. [NRS.E326.1.172]

FOGO, WILLIAM, a merchant, husband of Agnes Campbell, a burgess and guilds-brother of Glasgow in 1720, [GBR], 1745. [NRS.AC9.1672]

FOGO, Mrs, in Glasgow, 1753. [NRS.E326.1.172]

FORBES, WILLIAM, Professor of Law at the University of Glasgow, testaments, 1745/1751, Comm. Glasgow. [NRS]

The People of Glasgow, 1725-1775

FORREST, JOHN, a merchant in Glasgow, a deed, 1750. [NRS.RD3.210.393]

FORRESTER, AGNES, wife of Henry Oswald an Excise officer in Glasgow, testament, 1771, Comm. Glasgow. [NRS]

FORSYTH, HENRY, a sugar refiner in Glasgow, testament, 1759, Comm. Glasgow. [NRS]

FORSYTH, JOHN, a baxter, former apprentice to Robert McAulay a baxter, was admitted to the Baxter Incorporation, also as a burgess and guilds-brother of Glasgow in 1725. [IBG#119][GBR]

FORSYTH, JOHN, a weaver, former apprentice to John Walker a weaver, a burgess and guilds-brother of Glasgow in 1750, [GBR], heir to his father John Forsyth a comb-maker there in 1754. [NRS.SH.1754]

FOULIS, JAMES, son of Andrew Foulis in Glasgow, a clergyman educated at the University of Glasgow in 1734, emigrated to Virginia in 1750. [EMA.28][MAGU.13]

FOWLER, ALEXANDER, a baxter in Glasgow, testament, 1767, Comm. Glasgow. [NRS]

FRASER, JAMES, a cooper in Glasgow, testament, 1751, Comm. Glasgow. [NRS]

FREEBAIRN, ROBERT, a cordiner, former apprentice to Robert Finlay a cordiner, a burgess and guilds-brother of Glasgow in 1733, [GBR]; in 1763. [ERG.VII.116]

FREELAND, JOHN, overman of the weavers of Caltoun in the barony parish of Glasgow, testament, 1730, Comm. Glasgow. [NRS]

FRENCH, DAVID, only son of the late Robert French, a maltman in Glasgow, and his spouse Bethia Crawford, testament, 1739, Comm. Glasgow. [NRS]

FRENCH, JAMES, a merchant, husband of Eupham Scott, a burgess and guilds-brother of Glasgow in 1731, [GBR]; in Glasgow, 1753. [NRS.E326.1.172]

FULTON, HUGH, a surgeon apothecary in Neilson, a burgess and guilds-brother of Glasgow in 1701, [GBR], testament, 1728, Comm. Glasgow. [NRS]

FULTON, JAMES, a coppersmith, a burgess and guilds-brother of Glasgow in 1747, [GBR], testament, 1756, Comm. Glasgow. [NRS]

FULTON, JOHN, a baxter, husband of Elizabeth Allan, and former apprentice to William Findlay a baxter, was admitted to the Baxter Incorporation, and as a burgess and guilds-brother of Glasgow in 1730. [IBG#119][GBR]

FULTON, JOHN, a changekeeper in Glasgow, testament, 1757, Comm. Glasgow. [NRS]

The People of Glasgow, 1725-1775

FULTON, ROBERT, a copper-smith in Glasgow, 1725; testaments, 1744/1746/1749, Comm. Glasgow. [NRS] [ERG.V.232]

FYFE, JAMES, a barber in Anderstoun, barony parish of Glasgow, testament, 1734, Comm Glasgow. [NRS]

GALBRAITH, ARCHIBALD, from Glasgow, in Boston, 1758. [SCS]

GALBRAITH, JAMES, a baxter, former apprentice to James Gray, was admitted to the Baxter Incorporation, and as a burgess and guilds-brother of Glasgow in 1749. [IBG#120][GBR]; son of John Galbraith, a baxter from Glasgow, to Quebec before 1773. [NRS.CS.GMB.218; AC.GMB.40]

GALBRAITH, WILLIAM, in Glasgow, testament, 1742, Comm Glasgow. [NRS]

GALBREATH, THOMAS, a merchant from Glasgow, to New York before 1777. [NRS.B10.12.4]

GALIER, PATRICK, in Glasgow, 1753. [NRS.E326.1.172]

GALLOWAY, ALEXANDER, a baxter, former apprentice to William Ewing a baxter, was admitted to the Baxter Incorporation also as a burgess and guilds-brother of Glasgow in 1769. [IBG#120][GBR]; testament, 1773, Comm Glasgow. [NRS]

GALLOWAY, JAMES, a merchant in Glasgow, heir to his brother Robert Galloway a merchant there in 1750. [NRS.SH.1750]

GALLOWAY, ROBERT, a baxter, son in law of James Anderson a baxter, was admitted to the Baxter Incorporation and as a burgess and guilds-brother of Glasgow in 1772. [IBG#120][GBR]

GARDNER, ANDREW, in Glasgow, 1753. [NRS.E326.1.172]; a merchant in Glasgow, testament, 1760, Comm. Glasgow. [NRS]

GARDNER, JAMES, a mealman, sometime in Glasgow, testament, 1745, Comm Glasgow. [NRS]

GARDNER, JAMES, the elder, a merchant in Glasgow, testament, 1747, Comm Glasgow. [NRS]

GARDNER, JAMES, a horse-setter, son-in-law of Robert Young a skinner, was admitted to the Skinners Craft and as a burgess and guilds-brother of Glasgow in 1760. [SFG.268][GBR]

GARDNER, JOHN, a baxter, former apprentice to Andrew Scott a baxter, was admitted to the Baxter Incorporation, 1725. [IBG#119]; testament, 1742, Comm Glasgow. [NRS]

The People of Glasgow, 1725-1775

GARDNER, JOHN, son in law of Hugh Tennant a maltman, a freeman maltman in 1774, also as a burgess and guilds-brother of Glasgow in 1775. [MCG.136][GBR]

GARDNER, PETER, a merchant in Glasgow, testament, 1759, Comm Glasgow. [NRS]

GARDNER, ROBERT, a wigmaker from Glasgow, settled in Boston by 1729, in Boston, 1732. [Imm.NE.67][SCS]

GARDNER, THOMAS, a comb-maker in Glasgow, testament, 1773, Comm Glasgow. [NRS]

GARDNER, THOMAS, born in Glasgow 1772, son of James Gardner and his wife Margaret Wilson, a merchant in Savanna, Georgia, died in Sandhills, Augusta, Georgia, 1822. [Georgia Republican.27.8.1822][Glasgow Parish Register]

GARDNER, WILLIAM, born 1750, a wright from Glasgow, to Philadelphia, 1774. [NA.T47.12]

GARLAND, GEORGE, born 1750, a barber from Glasgow, to New York, 1775. [NA.T47.12]

GARLAND, WILLIAM, in Glasgow, an indenture, 1773. [NRS.RD4.218.33]

GARTSHORE, JOHN, a merchant, former apprentice to Laurence Dinwiddie a merchant, a burgess and guilds-brother of Glasgow in 1720, [GBR], there in 1730. [NRS.AC9.6415]

GARVEN, THOMAS, a barber in Glasgow, testament, 1767, Comm Glasgow. [NRS]

GAVIN, JAMES, a baxter, former apprentice to James Baird was admitted to the Baxter Incorporation, and a burgess and guilds-brother of Glasgow in 1737. [IBG#120][GBR]

GAVIN, JOHN, a baxter, eldest son of James Gavin a mealman, and former apprentice to John Wright was admitted to the Baxter Incorporation, and as a burgess and guilds-brother of Glasgow in 1739. [IBG#120][GBR]; testament, 1743, Comm Glasgow. [NRS]

GAY, MARION, relict of Robert Sym a hammerman in Glasgow, testament, 1727, Comm Glasgow. [NRS]

GEILLS, ANDREW, a merchant in Glasgow, to Virginia by 1744. [NRS.B10.15.5959]

GEMMILL, Dame LILIAS, in Glasgow, relict of Sir Hugh Montgomerie of Skermorlie, testament, 1756, Comm Glasgow. [NRS]

The People of Glasgow, 1725-1775

GEMMILL, WILLIAM, a weaver, husband of Agnes Armour, a burgess and guilds-brother of Glasgow in 1724, [GBR], testament, 1747, Comm Glasgow. [NRS]

GENTLEMAN, DAVID, a merchant, husband of Elizabeth Chrystie, a burgess and guilds-brother of Glasgow in 1731. [GBR]

GIBB, ARCHIBALD, a baxter, former apprentice to Thomas Scott a baxter, was admitted to the Baxter Incorporation and as a burgess and guilds-brother of Glasgow in 1773. [IBG#120][GBR]

GIBB, MARGARET, relict of William Tulip a mason in Glasgow, testament, 1766, Comm Glasgow. [NRS]

GIBSON, AGNES, relict of George Gilchrist a merchant in Glasgow, testament, 1753, Comm Glasgow. [NRS]

GIBSON, ANDREW, merchant and shipmaster in Glasgow, son of the late Walter Gibson a merchant and Provost of Glasgow, testament, 1728, Comm Glasgow. [NRS]

GIBSON, JAMES, a merchant from Glasgow, emigrated before 1731, settled at Pungataigue Creek, Accomack County, Virginia. [NRS.AC7.36/328]

GIBSON, JOHN, master weaver of the Incorporation of Weavers, 1725. [OGW#108]

GIBSON, JOHN, son in law of Patrick Johnston a maltman, a freeman maltman, 1736. [MCG.132]

GIBSON, JOHN, a merchant in Glasgow, testaments, 1752, Comm Glasgow. [NRS]

GIBSON, JOHN, a factor from Glasgow, settled in Colchester, Virginia, by 1770. [GA.779.21]

GIBSON, PATRICK, in Glasgow, a bond, 1758. [NRS.RD2.207.1252]

GILCHRIST, ANDREW, son of George Gilchrist and his wife Agnes Gibson, a merchant in Glasgow, emigrated to America by 1733, settled in Accomack County, Virginia, testament, Comm. Glasgow. [NRS.CC9.7.62]

GILCHRIST, JAMES, a merchant in Glasgow, testament, 1770, Comm. Glasgow. [NRS]

GILCHRIST, JOHN, son of George Gilchrist and his wife Agnes Gibson, in Glasgow, settled in Accomack County, Virginia, died 1751, probate 1751 Accomack County.

GILCHRIST, ROBERT, a merchant in Glasgow, later in Virginia, 1750. [NRS.AC9.1746/1764]

GILCHRIST, WILLIAM, in Glasgow, 1753. [NRS.E326.1.172]

GILFILLAN, WILLIAM, second son of the late James Gilfillan a merchant, a burgess and guilds-brother of Glasgow in 1766, testament, 1775, Comm. Glasgow. [NRS][GBR]

GILHAIGGIE, JANE, in Glasgow, 1753. [NRS.E326.1.172]

GILLHAGIE, WILLIAM, of Kennyhill, in Glasgow, 1725. [ERG.V.232]

GILLESPIE, ALEXANDER, a merchant, former apprentice to John Baxter a merchant, a burgess and guilds-brother of Glasgow in 1750. [GBR]

GILLESPIE, ALEXANDER, a cork-cutter in Glasgow, testament, 1765, Comm. Glasgow. [NRS]

GILLESPIE, JAMES, a merchant and a clerk of the Easter Sugar Works of Glasgow, testament, 1744, Comm. Glasgow. [NRS]

GILLESPIE, JAMES, a merchant in Glasgow, testament, 1774, Comm. Glasgow. [NRS]

GILLESPIE, JOHN, in Glasgow, 1753. [NRS.E326.1.172]; a merchant in Glasgow, testaments, 1762/1767, Comm. Glasgow. [NRS]

GILLIES, DAVID, a cow-feeder in Glasgow, testament, 1761, Comm. Glasgow. [NRS]

GILLIES, JOHN, born 1713 son of John Gillies minister at Careston, minister at The Blackfriars in Glasgow from 1742 to his death in 1796. [F.3.399]

GILLIES, MARY, wife of James Smith a weaver in Glasgow, and daughter of Thomas Gillies and his spouse Mary Smith in Gorbals, testament, 1769, Comm. Glasgow. [NRS]

GILLIES, ROBERT MCLAURIN, born 1754, son of Reverend John Gillies and his wife Elizabeth McLaurin, educated at Glasgow University, a merchant from Glasgow, settled in Jamaica, died there 1778. [MAGU][F.3.399][Car.4.15]

GILMOR, WILLIAM, a baxter, former apprentice to Zachary Allason a baxter, was admitted to the Baxter Incorporation, and as a burgess and guilds-brother of Glasgow in 1728/1730. [IBG#119][GBR]

GILMOUR, AGNES, spouse to William MacLean a merchant in Glasgow, testament, 1740, Comm. Glasgow. [NRS]

GILMOUR, ALEXANDER, born 1729, a weaver from Glasgow, to Philadelphia, 1774. [NA.T47.12]

GILMOUR, JOHN, late Deacon of the Fleshers in Glasgow, testaments, 1725/1735, Comm. Glasgow. [NRS]

GILMOUR, JOHN, a sailor in Glasgow, testament, 1736, Comm. Glasgow. [NRS]

GILMOUR, JOHN, in Glasgow, 1753. [NRS.E326.1.172]; a book-seller in Glasgow, 1759; a bookbinder in Glasgow, testament, 1773, Comm. Glasgow. [NRS] [ERG.VI.549]

GILMOUR, MATHEW, a hammerman, a guilds-brother of Glasgow in 1692, [GBR], a coppersmith and bailie of Glasgow, 1725; testament, 1730, Comm. Glasgow. [NRS] [ERG.V.243]

GILMOUR, MATTHEW, a hammerman, second son of the late Matthew Gilmour a hammerman, a burgess and guilds-brother of Glasgow in 1731, [GBR][HHG.294]; testament, 1755, Comm. Glasgow. [NRS]

GILZEAN, THOMAS, a merchant in Glasgow, son in law of Donald Govan a merchant, a burgess and guilds-brother of Glasgow in 1763, [GBR], testament, 1771, Comm. Glasgow. [NRS]

GIRDWOOD, ALEXANDER, a merchant in Glasgow, a burgess and guilds-brother of Glasgow in 1764, [GBR]; 1771. [NRS.CS16.1.143]

GLASSFORD, JAMES, a merchant, second son of the late James Glassford a merchant, a burgess and guilds-brother of Glasgow in 1734, [GBR], in Glasgow, 1753. [NRS.E326.1.172]

GLASSFORD, JAMES, a merchant from Glasgow, to Quebec in 1760, later in Boston by 1763 and in Norfolk, Virginia. [GA][SCS][NRS.CS16.1.98/168]

GLASSFORD, JOHN, a merchant, third son of the late James Glassford a merchant, a burgess and guilds-brother of Glasgow in 1737, [GBR], in Glasgow, 1753. [NRS.E326.1.172; CS16.1.168][NA.AO12.9.35]

GLASSFORD, JOHN, of Dougalston, born 1715, died 1783. [Ramshorn MI, Glasgow]

GLASSFORD, JOHN, born 1763, eldest son of John Glassford and his wife Anne Nisbet, died 1777. [Ramshorn MI, Glasgow]

GLASSFORD, REBECCA, born 1759, daughter of John Glassford and his wife Anne Nisbet, died 1780. [Ramshorn MI, Glasgow]

GLASSFORD, ROBERT, a merchant from Glasgow, settled in St Kitts and Grenada before 1764. [GA.T-MJ]

GLEN, ABIGAIL, relict of James Hunter a merchant in Glasgow, testament, 1729, Comm. Glasgow. [NRS]

GLEN, AGNES, relict of Robert Mauchline late Deacon of the Weavers in Glasgow, testament, 1736, Comm. Glasgow. [NRS]

GLEN, ALLAN, tailor and innkeeper in Glasgow, and his spouse Margaret Steven, testament, 1740, Comm. Glasgow. [NRS]

GLEN, ARCHIBALD, a merchant in Glasgow, testament, 1730, Comm. Glasgow. [NRS]

GLEN, ARCHIBALD, late Deacon of the Weavers in Glasgow, testament, 1735, Comm. Glasgow. [NRS]

GLEN, DAVID, son of George Glen at Ruchill, now in Glasgow, brother-german of the late Ninian Hill a merchant in Glasgow, testament, 1768, Comm. Glasgow. [NRS]

GLEN, JAMES, the younger, a baxter and messenger in Glasgow, testament, 1739, Comm. Glasgow. [NRS]

GLEN, JAMES, in Glasgow, 1753. [NRS.E326.1.172]; a goldsmith and bailie of Glasgow, testaments, 1759/1764, Comm. Glasgow. [NRS]

GLEN, JOHN, a merchant in Glasgow, testament, 1749, Comm. Glasgow. [NRS]

GLEN, NINIAN, a merchant, second son of William Glen in Ruchill, a burgess and guilds-brother of Glasgow in 1731, [GBR],testament, 1766, Comm. Glasgow. [NRS]

GORDON, ALEXANDER, in Glasgow, 1753; in Boston, 1754. [NRS.E326.1.172; AC7.46/101; CS16.1.107]

GORDON, GEORGE, a merchant in Glasgow, testament, 1766, Comm. Glasgow. [NRS]

GORDON, JOHN, a surgeon in Glasgow, 1725. [ERG.V.245]

GORDON, JOHN, in Glasgow, 1753. [NRS.E326.1.172]

GORDON, WILLIAM, a merchant in Glasgow, 1740s. [NRS.AC40.166]

GOSS, JANET, spouse of William Paterson a tobacconist in Glasgow, testament, 1744, Comm. Glasgow. [NRS]

GOVAN, ARCHIBALD, a merchant in Glasgow, testaments, 1743/1746, Comm. Glasgow. [NRS]

GOVAN, ARCHIBALD, a merchant in Glasgow, and his wife Janet Colhoun, testament, 1748, Comm. Glasgow. [NRS]

GOVAN, CHRISTIAN, from Glasgow, wife of James Grindlay, settled in Charleston, South Carolina, dead by 1777, testament, 1777, Comm. Glasgow. [NRS.CC9.7.70]

The People of Glasgow, 1725-1775

GOVAN, DONALD, of Cameron, a merchant in Glasgow, testament, 1736, Comm. Glasgow. [NRS]

GOVAN, GEORGE, a cooper in Glasgow, testament, 1726, Comm. Glasgow. [NRS]

GOVAN, GEORGE, a town officer of Glasgow, testament, 1767, Comm. Glasgow. [NRS]

GOVAN, JOHN, a workman in Glasgow, testament, 1740, Comm. Glasgow. [NRS]

GOVAN, MARTHA, relict of James Pollock a maltman in Glasgow, testament, 1747, Comm. Glasgow. [NRS]

GOW, JOHN, a merchant in Glasgow, testament, 1736, Comm. Glasgow. [NRS]

GOW, MARY, in Glasgow, testament, 1742, Comm. Glasgow. [NRS]

GOW, PETER, a baxter, former apprentice to John Watson a baxter, was admitted to the Baxter Incorporation, and as a burgess and guilds-brother of Glasgow in 1749. [IBG#120][GBR]

GRAHAME, ADAM, a jeweller and goldsmith, a burgess and guilds-brother of Glasgow in 1763, [GBR]; in Glasgow, 1770. [ERG.VII.311]

GRAHAME, ALEXANDER, from Glasgow, in Boston 1747. [SCS]

GRAHAME, ALEXANDER, late at the miln of Buchanan, then a vintner in Glasgow, 1770. [ERG.VII.311]

GRAHAM, ALLAN, a merchant in Glasgow, 1770. [ERG.VII.311]

GRAHAM, ANDREW, in Glasgow, 1753. [NRS.E326.1.172]; a manufacturer in Glasgow, testament, 1774, Comm. Glasgow. [NRS]

GRAHAM, ANN, spouse of John Oliphant a manufacturer in Glasgow, testament, 1771, Comm. Glasgow. [NRS]

GRAHAM, DANIEL, a workman in Glasgow, 1770. [ERG.VII.311]

GRAHAM, DUNCAN, a burgess and guilds-brother of Glasgow in 1757, [GBR]; a merchant in Glasgow, 1770. [ERG.VII.311]

GRAHAM, ELIZABETH, in Glasgow, 1753. [NRS.E326.1.172]

GRAHAME, GEORGE, an Episcopalian clergyman in Glasgow, 1730-1759. [NRS.NRAS.2704.43.60]

GRAHAM, GEORGE, a baxter, former apprentice to John Auchencloss a baxter, was admitted to the Baxter Incorporation, and a burgess and guilds-brother of Glasgow in 1740. [IBG#120][GBR]

GRAHAM, HENRY, a merchant in Glasgow, 1770; a former apprentice of Messrs Laurence Dinwiddie, Patrick Nisbet and Robert Dinwiddie jr, partners of the Delft Manufactory in Glasgow, a burgess and guilds-brother of Glasgow in 1773. [ERG.VII.311][GBR]

GRAHAM, JAMES, Deacon of the Cordiners in Glasgow, 1725. [ERG.V.237]

GRAHAM, JAMES, of Kilmannan, a resident of Glasgow, testament, 1746, Comm. Glasgow. [NRS]

GRAHAM, JAMES, of the Coffee House in Glasgow, 1753. [NRS.E326.1.172]

GRAHAM, JAMES, junior, a tailor in Glasgow, 1770. [ERG.VII.311]

GRAHAM, JAMES, a writer in Glasgow, 1770. [ERG.VII.311]

GRAHAM, JAMES, a vintner in Glasgow, 1770, [ERG.VII.311]; testaments, 1772/1779, Comm. Glasgow. [NRS]

GRAHAM, JAMES, a gardener in Glasgow, 1770. [ERG.VII.311]

GRAHAM, JAMES, a baxter, former apprentice to Walter Graham, was admitted to the Baxter Incorporation, 1773. [IBG#120]

GRAHAM, JOHN, in Glasgow, only son of the late John Graham, Provost of Glasgow, testament, 1731, Comm. Glasgow. [NRS]

GRAHAM, JOHN, a merchant and mason in Glasgow, a deed, 1750. [NRS.RD2.167.363]

GRAHAM, JOHN, son of Robert Graham and his wife Jean Luke, a tailor from Glasgow, emigrated by 1756, settled in Albemarle County, Virginia. [NRS.B10.15.6950][GA]

GRAHAM, JOHN, born 1752, a tailor from Glasgow, to New York, 1775. [NA.T47.12]

GRAHAM, JOHN, a baxter, son of George Graham, was admitted to the Baxter Incorporation, 1771. [IBG#120]

GRAHAM, RICHARD, a merchant in Glasgow, 1730. [NRS.AC9.6414/1131]

GRAHAM, ROBERT, a maltman in Glasgow, a deed, 1749. [NRS.RD3.210.45]

GRAHAM, ROBERT, a shipmaster in Glasgow, 1756. [NRS.S/H]

GRAHAME, ROBERT, of Auchincloch, a merchant in Glasgow, 1770. [ERG.VII.311]

GRAHAM, ROBERT, a vintner in Glasgow, 1770. [ERG.VII.311]

GRAHAM, SAMUEL, possibly from Glasgow, settled in Maryland, 1771. [GM.IX.422.48]

GRAHAM, THOMAS, a writer in Glasgow, 1770. [ERG.VII.311]

The People of Glasgow, 1725-1775

GRAHAM, WALTER, a baxter, former apprentice to John Watson, was admitted to the Baxter Incorporation, 1756. [IBG#120]

GRAHAM, Captain WALTER, late of General Guise's Regiment of Foot, a resident of Glasgow, testaments, 1760/1763/1765, Comm. Glasgow. [NRS]

GRAHAM, WALTER, a merchant in Glasgow, 1770. [ERG.VII.311]

GRAHAM, WALTER, a baxter, son of Walter Graham a baxter, was admitted to the Baxter Incorporation, 1775. [IBG#120]

GRAHAM, WILLIAM, of Gartur, a merchant in Glasgow, testament, 1768/1771, Comm. Glasgow. [NRS]

GRAHAME, WILLIAM, a coppersmith in Glasgow, 1770. [ERG.VII.311]

GRAY, ANDREW, senior, a merchant in Glasgow, 1730. [NRS.AC9.6415; AC7.35.354]

GRAY, ANDREW, a maltman in Glasgow, testament, 1741, Comm. Glasgow. [NRS]

GRAY, ANDREW, from Glasgow, in Boston, 1758. [SCS]

GRAY, ANDREW, a shipmaster and merchant in Glasgow, testament, 1772, Comm. Glasgow. [NRS]

GRAY, ARCHIBALD, a merchant in Glasgow, 1720s. [NRS.AC7.35.354; AC7.40.137; AC9.1116]

GRAY, JAMES, a baxter, eldest son of Robert Gray a baxter, was admitted to the Baxter Incorporation, also a burgess and guilds-brother of Glasgow in 1734. [IBG#120][GBR]

GRAY, JAMES, a baxter, son of James Gray, was admitted to the Baxter Incorporation, 1766. [IBG#120]

GRAY, JOHN, a merchant in Glasgow, 1720s. [NRS.AC7.33.433; AC7.34.697; AC7.36.328]

GRAY, JOHN, minister of St Andrew's, Glasgow, from 1700 until his death in 1729, testament, 1729, Comm. Glasgow. [NRS][F.3.432]

GRAY, JOHN, master weaver of the Incorporation of Weavers, 1725. [OGW#108]

GRAY, JOHN, a baxter, second son of Robert Gray a baxter, was admitted to the Baxter Incorporation, and a burgess and guilds-brother of Glasgow in 1734. [IBG#120][GBR]

GRAY, JOHN, son of John Gray a merchant in Glasgow, educated at Glasgow University in 1736, emigrated in 1748, settled in Port Royal, Caroline County,

The People of Glasgow, 1725-1775

Virginia, a Loyalist, died 1787.
[SM.50.362][MAGU.17][NRS.CC8.8.128][NA.AO13.30.398/424]
GRAY, Captain JOHN, in Glasgow, 1753. [NRS.E326.1.172]
GRAY, MARY, wife of John Ferguson a tailor in Glasgow, heir to her father Walter Gray a tailor there, also to her brother John Gray. [NRS.SH.1750]
GRAY, ROBERT, a cordiner in the Gallowgate of Glasgow, 1759; Deacon of the Cordiners of Glasgow, testament, 1767, Comm. Glasgow. [NRS] [ERG.VI.543]
GRAY, THOMAS, a merchant from Glasgow, settled in Boston by 1766. [NRS.B10.15.7234]
GRAY, WILLIAM, a merchant in Glasgow, 1733. [NRS.NRAS.2522/CA1/44]
GRAY, WILLIAM, from Glasgow, in Boston, 1747. [SCS]
GRAY, WILLIAM, senior, in Glasgow, 1753. [NRS.E326.1.172]; a merchant in Glasgow, testament, 1757, Comm. Glasgow. [NRS]
GREENLEES, JONAS, a saddler, eldest son of the late Thomas Greenlees a merchant, a hammerman, also a burgess and guilds-brother of Glasgow in 1728. [HHG.293][GBR]
GRIER, WILLIAM, a wright, husband of Agnes Herbison, a burgess and guilds-brother of Glasgow in 1720, [GBR], testament, 1738, Comm. Glasgow. [NRS]
GRIERSON, JOHN, a merchant, husband of Mary Luke, a burgess and guilds-brother of Glasgow in 1724, [GBR], testament, 1743, Comm. Glasgow. [NRS]
GRIERSON, WILLIAM, a merchant in Glasgow, testaments, 1771/1773, Comm. Glasgow. [NRS]
GRIERSON, Mrs, in Glasgow, 1753. [NRS.E326.1.172]
GRINTOUN, JAMES, a carrier in Glasgow, testament, 1754, Comm. Glasgow. [NRS]
GUN, DANIEL, a maltman or merchant, eldest son of Daniel Gun a merchant, a burgess and guilds-brother of Glasgow in 1717, [GBR], testament, 1735, Comm. Glasgow. [NRS]
GUN, ELIZABETH, daughter of the deceased Donald Gun in Glasgow, and relict of Andrew Thomson an Excise officer in Glasgow, testament, 1770, Comm. Glasgow. [NRS]
HADDIN, JOHN, a weaver in Glasgow, testament, 1728, Comm. Glasgow. [NRS]
HADDOW, ROBERT, a baxter, son in law of James Anderson, was admitted to the Baxter Incorporation, 1770. [IBG#121]

HALL, ALEXANDER, a merchant, husband of Isobel McAulay, a burgess and guilds-brother of Glasgow in 1738, [GBR], testament, 1743, Comm. Glasgow. [NRS]

HALL, CHRISTIAN, a resident of Glasgow, relict of Walter Aitchison of Ruchsolloch, testament, 1737, Comm. Glasgow. [NRS]

HALL, HUGH SYMONS, a mariner in Glasgow, last on board the Martha of Glasgow, testament, 1761, Comm. Glasgow. [NRS]

HALL, JOHN, in Glasgow, 1753. [NRS.E326.1.172]

HALL, MARY, relict of James McBrayer a shipmaster in Glasgow, testament, 1733, Comm. Glasgow. [NRS]

HALL, ROBERT, a writer in Glasgow, testament, 1748, Comm. Glasgow. [NRS]

HAMILTON, ALEXANDER, a merchant in Glasgow, testament, 1729, Comm. Glasgow. [NRS]

HAMILTON, ALEXANDER, H.M.Collector of Duties on stamped paper etc, in Glasgow, testament, 1748, Comm. Glasgow. [NRS]

HAMILTON, ALEXANDER, a merchant from Glasgow, settled in Pitscataway, Maryland, in 1760, died in Portobacco 1799. [MHS.ms1301][GC.1269][GA]

HAMILTON, ARCHIBALD, from Glasgow, in Boston, 1748. [SCS]

HAMILTON, ARCHIBALD, in Glasgow, 1753. [NRS.E326.1.172]

HAMILTON, ARCHIBALD, of Overton, a merchant from Glasgow, settled in Virginia before 1778. [NRS.CS16.1.173]

HAMILTON, ARCHIBALD, a merchant from Glasgow, partner in the firm of John Hamilton and Company, settled in Suffolk, North Carolina and Nansemond County, Virginia, from 1759 to 1776. [NA.AO13.95][NRS.CS16.1.170]

HAMILTON, GAVIN, a merchant from Glasgow, settled in Norfolk, Virginia, before 1750. [NRS.B10.15.6087; CS16.1.170]

HAMILTON, GEORGE, in Glasgow, 1753. [NRS.E326.1.172]

HAMILTON, GILBERT, a merchant in Glasgow, 1775. [NA.AO13.96.362]

HAMILTON, HELEN, wife of David Cochrane a merchant in Glasgow, heir to her brother William Hamilton late of Jamaica, [NRS.SH.1754]

HAMILTON, HUGH, a merchant in Glasgow, testament, 1738, Comm. Glasgow. [NRS]

HAMILTON, JAMES, of Newton, a surgeon in Glasgow, 1725, testament, 1755, Comm. Glasgow. [NRS] [ERG.V.242]

HAMILTON, JAMES, from Glasgow, in Boston, 1755. [SCS]

The People of Glasgow, 1725-1775

HAMILTON, JAMES, of Newton, a resident of Glasgow, testament, 1769, Comm. Glasgow. [NRS]

HAMILTON, JOHN, son of John Hamilton minister at Carmichael, educated at Glasgow University, minister of The Blackfriars, Glasgow, 1713 to 1741, died April 1741. [F.3.399]

HAMILTON, JOHN, a merchant in Glasgow, second son of the late James Hamilton of Aikenhead, testament, 1755, Comm. Glasgow. [NRS]

HAMILTON, JOHN, senior, in Glasgow, 1753. [NRS.E326.1.172]

HAMILTON, JOHN, a wright in Glasgow, testament, 1755, Comm. Glasgow. [NRS]

HAMILTON, JOHN, from Glasgow, settled in Nansemond, and Norfolk, Virginia, by 1765, later in New Brunswick. [NRS.NRAS.0620; T79.18][NA.AO13.95] [GA.T79.18]

HAMILTON, JOHN, the younger, a maltman and Convenor of the Trades of Glasgow, testament, 1756, Comm. Glasgow. [NRS]

HAMILTON, JOHN, a merchant in Glasgow, 1748, a deed, [NRS.RD2.167.229; RD2.168.301]; 1753. [NRS.E326.1.172] ; a merchant in Glasgow, testament, 1771, Comm. Glasgow. [NRS]

HAMILTON, JOHN, a stamp master in Glasgow, testament, 1773, Comm. Glasgow. [NRS]

HAMILTON, JOHN, a merchant from Glasgow, in North Carolina by 1770. [NA.AO12.47.92][GA.T79.18]

HAMILTON, PATRICK, born 1757 in Glasgow, son of Reverend John Hamilton and his wife Mary Bogle, died 1788 in Jamaica. [F.3.458]

HAMILTON, ROBERT, from Glasgow, in Boston, 1742. [SCS]

HAMILTON, THOMAS, tenant in Cowlairs, Glasgow, 1725. [ERG.V.243]

HAMILTON, THOMAS, a surgeon in Glasgow, 1725. [ERG.V.245]

HAMILTON, THOMAS, master weaver of the Incorporation of Weavers, 1725. [OGW#108]

HAMILTON, WILLIAM, master of Glasgow Grammar School, testaments, 1731/1738, Comm. Glasgow. [NRS]

HAMILTON, WILLIAM, a notary public in Glasgow, testament, 1754, Comm. Glasgow. [NRS]

HAMILTON, Mrs, in Glasgow, 1753. [NRS.E326.1.172]

The People of Glasgow, 1725-1775

HANNAY, THOMAS, son of the deceased Thomas Hannay, a merchant in Glasgow, testament, 1755, Comm. Glasgow. [NRS]

HANON, PATRICK, a vintner in Glasgow, 1770. [ERG.VII.311]

HARDIE, JOHN, a tobacco spinner in Glasgow, testament, 1734, Comm. Glasgow. [NRS]

HARDIE, ROBERT, a baxter, son in law of Gabriel Lochhead a baxter, was admitted to the Baxter Incorporation, and as a burgess and guilds-brother of Glasgow in 1770. [IBG#121][GBR]

HARLEY, ADAM, born 1763, a weaver from Glasgow, to New York, 1774. [NA.T47.12]

HARLEY, JAMES, born 1754, a weaver from Glasgow, to New York, 1774. [NA.T47.12]

HART, CHARLES, a weaver, son in law of Robert Fleming a weaver, a burgess and guilds-brother of Glasgow in 1730, [GBR], a deed, 1750. [NRS.RD3.210.52]

HART, JOHN, born 1743, a mason from Glasgow, to New York, 1775. [NA.T47.12]

HARVEY, WILLIAM, from Glasgow, in Boston, 1751. [SCS]

HARVIE, ALEXANDER, in Glasgow, 1753. [NRS.E326.1.172]

HARVIE, JAMES, in Glasgow, 1753. [NRS.E326.1.172]

HARVIE, JAMES, water bailie in Glasgow, 1775. [ERG.VII.455]

HARVIE, JOHN, a slater in Glasgow, testament, 1760, Comm. Glasgow. [NRS]

HARVIE, THOMAS, a merchant in Glasgow, testament, 1770, Comm. Glasgow. [NRS]

HARVIE, WILLIAM, a writing master in Glasgow, testament, 1748, Comm. Glasgow. [NRS]

HASWELL, CECILIA, relict of John Kennedy a merchant in Glasgow, testament, 1766, Comm. Glasgow. [NRS]

HAY, JAMES, a baxter, eldest son of John Hay and former apprentice to Thomas Scott a baxter, was admitted to the Baxter Incorporation, and as a burgess and guilds-brother of Glasgow in 1758. [IBG#121][GBR]

HAY, JOHN, a dyster in Glasgow, testament, 1729, Comm. Glasgow. [NRS]

HAY, JOHN, a merchant in Glasgow, 1728, [NRS.AC7.34.697]; testament, 1735, Comm. Glasgow. [NRS]

HAY, JOHN, a merchant in Glasgow, 1772; trading with Virginia in 1773. [NRS.NRAS.0623/3][GA.T76/6.3]

HAY, PETER, a merchant in Glasgow, 1772. [NRS.NRAS.0623/3]
HENDERSON, JAMES, a merchant in Glasgow, testament, 1753, Comm. Glasgow. [NRS]
HENDERSON, Captain JOHN, late in the military service of the English East India Company, later in Glasgow, testament, 1774, Comm. Glasgow. [NRS]
HENDERSON, PATRICK or PETER, a merchant in Glasgow, son of James Henderson a merchant there and sometime second mate aboard the Little Page of Glasgow, testament, 1734, Comm. Glasgow. [NRS]
HENDRY, FINDLAY, a baxter, son of William Hendry a baxter, was admitted to the Baxter Incorporation, and a burgess and guilds-brother of Glasgow in 1743. [IBG#121][GBR]
HENDSHAW, JOHN, a merchant in Glasgow, later in New York, 1755. [NRS.CS16.1.95]
HENRY, DAVID, a saddler, husband of Margaret Whitelaw, a burgess and guilds-brother of Glasgow in 1747, [GBR], possibly treasurer of Glasgow in 1759. [ERG.VI.546]
HENRY, WILLIAM, the younger, a merchant in Glasgow, testament, 1728, Comm. Glasgow. [NRS]
HENRY, WILLIAM, a merchant in Glasgow, testament, 1754, Comm. Glasgow. [NRS]
HEPBURN, CHARLES, a merchant from Glasgow, settled on Cape Fear, North Carolina, died 1741, testament, 1744, Comm. Edinburgh. [NRS]
HEPBURN, GAVIN, a baxter, son of the late John Hepburn a baxter, was admitted to the Baxter Incorporation, and as a burgess and guilds-brother of Glasgow in 1727. [IBG#121][GBR]
HEPBURN, GAVIN, a baxter, son of John Hepburn baxter, was admitted to the Baxter Incorporation, and as a burgess and guilds-brother of Glasgow in 1769. [IBG#121][GBR]
HEPBURN, JAMES, a merchant, husband of Christian McLimont a merchant, a burgess and guilds-brotherof Glasgow in 1755; in Glasgow, 1753, 1763. [NRS.E326.1.172][ERG.VII.116] [GBR]
HEPBURN, JOHN, a baxter, eldest son of Gavin Hepburn a baxter, was admitted to the Baxter Incorporation, and as a burgess and guilds-brother of Glasgow in 1748. [IBG#121][GBR]

The People of Glasgow, 1725-1775

HERBERTSON, JAMES, only son of John Herbertson junior a maltman, a freeman maltman, 1740. [MCG.136]

HERBERTSON, JAMES, a wright, eldest son of the late John Herbertson merchant, a burgess and guilds-brother of Glasgow in 1737, [GBR], late Deacon of the Wrights of Glasgow, testament, 1769, Comm. Glasgow. [NRS]

HERBERTSON, MATHEW, a merchant, husband of Isobel Dobbie, a burgess and guilds-brother of Glasgow in 1721, [GBR], testament, 1731, Comm. Glasgow. [NRS]

HERRIES, MICHAEL, a merchant in Glasgow, a deed, 1750. [NRS.RD2.168.10]; a merchant from Glasgow, land grants in Georgia, 1751, and East Florida, 1767. [NA.CO5.669][PCCol.v.591]

HERRIOT, WILLIAM, born 1753, a baxter from Glasgow, to New York or Georgia, 1775. [NA.T47.12]

HEYWOOD, JOHN, a writer in Glasgow, testament, 1760, Comm. Glasgow. [NRS]

HIGGINS, MARGARET, relict of John Craig late Deacon of the Wrights in Glasgow, testament, 1746, Comm. Glasgow. [NRS]

HILL, JANET, a rioter in Glasgow, transported to Barbados, 1726. [NA.T53.33.293; SP54.16.38/126]

HILL, LAURENCE, born 1700 son of Ninian Hill of Lambhill and his wife Mary Crawford, graduated MA from Glasgow University 1719, minister of barony parish of Glasgow from 1750 until his death in 1773. [F.3.394]

HILL, NINIAN, of Lambhill, barony parish of Glasgow, testament, 1727, Comm. Glasgow. [NRS]

HILL, NINIAN, a baxter, former apprentice to John Auchencloss a baxter, was admitted to the Baxter Incorporation, also a burgess and guilds-brother of Glasgow in 1730. [IBG#121][GBR]

HILL, NINIAN, Dean of Guild officer in Glasgow, 1759. [ERG.VI.546]

HILL, WALTER, eldest son of Walter Hill a land laborer and maltman, a burgess and guilds-brother of Glasgow in 1762; a wright in Glasgow, testament, 1768, Comm. Glasgow. [NRS][GBR]

HODGE, ELIZABETH, daughter of James Hodge a maltman in Glasgow, testament, 1764, Comm. Glasgow. [NRS]

The People of Glasgow, 1725-1775

HODGSON, JOHN, son of William Hodgson a merchant in Glasgow, to New England in 1762, a book-seller in Boston by 1772, died 1781. [NRS.S/H.1772][Imm.NE.88]

HOGGAN, JAMES, from Glasgow, a tobacco factor in Bladensburg, Virginia, by 1774. [GA]

HOGGAN, JOHN, a baxter, son in law of John Glen a baxter, was admitted to the Baxter Incorporation, and as a burgess and guilds-brother of Glasgow in 1743. [IBG#121][GBR]

HOLMES, PATRICK, schoolmaster at Glasgow Grammar School, a burgess and guilds-brother of Glasgow in 1765, dead by 1767. [GBR] [ERG.VII.240]

HOLMES, ROBERT, a weaver in Glasgow, testament, 1771, Comm. Glasgow. [NRS]

HONEYBULL, ANN, born 1741, a spinner from Glasgow, to New York, 1774. [NA.T47.12]

HOOD, ALEXANDER, born 1737 son of James Hood, a physician from Glasgow, settled in Montserrat before 1773. [MWI.48]

HOOD, JOHN, a merchant from Glasgow, to Virginia aboard the Joanna of Glasgow in 1760. [NRS.AC7.50; CS16.1.88/117]

HOOD, JOHN, a merchant from Glasgow in Flower d'Hundred, Va. by 1752, in Greenock, 1788. [NRS. CS16.1.88/117; CS17.1.7; AC7.50]

HOOK, JOHN, born 1745, son of Henry Hook, a merchant in Glasgow, emigrated in 1758, settled in Blandford and New London, Bedford County, Virginia, died 1808. [NRS.CS16.1.117][VSA.John Hook pp][VMHB.34.149][VaGaz#1050]

HOPE, JOHN, a merchant from Glasgow, emigrated before 1776, settled in Osborne and Halifax, Virginia. [GA.T79.25]

HOPKIRK, THOMAS, a merchant, eldest son of the late Francis Hopkirk a tailor, a burgess and guilds-brother of Glasgow in 1734, [GBR], in Glasgow, 1753. [NRS.E326.1.172]

HORSBURGH, ALEXANDER, a surgeon –apothecary, a burgess and guilds-brother of Glasgow in 1718, [GBR], there in 1725; husband of Lillias Marshall by 1735, [GBR], testament, 1745/1746, Comm. Glasgow. [NRS] [ERG.V.245]

HORSBURGH, ALEXANDER, a merchant from Glasgow, emigrated before 1776, settled in Brunswick and Petersburg, Virginia, a Loyalist, returned to

The People of Glasgow, 1725-1775

Glasgow aboard the Howe via New York in 1777. [GA.T79.1]

HORSBURGH, Mrs, in Glasgow, 1753. [NRS.E326.1.172]

HOSIE, ELIZABETH, relict of Archibald Halden a merchant in Glasgow, testament, 1728, Comm. Glasgow. [NRS]

HOUSTOUN, ALEXANDER, a merchant in Glasgow, deeds, 1750, 1753. [NRS.RD4.176/2.329; CS16.1.134][GA.B10.15.6183]

HOUSTOUN, GEORGE, a merchant, eldest son of the late Patrick Houstoun a merchant, burgess and guilds-brother of Glasgow in 1716, [GBR], testaments, 1724/1727/1731, Comm. Glasgow. [NRS]

HOUSTOUN, JAMES, a merchant from Glasgow, to Georgia, 1733. [NA.CO5.670.125]

HOUSTOUN, MARGARET, in Glasgow, relict of Mathew Crauford minister at Eastwood, testament, 1727, Comm. Glasgow. [NRS]

HOUSTOUN, PATRICK, from Glasgow, in Boston, 1750. [SCS]

HOWAT, WILLIAM, a workman in Glasgow, testament, 1732, Comm. Glasgow. [NRS]

HOWET, MARY, born 1749, a spinner from Glasgow, to New York, 1774. [NA.T47.12]

HOWIE, DANIEL, a merchant in Glasgow, a deed, 1750. [NRS.RD4.176/1.7]

HOWIE, JOHN, a skinner, eldest son of Matthew Howie a skinner, was admitted to the Skinners Craft, and as a burgess and guilds-brother of Glasgow in 1765. [SFG.268][GBR]

HOWIESON, JAMES, a tailor, eldest son of the late John Howieson a tailor, a burgess and guilds-brother in 1725, [GBR], testament, 1732, Comm. Glasgow. [NRS]

HUGH, MICHAEL, a baxter, son in law of William Alexander a baxter, was admitted to the Baxter Incorporation, and as a burgess and guilds-brother of Glasgow in 1754. [IBG#121][GBR]

HUGHES, MARY, born 1760, a servant from Glasgow, to Maryland, 1775. [NA.T47.11]

HUME, JAMES, from Glasgow, in Boston, 1741. [SCS]

HUME, WILLIAM, born 1735, a shipmaster from Glasgow, to Georgia, 1775. [NA.T47.12]

HUNTER, ELIZABETH, a resident of Glasgow, relict of John Baxter, testament, 1753, Comm. Glasgow. [NRS]

The People of Glasgow, 1725-1775

HUNTER, ISOBEL, in Glasgow, 1753. [NRS.E326.1.172]
HUNTER, JAMES, a merchant in Glasgow, testament, 1728/1737, Comm. Glasgow. [NRS]
HUNTER, JANET, relict of James Broun a bookbinder in Glasgow, testaments, 1736/1738, Comm. Glasgow. [NRS]
HUNTER, JANET, relict of John Wright a wright and glass-wright in Glasgow, testament, 1752, Comm. Glasgow. [NRS]
HUNTER, JOHN, a hammerman in Glasgow, testament, 1740, Comm. Glasgow. [NRS]
HUNTER, JOHN, a merchant in Glasgow, testaments, 1740/1742, Comm. Glasgow. [NRS]
HUNTER, JOHN, a merchant in Glasgow, a deed, 1750. [NRS.RD2.168.337]
HUNTER, JOHN, in Glasgow, testament, 1758, Comm. Glasgow. [NRS]
HUNTER, JOHN, a tobacconist in Glasgow, testament, 1757, Comm. Glasgow. [NRS]
HUNTER, JOHN, in Glasgow, 1753. [NRS.E326.1.172]
HUNTER, ROBERT, a weaver in Glasgow, testament, 1735, Comm. Glasgow. [NRS]
HUNTER, ROBERT, a dyer in Glasgow, testament, 1738, Comm. Glasgow. [NRS]
HUNTER, ROBERT, master of Glasgow Grammar School, testament, 1743, Comm. Glasgow. [NRS]
HUNTER, ROBERT, a butcher in Glasgow, a deed, 1749. [NRS.RD2.167.285]
HUNTER. THOMAS, a hammerman, and a burgess of Glasgow in 1728. [HHG.293][GBR]
HUTTON, CHARLES, a burgess and guilds-brother of Glasgow in 1762, a merchant from Glasgow, settled in Maryland before 1767, moved to Nevis by 1779. [NLS.ms8794][NRS.CS16.1.130][GBR]
HUTTON, JOHN, in Glasgow, 1753. [NRS.E326.1.172]
HYND, JAMES, a merchant, former apprentice to James Carlisle a merchant, a burgess and guilds-brother of Glasgow in 1731, [GBR], there in 1753. [NRS.E326.1.172]
HYNDMAN, WILLIAM, a merchant from Glasgow, settled in St Kitts before 1769. [NRS.SC36.63.13]
IMBRIE, WILLIAM, a chapman traveller in Glasgow, testament, 1751, Comm. Glasgow. [NRS]

INGLIS, JAMES, a tanner in Glasgow, testament, 1745, Comm. Glasgow. [NRS]

INGLIS, JAMES, a wright and town officer of Glasgow, a deed, 1750, [NRS.RD4.176/2.476]

INGLIS, JAMES, a merchant in Glasgow, testament, 1752, Comm. Glasgow. [NRS]

INGLIS, JOHN, a baxter, former apprentice to John Watson senior a baxter, was admitted to the Baxter Incorporation, and as a burgess and guilds-brother of Glasgow in 1764. [IBG#124]; testament, 1772, Comm. Glasgow. [NRS][GBR]

INGLIS, MARGARET, in Glasgow, relict of John Wardrop portioner of Dalmarnock, testament, 1733, Comm. Glasgow. [NRS]

INGLIS, ROBERT, in Glasgow, 1753. [NRS.E326.1.172]

INGLIS, WILLIAM, a merchant in Glasgow, testament, 1767, Comm. Glasgow. [NRS]

INGRAM, ARCHIBALD, a merchant, husband of Janet Simpson, a burgess and guilds-brother of Glasgow in 1728, [GBR], there in 1753. [NRS.E326.1.172; CS16.1.100; AC7.47.32]

IRELAND, JAMES, a merchant in Glasgow, testament, 1766, Comm. Glasgow. [NRS]

IRVINE, LAURENCE, born 1715, a cutler from Glasgow, to Jamaica in 1735. [CLRO/AIA]

JACK, JAMES, Precentor to the Associate Meeting in Glasgow, testament, 1747, Comm. Glasgow. [NRS]

JAFFREY, JOHN, in Glasgow, 1753. [NRS.E326.1.172]

JAMIESON, JOHN, a merchant in Glasgow, 1750, [NRS.RD2.167.288]; 1753. [NRS.E326.1.172; CS16.1.88]

JAMIESON, JOHN, a tinsmith from Glasgow, emigrated to Virginia before 1765. [VaGaz.30.10.1784]

JAMIESON, NEIL, a merchant from Glasgow, settled in Norfolk, Virginia, during 1760, a Loyalist who moved to London. [NRS.B10.15.7174; NRAS.0623; CS16.1.168][NA.AO13.6.72]

JAMIESON, THOMAS, a smith and ferrier in Glasgow, testament, 1755, Comm. Glasgow. [NRS]

JAMIESON, THOMAS, a tailor in Glasgow, testament, 1771, Comm. Glasgow. [NRS]

JAMIESON, THOMAS, a merchant in Glasgow, testament, 1773, Comm. Glasgow. [NRS]

JAMIESON, WILLIAM, a merchant in Glasgow, died 1771.[Ramshorn MI, Glasgow]

JARDEN, JOHN, a carter in Glasgow, testament, 1774, Comm. Glasgow. [NRS]

JARDIN, GEORGE, a hammerman, husband of Isobel Johnston, a burgess and guilds-brother of Glasgow in 1737, [GBR], a smith in Glasgow, 1759. [ERG.VI.540]

JOHNSON, JAMES, a merchant from Glasgow, a land grant in Georgia, 1751. [CRG]

JOHNSTONE, ABIGAIL, relict of James Cleland a maltman in Glasgow, and his daughters Abigail and Margaret Cleland, testaments, 1762/1772, Comm. Glasgow. [NRS]

JOHNSTONE, AGNES, relict of Robert Goodwine a land laborer in Glasgow, testament, 1744, Comm. Glasgow. [NRS]

JOHNSTONE, ANDREW, a merchant in Glasgow, testaments, 1725/1732, Comm. Glasgow. [NRS]

JOHNSTON, ANDREW, a merchant from Glasgow, settled in Petersburg, Virginia, in 1750, a Loyalist, died 1785. [NRS.CS16.1.84; CC8.8.127] [NA.AO13.33.153]

JOHNSTONE, JAMES, a dyer in Glasgow, testament, 1742, Comm. Glasgow. [NRS]

JOHNSTONE, JAMES, a merchant in Glasgow, testament, 1743, Comm. Glasgow. [NRS]

JOHNSTON, JAMES, a merchant from Glasgow, to Virginia in 1760 aboard the Joanna of Glasgow. [NRS.AC7.50]

JOHNSTONE, JOHN, a merchant and shopkeeper in Glasgow, testament, 1734, Comm. Glasgow. [NRS]

JOHNSTON, JOHN, son of John Johnston, a merchant from Glasgow, settled in Norfolk, Virginia, before 1748. [NRS.CS16.1.80/154/161]

JOHNSTONE, JOHN, a merchant and stamp-master in Glasgow, testament, 1751, Comm. Glasgow. [NRS]

JOHNSTONE, JOHN, in Glasgow, 1753. [NRS.E326.1.172]; a grocer in Glasgow, testament, 1758, Comm. Glasgow. [NRS]

JOHNSTONE, Dr JOHN, a physician and late Professor of Medicine at the University of Glasgow, testament, 1762, Comm. Glasgow. [NRS]

JOHNSTONE, JOHN, sometime a merchant in Nottingham thereafter a merchant in Glasgow, testament, 1770, Comm. Glasgow. [NRS]

JOHNSTON, ROBERT, a shipmaster in Glasgow, 1744. [NRS.S/H]

JOHNSTONE, ROBERT, a sailor in Glasgow, sometime mate of the Glasgow, testament, 1771, Comm. Glasgow. [NRS]

JOHNSTONE, THOMAS, a merchant, eldest son of James Johnston a merchant, a burgess and guilds-brother of Glasgow in 1749, [GBR], in Glasgow, 1753. [NRS.E326.1.172]; testament, 1772, Comm. Glasgow. [NRS.CS16.1.133]

JOHNSTONE, WALTER, a writer in Glasgow, testament, 1752, Comm. Glasgow. [NRS]

JONES, RICE, a tanner, burgess and guilds-brother of Glasgow in 1731, [GBR], testament, 1746, Comm. Glasgow. [NRS]

KEIR, or COLQUHOUN, AGNES, from Glasgow, guilty of assault, transported to the colonies, 1766. [AJ.958]

KEIR, COLIN, a huckster and shopkeeper in Bridgegate Street, Glasgow, testament, 1770, Comm. Glasgow. [NRS]

KELBURN, DAVID, a writer in Glasgow, testament, 1745, Comm. Glasgow. [NRS]

KELBURN, JAMES, servant to John McGilchrist a writer in Glasgow, 1725. [ERG.V.241]

KELBURN, JAMES, a writer in Glasgow, testaments, 1736/1737/1739/1743, Comm. Glasgow. [NRS]

KELBURN, JAMES, junior, a writer in Glasgow, 1727; [GA.D-TC13/603S]; testaments, 1730/1731/1732/1735/1737/1741, Comm. Glasgow. [NRS]

KELSO, ARCHIBALD, a merchant, a burgess and guilds-brother of Glasgow in 1734, [GBR], testament, 1751, Comm. Glasgow. [NRS]

KENNEDY, FERGUS, a former apprentice to David Stevenson a cordiner, a burgess and guilds-brother of Glasgow in 1751, [GBR]; in Glasgow, 1753. [NRS.E326.1.172]

KENNEDY, HUGH, a merchant from Glasgow, in Virginia by 1725. [NRS.AC9.925]

KENNEDY, HUGH, born 1768 in Glasgow, son of Daniel Kennedy and his wife Mary Brodie, died in Philadelphia in 1803. [GM.73.86]

KENNEDY, JOHN, a merchant in Glasgow, testament, 1750, Comm. Glasgow. [NRS]

KENNEDY, JOHN, in Glasgow, 1753. [NRS.E326.1.172]; a merchant in Glasgow, testament, 1758, Comm. Glasgow. [NRS]

KENNEDY, Dr THOMAS, a physician in Glasgow, testament, 1732, Comm. Glasgow. [NRS]

KENNEDY, THOMAS, a hammerman in Glasgow, testament, 1762, Comm. Glasgow. [NRS]

KENT, JOHN, a cabinet-maker from Glasgow, an indentured servant who absconded from Mathew Hopkins, Rock Creek, Prince George County, Maryland, 1748. [MdGaz.178]

KERR, AGNES, an innkeeper in Glasgow, testament, 1732, Comm. Glasgow. [NRS]

KERR, ANDREW, in Glasgow, letters, 1760, 1767. [NRS.NRAS.332C3/674/717.]

KERR, JOHN, was admitted to the Skinners Craft, 1753. [SFG.267]

KERR, WILLIAM, a mason, former apprentice of William Kerr a mason, a burgess and guilds-brother of Glasgow in 1726, [GBR], late Deacon of the Masons in Glasgow, testament, 1737, Comm. Glasgow. [NRS]

KERR, WILLIAM, a mealman in Glasgow, testament, 1741, Comm. Glasgow. [NRS]

KEY, JOHN, son of the late Robert Key a merchant in Glasgow, testament, 1738, Comm. Glasgow. [NRS]

KIBBLE, GAVIN, a hammerman, former apprentice to Robert Fukton a hammerman, a burgess and guilds-brother of Glasgow in 1729. [HHG.294] [GBR]; a coppersmith in Glasgow, testaments, 1742/1745, Comm. Glasgow. [NRS]

KILLOCH, WILLIAM, a weaver, husband of Anna Brown, a burgess and guilds-brother of Glasgow in 1739, [GBR], master of the Red Dye Society of Glasgow, 1759. [ERG.VI.547]

KILPATRICK, DAVID, a flesher, burgess and guilds-brother of Glasgow, 1750. [GBR]

KILPATRICK, JOHN, a merchant in Glasgow, a burgess and guilds-brother of Glasgow in 1751, [GBR]; in Glasgow, 1753. [NRS.E326.1.172]

KING, JOHN, a merchant in Glasgow, 1726, [NRS.AC9.1056; AC7.34.433]; a maltman and bailie of Glasgow, testaments, 1729/1743, Comm. Glasgow. [NRS]

KING, JOHN, a vintner and merchant in Glasgow, 1734, [NRS.AC7.40.137]; testament, 1748, Comm. Glasgow. [NRS]

KING, JOHN, eldest son of James King a maltman, a freeman maltman, 1760. [MCG.135]

KING, WILLIAM, the younger, a barber in Glasgow, testament, 1752, Comm. Glasgow. [NRS]

KING, WILLIAM, a sailor in Glasgow, late on board the Caesar of Glasgow, testament, 1761, Comm. Glasgow. [NRS]

KINNEAR, JOSEPH, a merchant in Glasgow, testament, 1732, Comm. Glasgow. [NRS]

KINNIBURGH, JAMES, a merchant, second son of James Kinniburgh a merchant, a burgess and guilds-brother of Glasgow in 1731/1741, [GBR], testament, 1750, Comm. Glasgow. [NRS]

KINNIBURGH, JAMES, born 1748, a laborer from Glasgow, to North Carolina, 1775. [NA.T47.12]

KINNINBURGH, JOHN, son of James Kinninburgh, a wright from Glasgow, settled in Virginia before 1751.[NRS.CS16.1.89; SH.1751]

KINNIBURGH, JOHN, born 1751, a laborer from Glasgow, to North Carolina, 1775. [NA.T47.12]

KINNIBURGH, ROBERT, a merchant, third son of James Kinniburgh a merchant, a burgess and guilds-brother of Glasgow in 1741, [GBR], testaments, 1750/1751, Comm. Glasgow. [NRS]

KIPPEN, GEORGE, in Glasgow, 1753. [NRS.E326.1.172] ; a merchant, eldest son of the late George Kippen a merchant, a burgess and guilds-brother of Glasgow in 1737, [GBR]; in Glasgow, testament, 1767, Comm. Glasgow. [NRS]

KIRKLAND, ANDREW, younger son of Mathew Kirkland a baxter, was admitted to the Baxter Incorporation, and as a burgess and guilds-brother of Glasgow in 1775. [IBG#125][GBR]

KIRKLAND, JAMES, a former apprentice to James Corse a wright, a burgess and guilds-brother of Glasgow in 1752. [GBR]

The People of Glasgow, 1725-1775

KIRKLAND, JAMES, a hammerman, eldest son of James Kirkland a wright, a burgess and guilds-brother of Glasgow in 1769, and a hammerman in 1775. [HHG.294][GBR]

KIRKLAND, MATHEW, a baxter, former apprentice to John Menzies a baxter, was admitted to the Baxter Incorporation, also as a burgess and guilds-brother of Glasgow in 1747. [IBG#125][GBR]

KIRKLAND, ROBERT, in Hall of Provan, barony parish of Glasgow, testament, 1725, Comm. Glasgow. [NRS]

KIRKLAND, WILLIAM, a barber, husband of Margaret Marshall, a burgess and guilds-brother of Glasgow in 1746, [GBR], testament, 1754, Comm. Glasgow. [NRS]

KIRKWOOD, ADAM, a tanner, eldest son of Adam Kirkwood a merchant, a burgess and guilds-brother of Glasgow in 1719, [GBR], and his spouse Ann Semple, testament, 1744, Comm. Glasgow. [NRS]

KIRKWOOD, ADAM, a tanner in Glasgow, testament, 1749, Comm. Glasgow. [NRS]

KNOX, JANET, a thief from Glasgow, transported to the colonies, 1758. [SM.20.328]

KNOX, WILLIAM, a merchant in Glasgow, testament, 1730, Comm. Glasgow. [NRS]

KNOX, WILLIAM, a weaver in Glasgow, testament, 1769, Comm. Glasgow. [NRS]

LADLEY, GRIZELL, in Glasgow, testament, 1773, Comm. Glasgow. [NRS]

LAING, WILLIAM, in Glasgow, 1753. [NRS.E326.1.172]; a merchant in Glasgow, 1764/1778. [NRS.CS16.1.117/174]

LAMONT, ARCHIBALD, a merchant in Glasgow, testament, 1763, Comm. Glasgow. [NRS]

LAMONT, JOHN, a hammerman in 1731. [HHG.294]

LAMONT, JOHN, a baxter, son in law of John Auchencloss a baxter, was admitted to the Baxter Incorporation, and as a burgess and guilds-brother of Glasgow in 1772. [IBG#126][GBR]

LANG, GEORGE, son of George Lang a barber, a barber from Glasgow, settled in Virginia before 1763. [NRS.CS16.1.117]

LANG, JAMES, a member of the Incorporation of Weavers, 1725. [OGW#108]

The People of Glasgow, 1725-1775

LANG, JEAN, relict of Alexander Barron a horse-setter in Glasgow, testament, 1773, Comm. Glasgow. [NRS]

LANG, JOHN, Deacon of the Weavers Incorporation, 1725. [OGW#108]

LANG, JOHN, a preacher in Glasgow, testament, 1729, Comm. Glasgow. [NRS]

LANG, JOHN, senior, a merchant in Glasgow, testament, 1742, Comm. Glasgow. [NRS]

LANG, JOHN, a baxter, former apprentice to William Weir, was admitted to the Baxter Incorporation, 1742. [IBG#126]

LANG, JOHN, a maltman in Glasgow, testament, 1756, Comm. Glasgow. [NRS]

LANG, JOHN, a merchant from Glasgow, died in Jamaica before 1761. [NRS.S/H.1761]

LANG, PATRICK, a baxter, former apprentice to John Garner a baxter, was admitted to the Baxter Incorporation, also a burgess and guilds-brother of Glasgow in 1739. [IBG#126][GBR]

LANG, ROBERT, a merchant in Glasgow, testament, 1726, Comm. Glasgow. [NRS]

LANG, ROBERT, a merchant, a burgess and guilds-brother of Glasgow in 1759, [GBR], HM Customs Controller in Glasgow, testament, 1766, Comm. Glasgow. [NRS]

LANG, WALTER, a hammerman, eldest son of John Lang a merchant, a burgess and guilds-brother of Glasgow in 1717, [GBR], a coppersmith in Glasgow, 1725; Convenor of the Trades in Glasgow, testament, 1740, Comm. Glasgow. [NRS] [ERG.V.222]

LANG, WALTER, a baxter, second son of the late Walter Lang a hammerman, and former apprentice to James Morison, was admitted to the Baxter Incorporation, and as a burgess and guilds-brother of Glasgow in 1748. [IBG#126][GBR]

LANG, WILLIAM, junior, a writer in Glasgow, testament, 1737, Comm. Glasgow. [NRS]

LANG, WILLIAM, a writer in Glasgow, testament, 1745/1746, Comm. Glasgow. [NRS]

LANG, WILLIAM, from Glasgow, a bookseller in Boston 1759, dead by 1765. [NRS.CS16.1.122/125/128]

LANG, WILLIAM, a shipmaster in Glasgow, son of Robert Lang a merchant there, 1772. [NRS.S/H]

The People of Glasgow, 1725-1775

LAURIE, JOHN, a merchant in Glasgow, 1769. [GA.B10.15.7233]
LAW, JOHN, Professor of Philosophy at the University of Glasgow, testament, 1735, Comm. Glasgow. [NRS]
LAW, ROBERT, son of Professor John Law of Glasgow University, testaments, 1734/1737, Comm. Glasgow. [NRS]
LAWSON, JAMES, a merchant from Glasgow, settled in Charles County, Maryland, before 1769. [MSA.Chancery.46/161][NA.AO13.33.367] [NRS.CS16.1.122; CS96.3186; GD103.2.442; NRAS.396/18]
LAWSON, JOHN, a tailor in Glasgow, testament, 1743, Comm. Glasgow. [NRS]
LAWSON, JOHN, a mason, eldest son of the late William Lawson a mason, a burgess and guilds-brother of Glasgow in 1733, [GBR], 1759, 1763. [ERG.VI.542; VII.115]
LAWSON, PATRICK, a workman in Glasgow, testament, 1771, Comm. Glasgow. [NRS]
LAWSON, WILLIAM, late Deacon of the Masons in Glasgow, testament, 1735, Comm. Glasgow. [NRS]
LECK, JOHN, in Glasgow, testament, 1746/1750, Comm. Glasgow. [NRS]
LECKIE, ANDREW, born 1756, a laborer from Glasgow, to New York, 1775. [NA.T47.12]
LECKIE, JANET, in Glasgow, daughter of the deceased Michael Leckie a merchant there, testament, 1771, Comm. Glasgow. [NRS]
LEECHMAN, WILLIAM, Principal of Glasgow College, a letter, 1770. [NRS.NRAS.332.C3.784]
LEES, JAMES, a merchant in Glasgow and his spouse Christian Corbet, testament, 1747, Comm. Glasgow. [NRS]
LEES, JOHN, a maltman, husband of Janet Woddrow a maltman, a burgess and guilds-brother of Glasgow in 1719, [GBR], testament, 1751, Comm. Glasgow. [NRS]
LEES, JOHN, transported to Virginia, landed at the James River, 1773. [NRS.JC27.10.3]
LEES, ROBERT, from Glasgow, in Boston, 1740. [SCS]
LEITCH, ROBERT, born 1746, a farmer from Glasgow, to New York, 1774. [NA.T47.12]
LEITH, ANN, in Glasgow, relict of James Boes late minister at Campbeltown, testament, 1758, Comm. Glasgow. [NRS]

The People of Glasgow, 1725-1775

LENNOX, CHARLES, born 1754, from Glasgow, settled in Prince William County, Virginia, before 1776. [VSL.23816]

LENNOX, ELIZABETH, in Glasgow, relict of John Kincaid of that Ilk, testaments, 1739/1740, Comm. Glasgow. [NRS]

LENNOX, WALTER, a baxter, son of Walter Lennox a baxter, was admitted to the Baxter Incorporation, and as a burgess and guilds-brother of Glasgow in 1763. [IBG#126][GBR]

LESLIE, GEORGE, master of Glasgow Grammar School, testament, 1766, Comm. Glasgow. [NRS]

LETHAM, JAMES, a wright, former apprentice to James Lochhead a wright, a burgess and guilds-brother of Glasgow in 1746, [GBR], testament, 1756, Comm. Glasgow. [NRS]

LETHEM, JOHN, a merchant in Glasgow, a burgess and guilds-brother of Glasgow in 1757, testament, 1760, Comm. Glasgow. [NRS][GBR]

LETHEM, LILIAS, daughter of John Lethem a merchant in Glasgow and spouse of Joseph McCaig a merchant there, testament, 1752, Comm. Glasgow. [NRS]

LETHEM, PATRICK, a maltman, son in law of Matthew Machen a maltman, a freeman maltman, and a burgess and guilds-brother of Glasgow in 1738, [GBR], [MCG.136]; a maltman in Glasgow, testament, 1749, Comm. Glasgow. [NRS]

LEWIS, JOHN, a tailor in Glasgow, testament, 1741, Comm. Glasgow. [NRS]

LINDSAY, JAMES, in Glasgow, 1753. [NRS.E326.1.172]

LINDSAY, JAMES, a baxter, former apprentice to James Anderson a baxter, was admitted to the Baxter Incorporation, and as a burgess and guilds-brother of Glasgow in1762. [IBG#126][GBR]

LINNING, ROBERT, a dyer in Glasgow, testament, 1742, Comm. Glasgow. [NRS]

LISTON, JOHN, a tanner, former apprentice to John Liston a tanner, a burgess and guilds-brother of Glasgow in 1707, [GBR], testaments, 1731/1736, Comm. Glasgow. [NRS]

LISTON, WILLIAM, a wright, former apprentice to Walter Barton a wright, a burgess and guilds-brother of Glasgow in 1716, [GBR], testament, 1759, Comm. Glasgow. [NRS]

LITTLE, HELEN, relict of John Johnston MD in Glasgow, testament, 1736, Comm. Glasgow. [NRS]

LIVINGSTON, PATRICK or PETER, son in law of James Gray a baxter, was admitted to the Baxter Incorporation, and as a burgess and guilds-brother of Glasgow in 1772. [IBG#126][GBR]

LOCH, ROBERT, a member of the Incorporation of Weavers, 1725. [OGW#108]

LOCHHEAD, AGNES, daughter of the deceased Walter Lochhead a merchant in Glasgow and late wife of David Smith a mason in Glasgow, testament, 1773, Comm. Glasgow. [NRS]

LOCHHEAD, GILBERT, a baxter, son of Walter Lochhead, was admitted to the Baxter Incorporation, 1747. [IBG#126]

LOCHHEAD, HENRY, a merchant, eldest son of James Lochhead a wright, a burgess and guilds-brother of Glasgow in 1735. [GBR]

LOCHHEAD, HENRY, born 1741, son of Henry Lochhead and his wife Jean Park, a merchant from Glasgow, to America by 1766, settled in Petersburg, Virginia. [NRS.CS16.1.125/183; CS17.1.3/354; B10.12.4; B10.15.7488]

LOCHHEAD, JAMES, a wright in Glasgow, 1725. [ERG.V.219]

LOCHHEAD, WALTER, a merchant in Glasgow, testament, 1743, Comm. Glasgow. [NRS]

LOCHHEAD, WALTER, second son of the late Walter Lochhead a baxter, was admitted to the Baxter Incorporation, and as a burgess and guilds-brother of Glasgow in1756. [IBG#126][GBR]

LOCHHEAD, WILLIAM, a baxter, son of John Lochhead, was admitted to the Baxter Incorporation, 1763. [IBG#126]

LOCKARD, HENRY, a merchant from Glasgow, settled in Alexandria, Virginia, by 1764. [NRS.CS16.1.117/125/171]

LOGAN, GEORGE, a merchant from Glasgow, settled at Kemp's Landing, Princess Anne County, Virginia, in 1746, a Loyalist, died in Glasgow 1781, probate 1781 PCC. [NRS.RD3.211.295; S/H.1799; NRAS.0934.488] [NA.AO13.30.71/2]

LOGAN, JOHN, a merchant in Glasgow, testament, 1730, Comm. Glasgow. [NRS]

LOGAN, JOHN, a merchant in Glasgow, testament, 1751, Comm. Glasgow. [NRS]

LOGAN, ROBERT, a merchant in Glasgow, testament, 1754, Comm. Glasgow. [NRS]

LOGAN, Mrs, in Glasgow, 1753. [NRS.E326.1.172]

LOMAX, JOHN, a merchant from Glasgow, settled in Maryland before 1754, probate 1757 PCC

LORIMER, DAVID, from Glasgow, in Boston, 1749. [SCS]

LORIMER, JAMES, a baxter, former apprentice to John Scott a baxter, was admitted to the Baxter Incorporation, also a burgess and guilds-brother of Glasgow in 1742. [IBG#126][GBR]

LORIMER, JANET, spouse of David Alexander a shipmaster in Glasgow, testament, 1760, Comm. Glasgow. [NRS]

LORIMER, NINIAN, a sailor in Glasgow, testament, 1728, Comm. Glasgow. [NRS]

LOUDOUN, ELIZABETH, in Glasgow, 1753. [NRS.E326.1.172]

LOUDOUN, FRANCIS, a distiller in Glasgow, testament, 1771, Comm. Glasgow. [NRS]

LOUDOUN, JAMES, a grocer in Glasgow, testament, 1771, Comm. Glasgow. [NRS]

LOUDOUN, JOHN, Professsor of Philosophy at the University of Glasgow, testament, 1750, Comm. Glasgow. [NRS]

LOW, JAMES, born 1750, a weaver from Glasgow, to New York, 1774. [NA.T47.12]

LUKE, CORNELIUS, a tailor, second son of David Luke a tailor, a burgess and guilds-brother of Glasgow in 1707, [GBR], there in 1725. [ERG.V.222]

LUKE, GEORGE, a printer in Glasgow, son of the deceased George Luke a merchant there, testament, 1754, Comm. Glasgow. [NRS]

LUKE, HENRY, a bookbinder or stationer, fifth son of James Luke a merchant, a burgess and guilds-brother of Glasgow in 1704, [GBR], testament, 1729, Comm. Glasgow. [NRS]

LUKE, JAMES, a merchant in Glasgow, testament, 1731, Comm. Glasgow. [NRS]

LUKE, JAMES, a merchant, eldest son of the late John Luke a merchant, a burgess and guilds-brother of Glasgow in 1752, [GBR], in Glasgow, 1753. [NRS.E326.1.172]; a testament, 1759, Comm. Glasgow. [NRS]

LUKE, JOHN, a goldsmith in Glasgow, and his brother german Walter Luke, sons of the late John Luke the younger, a merchant in Glasgow, testaments, 1734, Comm. Glasgow. [NRS]

LUKE, JOHN, of Claythorne, the elder, a merchant in Glasgow, testament, 1736, Comm. Glasgow. [NRS]

The People of Glasgow, 1725-1775

LUKE, JOHN, a baxter, eldest son of the late George Luke a merchant, and former apprentice to William Gilmor, was admitted to the Baxter Incorporation, and as a burgess and guilds-brother of Glasgow in 1748. [IBG#126][GBR]

LUKE, JOHN, in Glasgow, 1753. [NRS.E326.1.172]

LUKE, MARY, in Glasgow, 1753. [NRS.E326.1.172]

LUKE, ROBERT, a merchant in Glasgow, testament, 1729, Comm. Glasgow. [NRS]

LUKE, ROBERT, a merchant in Glasgow, 1739. [NRS.AC9.6449]

LUKE, ROBERT, of Greenfield, a goldsmith in Glasgow, testament, 1759, Comm. Glasgow. [NRS]

LUKE, WILLIAM, the elder, a merchant in Glasgow, testament, 1743, Comm. Glasgow. [NRS]

LUKE, Mrs, in Glasgow, 1753. [NRS.E326.1.172]

LUNDIE, HELEN, spouse to John Biggart a tailor in Glasgow, testament, 1737, Comm. Glasgow. [NRS]

LUNDIE, TOBIAS, a tailor, former apprentice to John Biggar a tailor, a burgess and guilds-brother of Glasgow in 1725, [GBR], Glasgow, 1753. [NRS.E326.1.172]

LYLE, JAMES, a writer in Glasgow, testament, 1762, Comm. Glasgow. [NRS]

LYMBURNER, JOHN, a weaver, formerly in Paisley, later in Glasgow, testament, 1755, Comm. Glasgow. [NRS]

LYON, JOHN, a merchant, eldest son of the late George Lyon a merchant, a burgess and guilds-brother of Glasgow in 1722, [GBR], 1731. [NRS.AC9.5455]

LYON, MATHEW, born 1726, a weaver from Glasgow, to North Carolina, 1775. [NA.T47.12]

MCALLASTER, THOMAS, born 1754, a shoemaker from Glasgow, to New York, 1774. [NA.T47.12]

MCALLISTER, GRISSELL, daughter of James McAllister a merchant in Campbeltown and spouse to James Hynd a merchant in Glasgow, testament, 1750, Comm. Glasgow. [NRS]

MCALLISTER, JOHN, a weaver, eldest son of the late Patrick McAllister a weaver, a burgess and guilds-brother of Glasgow in 1767, [GBR], testament, 1774, Comm. Glasgow. [NRS]

The People of Glasgow, 1725-1775

MCALLISTER, MARGARET, spouse to Patrick Lang a baxter in Glasgow, testaments, 1739/1746, Comm. Glasgow. [NRS]

MCALPIN, ARCHIBALD, born in Glasgow during 1772, settled in South Carolina and in Georgia, died in Savanna in 1822. ["Georgia for the Country, Savanna", 28 September 1822]

MCALPIN, DANIEL, younger son of John McAlpin a gardener, was admitted to the Baxter Incorporation, and as a burgess and guilds-brother of Glasgow in 1775. [IBG#131][GBR]

MCALPIN, JAMES, born 1761, a merchant from Glasgow, to Virginia before 1776, settled in Philadelphia, died 1847. [AP.236]

MCALPINE, JOHN, a merchant, a burgess and guilds-brother of Glasgow in 1737, [GBR], testament, 1742, Comm. Glasgow. [NRS]

MCALPINE, JOHN, a merchant and shopkeeper in Glasgow, testament, 1747/1750, Comm. Glasgow. [NRS]

MCALPINE, JOHN, a horse-setter in Glasgow, testament, 1753, Comm. Glasgow. [NRS]

MCALPIN, WALTER, from Glasgow, in Boston, 1744. [SCS]

MCALPINE, WALTER, a bookbinder from Glasgow, in America by 1776. [NRS.RS10.Dunbarton.11.256/278]

MCARTHUR, JAMES, senior, born 1731, a weaver from Glasgow, settled in Hampshire County, Virginia. [VSA.24296]

MCARTHUR, JOHN, a gardener in Glasgow, testament, 1730, Comm. Glasgow. [NRS]

MACAULAY, ALEXANDER, born 1754, a merchant from Glasgow, emigrated in 1775, settled in Yorktown, Virginia, died there in 1798. [WMQ.11/180; 2/22/235; 2/23/235; 2/23/509]

MACAULAY, JAMES, a baxter in Glasgow, testament, 1741, Comm. Glasgow. [NRS]

MCAULAY, WILLIAM, a rioter in Glasgow, transported to the colonies, 1749. [SM.11.252]

MCAUSLAND, ROBERT, a merchant in Glasgow, later in Newfoundland, 1783. [NRS.CS17.1.2/212]

MCBRAYER, JAMES, a shipmaster in Glasgow, testament, 1729, Comm. Glasgow. [NRS]

The People of Glasgow, 1725-1775

MCBRAYER, ROBERT, a mirror-maker in Glasgow, testament, 1744, Comm. Glasgow. [NRS]

MCCALL, ARCHIBALD, born 1734, son of Samuel McCall and his wife Margaret Adams, a merchant from Glasgow, emigrated in 1752, settled in Tappahannock, Essex County, Virginia, died 1814. [VMHB.73/313][NA.AO13.31.210][NRS.CS17.1.7/265]

MCCALL, GEORGE, born 1700, a merchant from Glasgow, settled in Philadelphia, died there 1740. [AP.237]

MCCALL, GEORGE, a merchant in Glasgow, 1775. [NRS.CS16.1.165; AC7.58]

MCCALL, JAMES, a storekeeper from Glasgow, to America by 1765, settled in New Glasgow, Essex County, Virginia. [GA.T79.41]

MCCALL, JOHN, in Glasgow, a marriage contract with Mary Crawford, 1763. [NRS.RD4.218.1059]

MCCALL, SAMUEL, a schoolmaster and planter from Glasgow, settled in Virginia before 1765. [NRS.CS16.1.120]

MCCALLUM, DANIEL, a merchant in Glasgow, testament, 1775, Comm. Glasgow. [NRS]

MCCALLUM, JOHN, a merchant, husband of Janet Miller, a burgess and guilds-brother of Glasgow in 1738, [GBR], testament, 1770, Comm. Glasgow. [NRS]

MCCAUL, ALEXANDER, a merchant from Glasgow, settled in Virginia by 1776, a Loyalist. [NA.AO13.32.116]

MCCAULL, HENRY, a merchant, husband of Janet Climey, a burgess and guilds-brother of Glasgow in 1720, [GBR], testaments, 1737/1739, Comm. Glasgow. [NRS]

MCCAULL, HENRY, a merchant in Glasgow, 1728, 1734, [NRS.AC7.34.708; AC40.166]; testament, 1763, Comm. Glasgow. [NRS]

MCCAULL, JAMES, a merchant from Glasgow, settled in Virginia before 1746, testament, 1747. [NRS.CS16.1.78]

MCCAULL, JOHN, a merchant in Glasgow, 1743, 1746. [NRS.E504.15.1/2; CS16.1.78]

MCCAULL, SAMUEL, a merchant in Glasgow, testament, 1770, Comm. Glasgow. [NRS]

MCCLAY, ISOBEL, spouse of John Dougall a merchant in Glasgow, testament, 1737, Comm. Glasgow. [NRS]

MCCLAY, JOHN, of Cathkin, a merchant in Glasgow, testament, 1740, Comm. Glasgow. [NRS]

MCCLAY, WILLIAM, a French teacher in Glasgow, testament, 1737, Comm. Glasgow. [NRS]

MCCLYMONT, WILLIAM, a merchant, husband of Agnes Fleming, a burgess and guilds-brother of Glasgow in 1730, [GBR], testaments, 1757/1758/1759/1770, Comm. Glasgow. [NRS]

MCCOLL, JOHN, of Glasdrum, a merchant in Glasgow, later in New York, 1787. [NAS.CS17.1.5/115]

MCCORKIE, JAMES, a sailor in Glasgow, testament, 1770, Comm. Glasgow. [NRS]

MCCREE, WILLIAM, a merchant in Glasgow, 1770. [NRS.AC7.53]

MCCROCKET, BOYD, a baxter, former apprentice to John Riddell a baxter, was admitted to the Baxter Incorporation, and as a burgess and guilds-brother of Glasgow in1763. [IBG#131][GBR]

MCCULLIE, JANET, in Glasgow, daughter of Duncan McCullie at the burn of Ardinprior, parish of Kippen, testament, 1729, Comm. Glasgow. [NRS]

MCCULLOCH, ISOBEL, relict of William Miller a tailor in Glasgow, testament, 1739, Comm. Glasgow. [NRS]

MCCULLOCH, JOHN, from Glasgow, in Boston, 1727. [SCS]

MCCULLOCH, LUDOVICK, a horse-setter in Glasgow, testament, 1773, Comm. Glasgow. [NRS]

MCCULLOCH, THOMAS, a merchant from Glasgow, settled in Gosport and Norfolk, Virginia, before 1776, returned to Glasgow in 1779. [NA.AO13.31.244] [NRS.NRAS.0623.T-MJ.363]

MCCULLOCH, WILLIAM, a merchant, a burgess and guilds-brother of Glasgow in 1762, [GBR], testament, 1766, Comm. Glasgow. [NRS]

MCCUNN, JOHN, a shipmaster in Glasgow, and his spouse Janet Gibson, testament, 1726, Comm. Glasgow. [NRS]

MCCUNN, WILLIAM, from Glasgow, in Boston, 1743. [SCS]

MCCUNN, WILLIAM, of Overnewton, a merchant in Glasgow, son of the deceased John McCunn a shipmaster there, testament, 1746, Comm. Glasgow. [NRS]

MCDONALD, CATHERINE, from Port Glasgow, an indentured servant in Philadelphia in 1772. [Records of Indentures in Philadelphia]

The People of Glasgow, 1725-1775

MCDONALD, DONALD, merchant, a burgess and guilds-brother of Glasgow in 1755, [GBR]; 1773. [Ramshorn MI, Glasgow]
MCDONALD, DUNCAN, gardener in Glasgow, 1771; a burgess and guilds-brother of Glasgow in 1780, [GBR]. [GA.D-TC13/603s]
MACDONALD, FELIX, a weaver in Glasgow, testaments, 1751/1752, Comm. Glasgow. [NRS]
MCDONALD JOHN, from Port Glasgow, an indentured servant in Philadelphia in 1772. [Records of Indentures in Philadelphia]
MCDOUGAL, ISOBEL, relict of John Ure a mealman in Glasgow, testament, 1771, Comm. Glasgow. [NRS]
MCDOUGALL, JAMES, in Glasgow, 1753. [NRS.E326.1.172]
MCDOUGALL, JOHN, in Glasgow, 1753. [NRS.E326.1.172]
MCDOWELL, JOHN, a merchant from Glasgow, settled in Hanover County, Virginia, 1750, a Loyalist, returned to Glasgow; a merchant, a burgess and guilds-brother of Glasgow in 1773, [GBR]; in Glasgow, a deed, 1775. [NRS.RD4.218.1077][NA.AO13.31.275][NRS.RD4.243; NRAS.0631.GDB4]
MCFADYEN, DANIEL, a lorimer, former apprentice of Robert Callendar a hammerman, a burgess and guilds-brother of Glasgow in 1777, [GBR]; settled in New York, probate 1781 PCC
MCFARLAND, WILLIAM, master of the Red Dye Society of Glasgow, 1759. [ERG.VI.547]
MCFARLANE, ALEXANDER, a factor from Glasgow, to America by 1761, settled in Chaptico, Maryland. [GA]
MACFARLANE, JANET, born 1756, a spinner from Glasgow, to New York, 1775. [NA.T47.12]
MCFARLANE, JOHN, a merchant in Glasgow, 1728, 1729. [NRS.AC7.24.710; AC7.34.708; AC10.138; AC9.1070]
MACFARLANE, JOHN, a barber in Glasgow, testament, 1742, Comm. Glasgow. [NRS]
MACFARLANE, JOHN, the younger, a workman in Glasgow, testament, 1749, Comm. Glasgow. [NRS]
MACFARLANE, JOHN, a house-breaker in Glasgow, transported to the colonies, 1772. [NRS.RH2.4.255]
MACFARLANE, JOHN, born 1755, a rope-maker from Glasgow, to New York, 1774. [NA.T47.12]

MACFARLANE, JOHN, born 1757, a hatter from Glasgow, to New York, 1774. [NA.T47.12]

MCFARLAN, PARLAN, born 1731, a merchant in Glasgow, died 1778, husband of Catherine Taylor. [Ramshorn MI, Glasgow]

MACFARLANE, ROBERT, a merchant, husband of Janet Mitchell, a burgess and guilds-brother of Glasgow in 1719, [GBR], testament, 1747, Comm. Glasgow. [NRS]

MACFARLANE, ROBERT, a horse-setter in Glasgow, testament, 1750, Comm. Glasgow. [NRS]

MCFARLANE, MARY, in Glasgow, 1753. [NRS.E326.1.172]

MCFEAT, JOHN, a baxter, former apprentice to John Morrison a baxter, was admitted to the Baxter Incorporation, also as a burgess and guilds-brother of Glasgow in 1754. [IBG#131][GBR]

MCFIE, JOHN, a causier in Glasgow, 1725. [ERG.V.208]

MACFIE, JOHN, a maltman in Glasgow, testament, 1756, Comm. Glasgow. [NRS]

MCFIE, THOMAS, a causier in Glasgow, 1725. [ERG.V.208]

MACGILCHRIST, ARCHIBALD, deputy town clerk of Glasgow, second son of the late James McGilchrist of Northbarr who was the eldest son of the deceased Donald McGilchrist of Northbarr a merchant, a burgess and guilds-brother of Glasgow in 1760, [GBR]; in Glasgow, a letter, 1769. [NRS.NRAS.332.C3.782]

MACGILCHRIST, CHRISTIAN, in Glasgow, 1753. [NRS.E326.1.172]

MACGILCHRIST, GEORGE, a merchant in Glasgow, testaments, 1735/1738, Comm. Glasgow. [NRS]

MACGILCHRIST, JOHN, a member of the Incorporation of Weavers, 1725. [OGW#108]

MACGILCHRIST, JOHN, in Glasgow, 1753. [NRS.E326.1.172]

MACGILCHRIST, LAWRENCE, a shipmaster in Glasgow, youngest son of James MacGilchrist of Northbarr, testament, 1749, Comm. Glasgow. [NRS]

MCGILCHRIST, ROBERT, son in law of Patrick Lethem a maltman, a freeman maltman, 1751. [MCG.136]

MCGILL, JAMES, born 1744, son of James McGill in Glasgow, educated at Glasgow University, to Canada before 1776, a fur trader in Montreal. [MAGU.55]

MCGILP, JOHN, a flesher, burgess and guilds-brother of Glasgow in 1750. [GBR]

The People of Glasgow, 1725-1775

MACGOMERY, PETER, from Glasgow, in Boston, 1748. [SCS]

MCGOVERN, WILLIAM, a merchant in Glasgow, 1767. [NRS.NRAS.2522/CA5/24]

MCGOWAN, MARION, in Glasgow, testament, 1758, Comm. Glasgow. [NRS]

MCGOWAN, ROBERT, a merchant in Glasgow, 1727. [NRS.AC7.36.328]

MCGOWAN, WILLIAM, a merchant in Glasgow and master of the Nelly and the Adventure of Glasgow, 1750. [NRS.AC9.1729]

MCGOWAN, WILLIAM, junior, sometime a merchant in Jamaica, thereafter in Glasgow, testament, 1770, Comm. Glasgow. [NRS]

MACHAN, WILLIAM, a maltman, eldest son of the late Matthew Machan a merchant, a burgess and guilds-brother of Glasgow in 1738, [GBR], testament, 1752, Comm. Glasgow. [NRS]

MCILDOE, CHRISTIAN, in Glasgow, 1753. [NRS.E326.1.172]

MCILDOE, SAMUEL, youngest son of the deceased John McIldoe a merchant in Glasgow, testament, 1749, Comm. Glasgow. [NRS]

MCILMORROW, THOMAS, a merchant, husband of Susanna Smith, a burgess and guilds-brother of Glasgow in 1743, [GBR], testament, 1751, Comm. Glasgow. [NRS]

MCILWHAM, MARGARET, relict of Caesar Burns a rope-maker in Glasgow, testament, 1757, Comm. Glasgow. [NRS]

MCILWHAM, WILLIAM, a mealman and maltman in Glasgow, testament, 1742, Comm. Glasgow. [NRS]

MCINDO, JAMES, a weaver in Glasgow, testament, 1761, Comm. Glasgow. [NRS]

MCINTYRE, DONALD, a merchant in Glasgow, testament, 1772, Comm. Glasgow. [NRS]

MCIVER, ALEXANDER, born 1753, a merchant in Glasgow, to New York, 1774. [NA.T47.12]

MACK, GEORGE, a merchant, husband of Margaret Broun, a burgess and guilds-brother of Glasgow in 1729, [GBR],testament, 1733, Comm. Glasgow. [NRS]

MCKAY, AGNES, from Glasgow, an indentured servant in Philadelphia in 1772. [Records of Indentures in Philadelphia]

MCKAY, ALEXANDER, from Glasgow, an indentured servant in Philadelphia in 1772. [Records of Indentures in Philadelphia]

The People of Glasgow, 1725-1775

MCKAY, ANGUS, from Port Glasgow, an indentured servant in Philadelphia in 1772. [Records of Indentures in Philadelphia]

MCKAY, ANNA, from Glasgow, an indentured servant in Philadelphia in 1772. [Records of Indentures in Philadelphia]

MCKAY, CATHERINE, from Glasgow, an indentured servant in Chester County, Pennsylvania in 1772. [Records of Indentures in Philadelphia]

MCKAY, CATHERINE, from Glasgow, an indentured servant in Philadelphia in 1772. [Records of Indentures in Philadelphia]

MCKAY, DONALD, from Glasgow, an indentured servant in Lancaster County, Pennsylvania, in 1772. [Records of Indentures in Philadelphia]

MACKAY, EBENEZER, a merchant from Glasgow, to Virginia by 1763, settled in Talbot County, Maryland.[NRS.16.1.115][Maryland Mag.2/375]

MCKAY, ISABELLA, from Glasgow, an indentured servant in Salem County, New Jersey, in 1772. [Records of Indentures in Philadelphia]

MCKAY, JAMES, from Port Glasgow, an indentured servant in Lancaster County, Pennsylvania, in 1772. [Records of Indentures in Philadelphia]

MCKAY, JEAN, from Port Glasgow, an indentured servant in Lancaster County, Pennsylvania, in 1772. [Records of Indentures in Philadelphia]

MCKAY, JOHN, from Glasgow, an indentured servant in Burlington, New Jersey, in 1772. [Records of Indentures in Philadelphia]

MCKAY, MARGARET, from Glasgow, an indentured servant in Philadelphia in 1772. [Records of Indentures in Philadelphia]

MCKAY, ROBERT, a merchant from Glasgow, to Virginia before 1761. [NRS.B10.15.6729]

MCKAY, SANDIE, from Port Glasgow, an indentured servant in Lancaster County, Pennsylvania, in 1772. [Records of Indentures in Philadelphia]

MCKAY, WILLIAM, from Port Glasgow, an indentured servant in Lancaster County, Pennsylvania, in 1772. [Records of Indentures in Philadelphia]

MCKEAN, JOHN, a smith in Cowcaddens, barony parish of Glasgow, testament, 1726, Comm. Glasgow. [NRS]

MCKEAN, WILLIAM, a tobacconist from Glasgow, at Charles Wharf, North End, Boston, in 1764, [Boston Gazette:8 October 1764]; in Boston, 1767. [SCS]

MCKECHNIE, ALEXANDER, a merchant in Glasgow, testament, 1771, Comm. Glasgow. [NRS]

The People of Glasgow, 1725-1775

MCKECHNIE, JAMES, a tailor, former apprentice to Nathaniel Colquhoun a tailor, a burgess and guilds-brother of Glasgow in 1732, [GBR], testament, 1766, Comm. Glasgow. [NRS]

MCKECHNIE, JANET, a shop-keeper in Glasgow, daughter of the deceased Charles McKechnie a maltman in Rothesay, testament, 1744, Comm. Glasgow. [NRS]

MCKECHNIE, JOHN, a merchant, husband of Janet Humphrey, a burgess and guilds-brother of Glasgow in 1745, [GBR], there in 1769. [NRS.CS16.1.107]

MCKECHNIE, WILLIAM, a barber, eldest son of William McKechnie a barber, a burgess and guilds-brother of Glasgow in 1757, [GBR], testament, 1758, Comm. Glasgow. [NRS]

MCKENNIE, ANDREW, a merchant in Glasgow, testaments, 1730/1731, Comm. Glasgow. [NRS]

MCKENNIE, JOHN, senior, a merchant in Glasgow, testament, 1742, Comm. Glasgow. [NRS]

MCKENNOT, JAMES, born 1756, a copper-smith from Glasgow, to New York, 1774. [NA.T47.12]

MCKENZIE, AGNES, a thief from Glasgow, daughter of Agnes McDonald, transported to the colonies, 1775. [SM.37.405]

MCKENZIE, ANDREW, from Glasgow, in Boston, 1748. [SCS]

MCKENZIE, JAMES, a merchant from Glasgow, died in Maryland 1748. [MdGaz.21.9.1748; #178]

MCKENZIE, JOHN, a merchant in Glasgow, testaments, 1751/1752, Comm. Glasgow. [NRS][NRS.AC9.1697-8]

MCKENZIE, JOHN, a merchant, eldest son of the late John McKenzie a merchant, a burgess and guilds-brother of Glasgow in 1764, [GBR], in Glasgow, 1771. [NRS.CS96.3176]

MACKENZIE, Lady MARGARET, daughter of George, Earl of Cromarty, third wife of John Glassford of Dougalston, died 1773. [Ramshorn MI, Glasgow]

MCKENZIE, WILLIAM, in Glasgow, 1753. [NRS.E326.1.172]

MCKERROW, JAMES, a mason, a burgess and guilds-brother of Glasgow in 1765, [GBR], testament, 1772, Comm. Glasgow. [NRS]

MACKIE, ALEXANDER, a merchant from Glasgow, settled in Maryland by 1748, testament, 1766, Comm. Glasgow; probate 1766 Maryland. [NRS.B10.5959/6653; 15.7019]

MACKIE, ALEXANDER, a forger in Glasgow, was transported to the colonies, 1773. [SM.35.334]

MACKIE, ANDREW, son of Andrew Mackie of Lerbor, a dyer and merchant from Glasgow, a burgess and guilds-brother of Glasgow in 1762, [GBR]; settled in Virginia, testament, 1766, Comm. Glasgow. [NRS.B10.15.7019]

MCKINDLAY, JAMES, a baxter, eldest son of the late John McKindlay a baxter, was admitted to the Baxter Incorporation, and as a burgess and guilds-brother of Glasgow in 1744. [IBG#131][GBR]

MCKINDLAY, JOHN, a baxter, second son of John McKindlay, was admitted to the Baxter Incorporation, and as a burgess and guilds-brother of Glasgow in 1735. [IBG#131][GBR]

MCKINLAY, DAVID, a baxter, son of John McKinlay a baxter, was admitted to the Baxter Incorporation, and as a burgess and guilds-brother of Glasgow in 1758. [IBG#131][GBR]

MCKINLAY, JOHN, a vintner in Glasgow, testament, 1767, Comm. Glasgow. [NRS]

MCKINLAY, PETER, born 1751, a wright from Glasgow, to New York, 1775. [NA.T47.12]

MCKINNON, JOHN, in Glasgow, a deed, 1775. [NRS.RD2.217/1.778]

MCKINNON, Mrs, in Glasgow, 1753. [NRS.E326.1.172]

MCKINVEN, JOHN, a journeyman wright in Glasgow, testament, 1755, Comm. Glasgow. [NRS]

MACKLEM, JAMES, a baxter, eldest son of William Macklem a baxter, was admitted to the Baxter Incorporation, and as a burgess and guilds-brother of Glasgow in 1775. [IBG#127][GBR]

MCLACHLAN, JAMES, born 1727, eldest son of the late John McLachlan, a wright, and his wife Elizabeth Luke in Glasgow, a burgess and guilds-brother of Glasgow in 1769, [GBR], a tailor from Glasgow, emigrated to America, 1756. [NRS.B10.15.6682]

MCLAREN, JOHN, a minister in Glasgow, testament, 1756, Comm. Glasgow. [NRS]

MCLAUGHLAN, Captain HUGH, from Glasgow, died 1755 in Jamaica. [GJ.752]

MCLAUCHLAN, HUGH, of Cameron, a merchant in Kingston, Jamaica, [NRS.S/H.1756], later in Glasgow, testaments, 1757/1760/1762, Comm. Glasgow. [NRS]

The People of Glasgow, 1725-1775

MCLAUCHLAN, LACHLAN, a felt-maker in Glasgow, testament, 1729, Comm. Glasgow. [NRS]

MCLAUCHLAN, WALTER, a journeyman shoemaker in Glasgow, and Andrew McLauchlan a sailor in Port Glasgow, sons of the deceased Andrew McLauchlan of Drumland, testament, 1751, Comm. Glasgow. [NRS]

MCLAURIN, JOHN, born in Glendaruel in 1693, minister of Ramshorn, Glasgow, from 1723 until his death in 1754. [F.3.439]

MCLEA, JOHN, a flesher, husband of Margaret Marshall, a burgess and guilds-brother of Glasgow in 1768, [GBR], a thief from Glasgow, transported to the West Indies, 1775. [SM.37.523]

MCLEAN, ARCHIBALD, a baxter, former apprentice to Patrick Whyte a baxter, was admitted to the Baxter Incorporation, and as a burgess and guilds-brother of Glasgow in 1769. [IBG#131][GBR]

MCLEAN, DANIEL, a merchant in Glasgow, husband of Mary Dickson, a burgess and guilds-brother of Glasgow in 1751, [GBR]; letters 1756-1765, in America, 1773. [NRS.NRAS.3283, bundle 391; CS16.1.154]

MCLEAN, HUGH, a writer in Glasgow, 1772. [LC#3233]

MCLEAN, JAMES, sometime a waiter in Port Glasgow, thereafter in Glasgow, testament, 1744, Comm. Glasgow. [NRS]

MCLEAN, LACHLAN, in Glasgow, 1753. [NRS.E326.1.172]

MCLEAN, MARGARET, in Glasgow, 1753. [NRS.E326.1.172]

MCLEDOE, PATRICK, a merchant in Glasgow, testaments, 1728/1729, Comm. Glasgow. [NRS]

MCLELLAN, JOHN, born 1748, a laborer from Glasgow, to New York, 1775. [NA.T47.12]

MCLEOD, JOHN, senior, a tailor, eldest son of the late John McLeod a tailor, a burgess and guilds-brother of Glasgow in 1756, [GBR]; from Glasgow, to New York, 1774. [NA.T47.12]

MCLUM, JANET, spouse to Robert Gibson a weaver in Glasgow, testament, 1753, Comm. Glasgow. [NRS]

MCLUM, WILLIAM, a baxter, former apprentice to John Menzies a baxter, was admitted to the Baxter Incorporation, 1745. [IBG#127]

MCMARTINE, MARY, born 1752, a brush-maker from Glasgow, to New York, 1775. [NA.T47.12]

The People of Glasgow, 1725-1775

MCNAIR, JAMES, a shipmaster in Glasgow, son of Robert McNair a merchant in Glasgow, 1751. [NRS.AC16.2.277-407]

MCNAIR, ROBERT, a sugar baxter in Glasgow, 1753, 1763. [NRS.E326.1.172] [ERG.VII.116]

MCNAUGHT, JOHN, H.M. Excise Supervisor in Glasgow, testament, 1731, Comm. Glasgow. [NRS]

MCNEILL, NEILL, late of Hanover, Jamaica, thereafter in Glasgow, testament, 1749, Comm. Glasgow. [NRS]

MCNICOLL, DONALD, a merchant and factor from Glasgow, emigrated by 1760, settled in Pittsylvania County, Virginia. [GA]

MCPHADYEN, HUGH, a baxter, former apprentice to John Ure a baxter, was admitted to the Baxter Incorporation, and admitted as a burgess and guilds-brother of Glasgow in 1775. [IBG#131][GBR]

MCPHEE, DANIEL, born 1754, a joiner from Glasgow, to Maryland, 1775. [NA.T47.9-11]

MCTAVISH, DOUGALL, a boatman in Glasgow, testament, 1764, Comm. Glasgow. [NRS]

MCTEIR, WILLIAM, a merchant in Glasgow, testament, 1746, Comm. Glasgow. [NRS]

MCURE, ROBERT, a writer in Glasgow, testament, 1728, Comm. Glasgow. [NRS]

MCVEY, THOMAS, a student of Divinity in Glasgow, testament, 1732, Comm. Glasgow. [NRS]

MCVICAR, DUNCAN, born 1741, son of Archibald and Florence McVicar in Glasgow, a merchant from Glasgow, to America before 1758, settled in Charleston and in New York. [GA.T-MJ427.140]

MCVICAR, JOHN, born 1738, a tailor from Glasgow, to Wilmington, North Carolina, 1774. [NA.T47.9-11]

MAIN, ALEXANDER, a shipmaster in Glasgow, testament, 1725, Comm. Glasgow. [NRS]

MAIN, DAVID, a maltman in Glasgow, testament, 1752, Comm. Glasgow. [NRS]

MAIN, JAMES, from Glasgow, in Boston, 1747. [SCS]

MAIN, MARGARET, in Glasgow, relict of Alexander Cunningham of Capiston, testament, 1768, Comm. Glasgow. [NRS]

The People of Glasgow, 1725-1775

MAIN, WILLIAM, an indentured servant from Glasgow, absconded from the Commerce in New York on 22 June 1774. [NY Gazette & Weekly Mercury, 27.6.1774]

MAIR, DANIEL, born 1739, a weaver from Glasgow, to New York, 1774. [NA.T47.12]

MAIR, JAMES, a merchant grocer in Glasgow, testament, 1769, Comm. Glasgow. [NRS]

MAITLAND, WILLIAM, a baxter, former apprentice to William Alexander a baxter, was admitted to the Baxter Incorporation, 1756. [IBG#127]

MANN, JOSEPH, a merchant in Glasgow, testament, 1768, Comm. Glasgow. [NRS]

MAN, ROBERT, a wright, younger son of Joseph Man a merchant, a burgess and guilds-brother of Glasgow in 1767, [GBR], in Glasgow, 1775. [ERG.VII.448]

MARJORYBANKS, THOMAS, born 1749, a baxter, son in law of John Auchincloss a baxter, was admitted into the Baxter Incorporation, also as a burgess and guilds-brother of Glasgow in 1760, [IBG#127][GBR]; a baxter from Glasgow, to Philadelphia, 1774. [NA.T47.12]

MARSHALL, GEORGE, a weaver in Glasgow, testament, 1773, Comm. Glasgow. [NRS]

MARSHALL, HENRY, a surgeon in Glasgow, testaments, 1729/1730, Comm. Glasgow. [NRS]

MARSHALL, HENRY, son of the deceased John Marshall, a surgeon in Glasgow, and his spouse Margaret Baillie, testament, 1749, Comm. Glasgow. [NRS]

MARSHALL, JAMES, a factor from Glasgow, to America in 1747, died 1803 in Frederick County, Maryland. [DPCA.71][UNC; Williams pp][AJ.2918]

MARSHALL, JAMES, master of the Red Dye Society of Glasgow, 1759. [ERG.VI.547]

MARSHALL, JOHN, a dyer in Glasgow, testament, 1740, Comm. Glasgow. [NRS]

MARSHALL, JOHN, in Glasgow, a deed, 1765. [NRS.RD4.218.697]

MARSHALL, LILLIAS, in Glasgow, 1753. [NRS.E326.1.172]

MARSHALL, PETER, a frame-smith in Glasgow, testament, 1764, Comm. Glasgow. [NRS]

MARSHALL, ROBERT, a merchant, a burgess and guilds-brother of Glasgow in 1769, [GBR]; in Glasgow, 1774. [NRS.CS16.1.161]

The People of Glasgow, 1725-1775

MARSHALL, ROBERT, born 1746, a hammerman, son in law of James Dunlop of Garnkirk, a burgess and guilds-brother of Glasgow in 1769, [GBR], a wright from Glasgow, to New York, 1775. [NA.T47.12]

MARSHALL, WILLIAM, a quarter master in Glasgow, 1725. [ERG.V.247]

MARSHALL, WILLIAM, a student of Divinity in Glasgow, testament, 1730, Comm. Glasgow. [NRS]

MARTIN, ANDREW, of Eisenyards, a preacher in Glasgow, testament, 1730, Comm. Glasgow. [NRS]

MARTIN, or MCCANDLISH, GRIZEL, from Mill of Aries, Glasgow, settled in Janefield, New York, died 1770, testament, 1777, Comm. Edinburgh. [NRS]

MARTINE, ROBERT, in Glasgow, 1753. [NRS.E326.1.172]

MARTINE, WILLIAM, in Glasgow, 1753. [NRS.E326.1.172]

MASSON, ADAM, a tailor in Glasgow, testament, 1736, Comm. Glasgow. [NRS]

MASSON, MARGARET, relict of Patrick Gilmore a tailor and merchant in Glasgow, testament, 1737, Comm. Glasgow. [NRS]

MASSON, MARY, widow of Alexander Wardrop a shoemaker in Glasgow, testament, 1771, Comm. Glasgow. [NRS]

MASSON, ROBERT, a maltman in Glasgow, testament, 1734, Comm. Glasgow. [NRS]

MATHIE, ALEXANDER, a plumber in Glasgow, 1759. [ERG.VI.549]

MATHIE, WILLIAM, third son of William Mathie a maltman, a freeman maltman, 1744. [MCG.133]

MATTHEWSON, NEIL, from Glasgow, an indentured servant in Philadelphia, in 1772. [Records of Indentures in Philadelphia]

MAXWELL, JAMES, from Glasgow, in Boston, 1726, 1733. [SCS]

MAXWELL, Captain JAMES, a merchant in Glasgow, testament, 1756, Comm. Glasgow. [NRS]

MAXWELL, JOHN, a glazier in Glasgow, 1725. [ERG.V.220]

MAXWELL, JOHN, was admitted to the Skinners Craft, 1759. [SFG.268]

MAXWELL, MARGARET, relict of John Govan of Hogginfield sometime in Liverpool, thereafter in Glasgow, testament, 1733, Comm. Glasgow. [NRS]

MAXWELL, PATRICK, in Bridgegate, Glasgow, 1759. [ERG.VI.554]

MAXWELL, ROBERT, a merchant in Glasgow, testaments, 1737/1738, Comm. Glasgow. [NRS]

MAXWELL, THOMAS, a merchant, second son of the late Thomas Maxwell a merchant, a burgess and guilds-brother of Glasgow in 1737, [GBR], testament, 1750, Comm. Glasgow. [NRS]

MAXWELL, WILLIAM, born 1700, a clergyman from Glasgow, emigrated in 1726, settled in Charleston from 1724 to 1730, later on Edisto Island, and Barnsted Downs, South Carolina, died in Scotland 1780. [F.7.664; F.3.488]

MAXWELL, WILLIAM, from Glasgow, guilty of assault, transported to the colonies, 1725. [NRS.JC27]

MAXWELL, Mrs, in Glasgow, 1753. [NRS.E326.1.172]

MEFFAN, ALEXANDER, a surgeon in Glasgow, testament, 1725, Comm. Glasgow. [NRS]

MEFFAN, GRIZELL, daughter of the deceased John Meffan a surgeon in Glasgow, testaments, 1748/1750, Comm. Glasgow. [NRS]

MEIKLE, JAMES, son in law of John Weinzat a maltman, a freeman maltman, 1738. [MCG.134]

MELVILLE, JOHN, a merchant and tobacconist in Glasgow, testament, 1767, Comm. Glasgow. [NRS]

MELVILLE, WILLIAM, a dyer and bonnet-maker, husband of Elizabeth Mackie, a burgess and guilds-brother of Glasgow in 1748, [GBR], a deed, 1750. [NRS.RD2.168.146]

MENZIES, ANDREW, a baxter, eldest son of John Menzies a baxter, was admitted to the Baxter Incorporation, and as a burgess and guilds-brother of Glasgow in 1754. [IBG#127][GBR]

MENZIES, JOHN, a weaver in Glasgow, testament, 1725, Comm. Glasgow. [NRS]

MENZIES, JOHN, a baxter, former apprentice to Thomas Findlay a baxter, was admitted to the Baxter Incorporation, and a burgess and guilds-brother of Glasgow in 1731. [IBG#127][GBR]

MENZIES, JOHN, a weaver in Glasgow, testament, 1773, Comm. Glasgow. [NRS]

MENZIES, NINIAN, a merchant from Glasgow, settled in Richmond, Virginia, before 1775, a Loyalist, died in St Eustatia 1781. [NRS.CC8.8.131][NA.AO13.33.297][SM.43.223][NRS.NRAS.0623/3; CS16.1.165]

MENZIES, WILLIAM, a cordiner, former apprentice to James Montgomery a cordiner, a burgess and guilds-brother of Glasgow in 1723, [GBR], testament, 1728, Comm. Glasgow. [NRS]

MILLER, ALEXANDER, a book-binder in Glasgow, testament, 1745, Comm. Glasgow. [NRS]

MILLER, ANDREW, a maltman in Glasgow, testament, 1741, Comm. Glasgow. [NRS]

MILLER, CHARLES, a wright in Glasgow, testament, 1770, Comm. Glasgow. [NRS]

MILLER, DANIEL, in Glasgow, 1753. [NRS.E326.1.172]

MILLER, ELIZABETH, relict of James Miller late Visitor of the Maltmen in Glasgow, testament, 1744, Comm. Glasgow. [NRS]

MILLER, GAVIN, a merchant in Glasgow, husband of Isobel Hodge, a burgess and guilds-brother of Glasgow in 1770, [GBR], testament, 1772, Comm. Glasgow. [NRS]

MILLER, GEORGE, a merchant in Glasgow, deeds, 1750. [NRS.RD2.167.153/286; RD4.176/1.406]

MILLER, JANET, relict of James Grahame a cordiner in Glasgow, testament, 1726, Comm. Glasgow. [NRS]

MILLER, JOHN, of Westertoun, a maltman in Glasgow, testament, 1737, Comm. Glasgow. [NRS]

MILLER, JOHN, a weaver in the Caltoun of Glasgow, testament, 1743, Comm. Glasgow. [NRS]

MILLER, JOHN and JEAN, children of the deceased John Miller a merchant in Glasgow, testament, 1766, Comm. Glasgow. [NRS]

MILLER, JOHN, in Glasgow, 1753. [NRS.E326.1.172]; a merchant in Glasgow, testament, 1768, Comm. Glasgow. [NRS]

MILLER, JOSEPH, from Glasgow, in Boston, 1739. [SCS]

MILLER, MARGARET, sometime spouse of the deceased Andrew Adam a maltman in Glasgow, and thereafter spouse of the deceased James Rankine also a maltman there, testament, 1750, Comm. Glasgow. [NRS]

MILLER, MARION, spouse of William Tait a merchant in Glasgow, testament, 1760, Comm. Glasgow. [NRS]

MILLER, MARTHA, in Glasgow, 1753. [NRS.E326.1.172]; widow of John Luke of Claythorn a merchant in Glasgow, testament, 1762, Comm. Glasgow. [NRS]

The People of Glasgow, 1725-1775

MILLER, ROBERT, eldest son of Andrew Miller a merchant, a burgess and guilds-brother of Glasgow in 1754, [GBR], a coppersmith in Glasgow, 1759. [ERG.VI.540/549]

MILLER, THOMAS, a baxter, son in law of Alexander Buchanan a baxter, was admitted to the Baxter Incorporation, also as a burgess and guilds-brother of Glasgow in 1769. [IBG#127][GBR]

MILLER, THOMAS, a baxter, son in law of William Macklem a baxter, was admitted to the Baxter Incorporation, also as a burgess and guilds-brother of Glasgow in 1774. [IBG#127][GBR]

MILLER, WILLIAM, miller at the town milne of Glasgow, testament, 1747, Comm. Glasgow. [NRS]

MILLER, WILLIAM, a merchant from Glasgow, settled in Virginia before 1749. [NRS.CS16.1.81]

MILLER, WILLIAM, a merchant in Glasgow, deeds, 1750. [NRS.RD3.210.450; RD4.176/1.251]

MILLER, WILLIAM, in Glasgow, 1753. [NRS.E326.1.172]

MILLER, WILLIAM, from Glasgow, in Boston, 1765. [SCS]

MILLIKEN, HUGH, merchant in Glasgow, 1731. [NRS.AC9.5455]

MILNE, JOHN, a tailor in Glasgow, testament, 1729, Comm. Glasgow. [NRS]

MITCHELL, ALEXANDER, a baxter, former apprentice to Thomas Mitchell a baxter, was admitted to the Baxter Incorporation, and as a burgess and guilds-brother of Glasgow in 1750. [IBG#127][GBR]

MITCHELL, GEORGE, born 1747, a joiner from Glasgow, to Philadelphia, 1775. [NA.T47.12]

MITCHELL, GILBERT, born 1753, a rope-maker from Glasgow, to New York, 1774. [NA.T47.12]

MITCHELL, HENRY, a merchant from Glasgow, to America in 1757, settled in Fredericksburg, Virginia, a Loyalist, returned to Glasgow. [NA.AO13.31.635]

MITCHELL, HUGH, from Glasgow, settled in Charlestown, Charles County, Maryland, in 1760. [MSA.Charles Deeds G3.435/L536]

MITCHELL, JAMES, born in Glasgow 1705, to New England, 1730, settled in Weathersfield, Connecticut. [NRS.RD4.178.198][NNQ.7.89]

MITCHELL, JAMES, a baxter, second son of the late James Mitchell a maltman, also former apprentice to John Charity a baxter, was admitted to the Baxter

Incorporation, and as a burgess and guilds-brother of Glasgow in 1744. [IBG#127][GBR]

MITCHELL, JAMES, eldest son of James Mitchell a maltman, a freeman maltman, 1748. [MCG.132]

MITCHELL, JAMES, senior, in Glasgow, 1753. [NRS.E326.1.172]; a merchant in Glasgow, testament, 1763, Comm. Glasgow. [NRS]

MITCHELL, JAMES, a merchant from Glasgow, to Virginia by 1761. [NRS.B10.15.7118]

MITCHELL, JANET, relict of James Key of Edinbelly, resident in Glasgow, testament, 1763, Comm. Glasgow. [NRS]

MITCHELL, JOHN, the elder, a maltman in Glasgow, testament, 1727/1729, Comm. Glasgow. [NRS]

MITCHELL, JOHN, a merchant in Glasgow, testaments, 1736, Comm. Glasgow. [NRS]

MITCHELL, JOHN, a merchant in Glasgow, deeds, 1750. [NRS.RD3.210.52; RD4.176/2.67/108/257/476]

MITCHELL, JOHN, a merchant from Glasgow, settled in Charles County, Maryland, by 1761. [MSA.Charles County Deeds G3.435/L536]

MITCHELL, JOHN, a tanner in Glasgow, testament, 1766, Comm. Glasgow. [NRS]

MITCHELL, JOHN, a baxter, younger son of Thomas Mitchell a baxter, was admitted to the Baxter Incorporation, also as a burgess and guilds-brother of Glasgow in 1769. [IBG#127][GBR]

MITCHELL, JOHN, son of John Mitchell and his wife Janet Warden, a merchant and tobacco factor from Glasgow, settled in Fredericksburg and Culpepper Counties, Virginia, before 1776. [NRS.RD2.241.382; CS17.1.1][GA.T79.32]

MITCHELL, JOHN, born 1749, a farmer from Glasgow, to New York, 1774. [NA.T47.12]

MITCHELL, MARK, born 1755, a peruke-maker from Glasgow, emigrated via London aboard the <u>Planter</u> in 1774, landed at Hampton, Virginia. [NA.T47.9/11]

MITCHELL, PATRICK, a merchant in Glasgow, testaments, 1730/1736, Comm. Glasgow. [NRS]

MITCHELL, PATRICK, a merchant in Glasgow, testaments, 1746/1747, Comm. Glasgow. [NRS]

MITCHELL, PATRICK, a merchant in Glasgow, trading in Virginia after 1757. [GA.B10.15.7036]

MITCHELL, PATRICK, quartermaster of Glasgow, 1775. [ERG.VII.442]

MITCHELL, THOMAS, a baxter, former apprentice to James Algie a baxter, was admitted to the Baxter Incorporation, also as a burgess and guilds-brother of Glasgow in 1738. [IBG#127][GBR]

MITCHELL, THOMAS, junior, a baxter, son in law of John McKinlay a baxter, was admitted to the Baxter Incorporation, also as a burgess and guilds-brother of Glasgow in 1764. [IBG#127][GBR]

MITCHELL, WILLIAM, a writer in Glasgow, testament, 1728, Comm. Glasgow. [NRS]

MITCHELL, WILLIAM, a merchant in Glasgow, testaments, 1725/1729, Comm. Glasgow. [NRS]

MITCHELL, WILLIAM, born 1703 in Glasgow, son of John Mitchell and his wife Janet McLauchlan, to New England 1755, settled in Weatherfield and Chester, Connecticut. [NNQ.VII.89]

MITCHELL, WILLIAM, of Blairgotts, a merchant in Glasgow, testaments, 1738/1739/1740/1742/1747, Comm. Glasgow. [NRS]

MITCHELL, WILLIAM, a lint-dresser and lint-heckler in Glasgow, testament, 1750, Comm. Glasgow. [NRS]

MOCHLINE, WILLIAM, a planter from Glasgow, emigrated 1749, settled in St Andrew's, Brunswick County, Virginia. [NRS.RD2.168.10]

MOFFAT,......, born 1766 in Glasgow, died at Montego Bay, Jamaica, 1814. [Montego Bay MI]

MOLL, JOHN, a merchant, husband of Maly Ronald, a burgess and guilds-brother of Glasgow in 1701, [GBR], testament, 1727, Comm. Glasgow. [NRS]

MONNOCH, ANDREW, a distiller in Glasgow, testament, 1742, Comm. Glasgow. [NRS]

MONRO, ALEXANDER, a merchant in Glasgow, 1771. [NA.AO13.31.642]

MONROE, DANIEL, in Glasgow, 1753. [NRS.E326.1.172]

MONTEATH, ISABELLA, in Glasgow, testament, 1758, Comm. Glasgow. [NRS]

MONTEATH, WALTER, a merchant, eldest son of Walter Monteath of Kepps, a burgess and guilds-brother of Glasgow in 1760, [GBR], in Glasgow, 1765, 1774, a bond, 1773. [NRS.CS16.1.122/157; AC40.166; RD4.218.731]

MONTGOMERY, ADAM, a merchant and late Dean of Guild in Glasgow, testament, 1744, Comm. Glasgow. [NRS]

MONTGOMERY, CHRISTIAN, relict of James Clark a minister in Glasgow, and sister-german of the deceased Sir Hugh Montgomery of Skermorlie, testament, 1756, Comm. Glasgow. [NRS]

MONTGOMERY, Dr GEORGE, a physician, eldest son of the late Daniel Montgomery a merchant, a burgess and guilds-brother of Glasgow in 1752, [GBR], in Glasgow, 1753. [NRS.E326.1.172]

MONTGOMERT, Sir HUGH, of Skermorlie, in Glasgow, testament, 1735, Comm. Glasgow. [NRS]

MONTGOMERY, JAMES, from Glasgow, in Boston, 1733. [SCS]

MONTGOMERY, JAMES, of Pearston, a merchant and bailie of Glasgow, testament, 1742, Comm. Glasgow. [NRS]

MONTGOMERY, JAMES, a shipmaster in Glasgow, testament, 1753, Comm. Glasgow. [NRS]

MONTGOMERY, JAMES, a merchant in Glasgow, a deed, 1750, [NRS.RD2.168.148]; testaments, 1768/1771/1774, Comm. Glasgow. [NRS]

MONTGOMERY, JOHN, from Glasgow, to Boston, 1758. [SCS]

MONTGOMERY, PATRICK, a merchant, eldest son of James Montgomery, a burgess and guilds-brother of Glasgow in 1729, [GBR], testament, 1767/1768, Comm. Glasgow. [NRS]

MONTGOMERY, PETER, a merchant in Glasgow, 1734. [NRS.AC40.166]

MONTIER, JAMES, a merchant from Glasgow, 1734, [NRS.AC40.166]; in Boston, 1739. [SCS]

MONTIRE, ELIZABETH, in Glasgow, 1753. [NRS.E326.1.172]; a shopkeeper in Glasgow, daughter of the late William Montire alias McTyre a merchant in Glasgow, testament, 1760, Comm. Glasgow. [NRS]

MONTIRE, LILIAS, relict of George Stirling a maltman in Glasgow, testament, 1765, Comm. Glasgow. [NRS]

MOODY, HUGH, from Glasgow, in Boston, 1758. [SCS]; a shipmaster in Glasgow, a burgess of Irvine, Ayrshire, 1763. [AA]

MOODY, JOHN, visitor of the maltmen in Glasgow, 1725, [ERG.V.243]

MOODY, ROBERT, gardener, second son of the late John Moody a gardener, a burgess and guilds-brother of Glasgow in 1728, [GBR], in Glasgow, 1753. [NRS.E326.1.172]; testament, 1773, Comm. Glasgow. [NRS]

The People of Glasgow, 1725-1775

MOORE, JOHN, a messenger in Glasgow, a deed, 1750, [NRS.RD4.176/2.476]; testament, 1754, Comm. Glasgow. [NRS]

MORRIS, LOUDEN, eldest son of Andrew Morris a surgeon in Glasgow, educated at Glasgow University, a surgeon in Jamaica 1788. [MAGU]

MORRISON, AGNES, widow of Roderick McLeod a merchant in Glasgow, testament, 1775/1779, Comm. Glasgow. [NRS]

MORRISON, ALEXANDER, a baxter, former apprentice to Thomas Mitchell a baxter, was admitted to the Baxter Incorporation, also as a burgess and guilds-brother of Glasgow in 1766. [IBG#127][GBR]

MORRISON, ALEXANDER, a merchant in Glasgow, testament, 1773, Comm. Glasgow. [NRS]

MORRISON, CHRISTIAN, spouse of David Anderson a servant to Lawrence Dinwiddie a merchant in Glasgow, testament, 1764, Comm. Glasgow. [NRS]

MORRISON, DAVID, a wright and plumber, eldest son of George Morrison a wright, a burgess and guilds-brother of Glasgow in 1725. [GBR][ERG.V.220]

MORRISON, DAVID, born 1749, a wright from Glasgow, to New York, 1774. [NAS.T47.12]

MORRISON, JAMES, the elder, a baxter in Glasgow, testament, 1730, Comm. Glasgow. [NRS]

MORRISON, JAMES, a baxter, former apprentice and eldest son of James Morrison a baxter, was admitted to the Baxter Incorporation, and a burgess and guilds-brother of Glasgow in 1727. [IBG#127][GBR]

MORRISON, ROBERT, a merchant in Glasgow, testament, 1732, Comm. Glasgow. [NRS]

MORRISON, WILLIAM, a baxter, eldest son of James Morrison a baxter, was admitted to the Baxter Incorporation, also as a burgess and guilds-brother of Glasgow in 1763. [IBG#127][GBR]

MORSON, ARTHUR, a merchant from Glasgow, settled in Falmouth, Virginia, before 1768. [NRS.B10.15.7174]

MORTHLAND, ROBERT, Collector of the Weavers Incorporation, 1725. [OGW#108]

MORTON, JOHN, a maltman, burgess and guilds-brother of Glasgow in 1771, [GBR], a brewer in Glasgow, testament, 1775, Comm. Glasgow. [NRS]

MOUSIE, GILBERT, in Glasgow, testament, 1744, Comm. Glasgow. [NRS]

The People of Glasgow, 1725-1775

MOWBRAY, JAMES, a merchant in Vienna, Maryland, around 1763. [GA.B10.15.6863]

MUIR, ABIGAIL, relict of Alexander Dunlop the Professor of Greek in the University of Glasgow, testament, 1763, Comm. Glasgow. [NRS]

MUIR, CHRISTIAN, in Glasgow, 1753. [NRS.E326.1.172]

MUIR, FRANCIS, a coppersmith, a burgess and guilds-brother of Glasgow in 1753, [GBR], later was admitted to the Skinners Craft, 1758. [SFG.267]

MUIR, JAMES, a mason in Glasgow, 1725. [ERG.V.220]

MUIR, JAMES, a merchant in Glasgow, a deed, 1750. [NRS.RD3.210.585]

MUIR, JAMES, late Deacon of the Masons in Glasgow, testament, 1754, Comm. Glasgow. [NRS]

MUIR, JAMES, in Glasgow, 1753. [NRS.E326.1.172]; a tobacconist in Glasgow, testament, 1765, Comm. Glasgow. [NRS]

MUIR, JAMES, a surgeon in Glasgow, testament, 1770, Comm. Glasgow. [NRS]

MUIR, MARGARET, in Glasgow, 1753. [NRS.E326.1.172]

MUIR, ROBERT, Deacon of the Tailors in Glasgow, testament, 1738, Comm. Glasgow. [NRS]

MUIR, ROBERT, a mason in Glasgow, 1759. [ERG.VI.543]

MUIR, WILLIAM, in Glasgow, 1753. [NRS.E326.1.172]; a merchant in Glasgow, testament, 1753, Comm. Glasgow. [NRS]

MUIR, WILLIAM, a maltman in Glasgow, former Provost of Rutherglen, testament, 1770, Comm. Glasgow. [NRS]

MUIR, WILLIAM, a hatter in Glasgow, and his spouse Janet Kerr, testaments, 1771/1773, Comm. Glasgow. [NRS]

MUIRHEAD, BETTY, in Glasgow, 1753. [NRS.E326.1.172]

MUIRHEAD, GEORGE, Professor of Humanity in the University of Glasgow, testaments, 1773/1774, Comm. Glasgow. [NRS]

MUIRHEAD, JAMES, a baxter, nephew of James Muirhead, was admitted to the Baxter Incorporation, 1728. [IBG#127]

MUIRHEAD, JAMES, a rope-maker in Glasgow, testament, 1772, Comm. Glasgow. [NRS]

MUIRHEAD, JOHN, a maltman in Glasgow, testament, 1728, Comm. Glasgow. [NRS]

MUIRHEAD, JOHN, a baxter, former apprentice to William Hanna a baxter, was admitted to the Baxter Incorporation, 1738. [IBG#127]

The People of Glasgow, 1725-1775

MUIRHEAD, JOHN, a wright, husband of Margaret Donaldson, a burgess and guilds-brother of Glasgow in 1739, [GBR], a contract. 1749. [NRS.RD2.167.63]

MUIRHEAD, ROBERT, a merchant in Glasgow, trading with Virginia, 1773. [GA.T76/6.3]

MUIRHEAD, THOMAS, of Wester Borland, a wright in Glasgow, testaments, 1767/1769/1773, Comm. Glasgow. [NRS]

MUNN, JOHN, a carter in Glasgow, testament, 1756, Comm. Glasgow. [NRS]

MUNNOCH, ROBERT, a wright in Glasgow, testament, 1743, Comm. Glasgow. [NRS]

MUNNOCH, ROBERT, only son of the late Robert Munnoch a wright in Glasgow, testament, 1743, Comm. Glasgow. [NRS]

MUNRO, DANIEL, a tailor and bailie of Glasgow, testament, 1764, Comm. Glasgow. [NRS]

MUNRO, EBENEZER, a burgess and guilds-brother of Glasgow in 1756, [GBR], a merchant in Glasgow, 1756, testaments, 1765/1768, Comm. Glasgow. [NRS.CS16.1.95]

MUNRO, FLORENCE, born 1754, a spinner from Glasgow, to New York 1774. [NA.T47.12]

MUNRO, GEORGE, born 1745, a wright from Glasgow, to New York, 1775. [NA.T47.12]

MURDOCH, ELIZABETH, in Glasgow, 1753. [NRS.E326.1.172]

MURDOCH, GEORGE, late Provost of Glasgow, 1759. [ERG.VI.549]

MURDOCH, GEORGE, son of George Murdoch in Glasgow, died in Grenada, 1771. [SM.34.109]

MURDOCH, JAMES, a merchant in Glasgow, testament, 1754, Comm. Glasgow. [NRS]

MURDOCH, JAMES, born 1743, a gardener from Glasgow, to New York, 1774. [NA.T47.12]

MURDOCH, JOHN, husband of Marion, daughter of James Scott, . a hammerman burgess of Glasgow, 1726. [HHG.293][GBR]

MURDOCH, JOHN, a tailor in Glasgow, testament, 1745, Comm. Glasgow. [NRS]

MURDOCH, JOHN, a merchant in Glasgow, deeds, 1747/1749. [NRS.RD2.167.57; RD4.176/1.399]

MURDOCH, JOHN, a writing master in Glasgow, a deed of factory, 1748. [NRS.RD2.168.145]

MURDOCH, MARGARET, relict of James Cross a mason in Glasgow, 1759. [ERG.VI.547]

MURDOCH, MARY, in Glasgow, 1753. [NRS.E326.1.172]; relict of William Crawford, junior, a merchant in Glasgow, testament, 1767, Comm. Glasgow. [NRS]

MURDOCH, MARY, in Glasgow, 1753. [NRS.E326.1.172]

MURDOCH, PETER, a merchant in Glasgow, 1753, 1763. [NRS.E326.1.172] [NA.AO12.109.212][GA.B10.15.6863]

MURDOCH, ROBERT, a writer in Glasgow, deeds, 1750. [NRS.RD4.176/1.57/101]

MURDOCH, SUSANNA, spouse of Robert Robertson, junior, a cooper in Glasgow, and daughter of the deceased George Murdoch of Greenside and his spouse Margaret Forrester, testament, 1773, Comm. Glasgow. [NRS]

MURDOCH, ZACHARY, in Glasgow, 1753. [NRS.E326.1.172]

MURDOCH, Mrs, in Glasgow, 1753. [NRS.E326.1.172]

MURRAY, AGNES, relict of John Baxter a maltman in Glasgow, testament, 1758, Comm. Glasgow. [NRS]

MURRAY, ALEXANDER, a merchant in Glasgow, testaments, 1727/1729, Comm. Glasgow. [NRS]

MURRAY, ALEXANDER, a merchant in Glasgow, testament, 1738, Comm. Glasgow. [NRS]

MURRAY, ALEXANDER, born 1734, a merchant-skipper from Glasgow, settled in Osburne, Virginia, 1762, a Loyalist, removed to Shelburne, Nova Scotia, in 1783. [NA.AO12.55.61; AO12.109.218]

MURRAY, CHARLES, son in law of John Carss a maltman, a freeman maltman, 1770. [MCG.132]

MURRAY, DAVID, born 1708, a merchant, died 1 November 1771. [Ramshorn MI, Glasgow]

MURRAY, HELEN, from Glasgow, an indentured servant in Burlington, New Jersey, in 1772. [Records of Indentures in Philadelphia]

MURRAY, JAMES, from Glasgow, settled in Joppa, Maryland, died 1762. [NRS.S/H]

The People of Glasgow, 1725-1775

MURRAY, JOHN, a merchant in Glasgow, testament, 1726, Comm. Glasgow. [NRS]

MURRAY, JOHN, a hammerman, and a burgess and guilds-brother of Glasgow in 1725. [HHG.293][GBR]

MURRAY, JOHN, in Glasgow, 1753. [NRS.E326.1.172]

MURRAY, JOHN, born 1708, a merchant, died 12 January 1769. [Ramshorn MI, Glasgow]

MURRAY, JOHN, in Glasgow, a bond, 1772. [NRS.RD2.217/1.838]

MURRAY, JOHN, a tobacco factor from Glasgow, settled in Aquia, Virginia, by 1770. [GA.T79.21]

MURRAY, JOHN, from Glasgow, an indentured servant in Philadelphia, in 1772. [Records of Indentures in Philadelphia]

MURRAY, ROBERT, from Glasgow, an indentured servant in Lancaster County, Pennsylvania, in 1772. [Records of Indentures in Philadelphia]

MUSHETT, WILLIAM, of Glassingall, resident of Glasgow, testaments, 1727/1740, Comm. Glasgow. [NRS]

MUSHETT, WILLIAM, a merchant in Glasgow, a deed, 1750. [NRS.RD2.167.137]

NAISMITH, HENRIETTA, spouse of John Ballantyne a shoemaker in Glasgow, a sasine, 1762. [NRS.RS.Lanark.xvii.397]

NAPIER, GEORGE, a writer in Glasgow, husband of Janet, daughter of Robert Scott a tailor, a burgess and guilds-brother of Glasgow in 1744, [GBR]; testament, 1772, Comm. Glasgow. [NRS]

NAPIER, JAMES, a hammerman, 1732. [HHG.294]; a goldsmith, second son of Peter Napier a merchant, a burgess and guilds-brother of Glasgow, 1732. [GBR]

NAPIER, THOMAS, a watchmaker, husband of Christian daughter of Thomas Buchanan a surgeon, a burgess and guilds-brother of Glasgow, 1746, [GBR]; in Glasgow, 1753. [NRS.E326.1.172]

NAPIER, WILLIAM, a merchant and late Provost of Glasgow, testament, 1731, Comm. Glasgow. [NRS]

NAPIER, WILLIAM, son of Peter Napier of Napierston, a surgeon from Glasgow, settled in Charleston, South Carolina, dead by 1735. [NRS.S/H.1735]

NEILSON, ISABEL, relict of James Gilmour a flesher in Glasgow, testament, 1732, Comm. Glasgow. [NRS]

NEILSON, JOHN, in Glasgow, 1753. [NRS.E326.1.172]

The People of Glasgow, 1725-1775

NEILSON, WILLIAM, a barber in Glasgow, testament, 1727, Comm. Glasgow. [NRS]

NEWALL, JAMES, a merchant in Glasgow, testament, 1738/1741, Comm. Glasgow. [NRS]

NEWLANDS, RICHARD, in Glasgow, 1753. [NRS.E326.1.172]

NICHOLLS, JAMES, from Glasgow, in Boston, 1733. [SCS]

NICOLLS, JOHN, from Glasgow, in Boston, 1748. [SCS]

NICOLSON, DANIEL, a merchant in Glasgow, testament, 1753, Comm. Glasgow. [NRS]

NICOLSON, HELEN, spouse to Archibald Brown a workman in Glasgow, testament, 1743, Comm. Glasgow. [NRS]

NICOLSON, JOHN, a merchant in Glasgow, testament, 1750, Comm. Glasgow. [NRS]

NIMMO, JOHN, a merchant in Glasgow, testament, 1765, Comm. Glasgow. [NRS]

NISBET, ANNE, second daughter of Sir John Nisbet of Dean, second wife of John Glassford of Dougalston, died 1766. [Ramshorn MI, Glasgow]]

NISBET, DAVID, in Glasgow, 1753. [NRS.E326.1.172]

NISBET, GEORGE, a gaoler in Glasgow, dead by 1725. [ERG.V.244]

NISBET, GEORGE, a wright in Glasgow, 1759. [ERG.VI.540]

NISBET, JAMES, a glazier, 1725. [ERG.V.206]

NISBET, JAMES, in Glasgow, 1753. [NRS.E326.1.172]

NISBET, JOHN, born 1757, a wright from Glasgow, to Jamaica, 1775. [NA.T47.12]

NISBET, JOHN, a wright, husband of Katherine Buchanan, a burgess and guildsbrother of Glasgow in 1769. [GBR]

NISBET, PATRICK, a merchant in Glasgow, trading in Virginia after 1757. [NRS.B10.15.7036]

NIVEN, DUNCAN, in Glasgow, 1753. [NRS.E326.1.172]

NIVEN, JAMES, junior, in Glasgow, 1753. [NRS.E326.1.172] ; a merchant in Glasgow, testament, 1760/1771, Comm. Glasgow. [NRS]

NORRIE, JOHN, a merchant in Glasgow, 1725. [ERG.V.222]

NORRIE, MARION, a shopkeeper in Glasgow, testament, 1735, Comm. Glasgow. [NRS]

NORRIS, JOHN, a merchant in Glasgow, testament, 1764, Comm. Glasgow. [NRS]

OLIPHANT, JOHN, from Glasgow, emigrated to Virginia in 1775. [NRS.GD136]

OLIPHANT, ROBERT, a cordiner in Glasgow, testament, 1754, Comm. Glasgow. [NRS]

ORR, HEW, a maltman in Glasgow, testament, 1730, Comm. Glasgow. [NRS]

ORR, HUGH, a merchant, late in Albany, New York, died in Anderston, Glasgow, 1789, testament, 1790, Comm. Glasgow. [NRS.CC9.7.74]

ORR, JOHN, of Jamphrallstock, a maltman in Glasgow, testament, 1736, Comm. Glasgow. [NRS]

ORR, THOMAS, a barber in Port Glasgow, thereafter in Glasgow, testament, 1730, Comm. Glasgow. [NRS]

ORR, THOMAS, procurator fiscal of Glasgow, 1725; a writer in Glasgow, testaments, 1737/1739, Comm. Glasgow. [NRS] [ERG.V.243]

ORR, THOMAS, a merchant in Glasgow, testament, 1762, Comm. Glasgow. [NRS]

OSWALD, ALEXANDER, a merchant in Glasgow, 1748. [NRS.AC9.6455]; deeds, 1747-1740, [NRS.RD2.167.32; RD3.210.235; RD4.176/1.146/457]

OSWALD, GEORGE, of Scotstoun, a burgess and guilds-brother of Glasgow in 1760, [GBR], a merchant in Glasgow, 1763. [NRS.GD1.618.1]

OSWALD, HENRY, a surgeon from Glasgow, settled in Essex County, Virginia, a burgess and guilds-brother of Glasgow in 1725, [GBR], died 1726, probate 1726 Essex County, Virginia.

OSWALD, RICHARD, a merchant in Glasgow, 1739, 1748. [NRS.AC7.44.488; AC9.6455]; deeds, 1747/1749, [NRS.RD2.167.32; RD3.210.235; RD4.176/1.457; RD4.176/1.146]; land grant in Georgia, 1751. [NA.CO5.669]

OUSTINE, ROBERT, an Excise officer in Glasgow, testament, 1729, Comm. Glasgow. [NRS]

PAGAN, DAVID, a merchant in Glasgow, testament, 1769, Comm. Glasgow. [NRS]

PAGAN, DAVID, son of William Pagan, a sugar boiler in Glasgow, testament, 1772, Comm. Glasgow. [NRS]

PAGAN, GEORGE, in Glasgow, 1753. [NRS.E326.1.172] ; a merchant in Glasgow, testament, 1771, Comm. Glasgow. [NRS]

PAGAN, JOHN, second son of the late David Pagan a merchant, a burgess and guilds-brother of Glasgow in 1754, [GBR], a merchant in Glasgow, 1763. [ERG.VII.125]

PAGAN, MARY, relict of Andrew Lees a merchant in Glasgow, testament, 1737, Comm. Glasgow. [NRS]

PAGAN, WILLIAM, in Glasgow, 1753. [NRS.E326.1.172]; eldest son of the late David Pagan a merchant, a burgess and guilds-brother of Glasgow in 1754. [GBR]

PAGET, JOHN, a comb-maker in Glasgow, eldest son of the late Richard Paget a tanner, a burgess and guilds-brother of Glasgow in 1762, [GBR], testament, 1775, Comm. Glasgow. [NRS]

PAGET, RICHARD, a tanner in Glasgow, testaments, 1763/1765/1773/1775, Comm. Glasgow. [NRS]

PAISLEY, JOHN, a surgeon in Glasgow, testament, 1741, Comm. Glasgow. [NRS]

PARK, JOHN, senior, a merchant in Glasgow, testament, 1743, Comm. Glasgow. [NRS]

PARK, JOHN, a merchant in Glasgow, testament, 1746, Comm. Glasgow. [NRS]

PARK, JOHN, a carter and land-laborer in Glasgow, testament, 1771, Comm. Glasgow. [NRS]

PARK, MARY, relict of Robert Winning, the elder, a weaver in Glasgow, testament, 1739, Comm. Glasgow. [NRS]

PARK, WILLIAM, born in Glasgow 1704, son of James Park and his wife Lilias Liddle, to Boston 1756, died in Groton, Massachusetts, 1788. [ImmNE.151]

PARLAN, Mrs, in Glasgow, 1753. [NRS.E326.1.172]

PARR, ROBERT, in Glasgow, 1753. [NRS.E326.1.172]

PATERSON, ARCHIBALD, a hammerman, 1733. [HHG.294]

PATERSON, JAMES, in Glasgow, 1753. [NRS.E326.1.172]

PATERSON, JAMES, a vintner in Glasgow, 1770. [ERG.VII.311]

PATERSON, JEAN, relict of Alexander Thomson a maltman in Glasgow, testament, 1744, Comm. Glasgow. [NRS]

PATERSON, JAMES, a baxter, eldest son of John Paterson a baxter, was admitted to the Baxter Incorporation, also as a burgess and guilds-brother of Glasgow in 1752. [IBG#133][GBR]

The People of Glasgow, 1725-1775

PATERSON, JAMES, a baxter, former apprentice to Patrick Whyte a baxter, was admitted to the Baxter Incorporation, and as a burgess and guilds-brother of Glasgow in 1774. [IBG#133][GBR]

PATERSON, JOHN, a baxter, former apprentice to Robert MacAuley a baxter, was admitted to the Baxter Incorporation, 1730. [IBG#133]

PATERSON, JOHN, a baxter, son in law of Zacherias Alison, former apprentice to was admitted to the Baxter Incorporation, 1772. [IBG#133]

PATERSON, MARGARET, daughter of the late Robert Paterson a shoemaker in Glasgow, testament, 1766, Comm. Glasgow. [NRS]

PATERSON, PETER, a writer in Glasgow, 1765. [NRS.AC7.51]

PATERSON, ROBERT, a cordiner in Glasgow, testament, 1736, Comm. Glasgow. [NRS]

PATERSON, WILLIAM, born 1746, a coppersmith from Glasgow, to New York, 1775. [NA.T47.12]

PATON, ALEXANDER, in Glasgow, 1753. [NRS.E326.1.172]

PATON, JOSEPH, born 1745, a farmer from Glasgow, to New York, 1774. [NA.T47.12]

PATRICK, ALEXANDER, merchant in Glasgow, 1726. [GA.D-TC13/603S]

PATRICK, MARGARET, in Glasgow, a tack, 1774. [NRS.RD2.217/1.1035]

PATTISON, JOHN, a shoemaker or cordiner in Glasgow, testament, 1756, Comm. Glasgow. [NRS]

PATTON, ROBERT, a merchant and factor from Glasgow, settled in Culpepper County, Virginia, before 1776. [GA]

PAUL, ANDREW, Commissary officer of Glasgow, testament, 1754, Comm. Glasgow. [NRS]

PAUL, JOHN, born 1745, a farmer from Glasgow, to New York, 1774. [NA.T47.12]

PAUL, WILLIAM, in Blochairne, barony parish of Glasgow, testament, 1736/1737, Comm. Glasgow. [NRS]

PAUL, WILLIAM, a farmer in Glasgow, testament, 1763, Comm. Glasgow. [NRS]

PEACOCK, AGNES, widow of John Rowand late Deacon of the Coopers in Glasgow, testament, 1769, Comm. Glasgow. [NRS]

PEACOCK, FRANCIS, a merchant, third son of the late James Peacock a cordiner, a burgess and guilds-brother of Glasgow in 1754, [GBR], a merchant in Glasgow, testament, 1770, Comm. Glasgow. [NRS]

PEACOCK, JAMES, son of John Peacock in Glasgow, a shipmaster in Havannah bound for Japan, 1752. [A J#257]

PEADIE, JAMES, of Ruchill, Dean of Guild, 1725; Provost of Glasgow, and John Peadie his only son, in Glasgow, testament, 1731/1740, Comm. Glasgow. [NRS] [ERG.V.243]

PEASLY, ROBERT, from Glasgow, in Boston, 1737. [SCS]

PEDDIE, JAMES, from Glasgow, in Boston, 1743. [SCS]

PEDDIE, JOHN, a merchant in Glasgow, testament, 1746, Comm. Glasgow. [NRS]

PEDDIE, MARY, in Glasgow, 1753. [NRS.E326.1.172]

PEDDIE, THOMAS, a skinner in Glasgow, testament, 1747, Comm. Glasgow. [NRS]

PETER, JOHN, born 1722, a merchant from Glasgow, settled in Surrey County, Virginia, before 1760, died 1763. [CD.43]

PETER, THOMAS, of Crossbasket, in Glasgow, 1753. [NRS.E326.1.172]; a merchant in Glasgow, testament, 1774, Comm. Glasgow. [NRS]

PETER, WALTER, son of Thomas Peter, a merchant from Glasgow, settled in Surrey County, Virginia, before 1763, died 1787. [NRS.CS16.1.122/126/174/185; SH.1787; GD180.348; CS17.1.6/358]

PETTIGREW, JAMES, a member of the Incorporation of Weavers, 1725. [OGW#108]

PETTIGREW, JOHN, a merchant from Glasgow, settled in Augusta, Georgia, by 1756, died in Savannah 1775, probate 1775 Georgia. [NA.CO5.646/C10; AO12.101.190]

PETTIGREW, WILLIAM, a plumber in Glasgow, 1759, [ERG.VI.549]

PICKEN, ROBERT, master weaver of the Incorporation of Weavers, 1725. [OGW#108]

PITCAIRN, JAMES, a wright in Glasgow, son of the deceased James Pitcairn, a slater in Glasgow, and his spouse Agnes Forrest, testament, 1730, Comm. Glasgow. [NRS]

PITTIGREW, JAMES, born 1746, a merchant from Glasgow, to Charleston, South Carolina, in 1774. [NA.T47.12]

POLLOCK, ANNABELLA, spouse of James Hamilton of Newton a surgeon in Glasgow, testaments, 1745, Comm. Glasgow. [NRS]

POLLOCK, JOHN, a tailor in Glasgow, 1725. [ERG.V.219]

The People of Glasgow, 1725-1775

POLLOCK, JOHN, a tailor in Glasgow, testament, 1728, Comm. Glasgow. [NRS]

POLLOCK, WILLIAM, a servant to Robert Finlay and Company, tanners in Glasgow, testament, 1762, Comm. Glasgow. [NRS]

POLLOCK, WILLIAM, a horse-hirer and brandy dealer in Glasgow, a murderer, transported to the colonies in 1763. [NRS.HCR.I.94]

POLSON, MADGALEN, in Glasgow, widow of Captain John Brown of General Richbell's Regiment of Foot, testament, 1755, Comm. Glasgow. [NRS]

PORTEOUS, GEORGE, born 1766 in Glasgow, son of Reverend William Porteous and his wife Grizel Lindsay, died in Spring Valley, Jamaica, 1793. [F.3.443]

PORTEOUS, JAMES, born 1761 in Glasgow, son of Reverend William Porteous and his wife Grizel Lindsay, settled at Bonhill, Jamaica, a letter 1817. [F.3.443] [NRS.RD5.119.63]

PORTER, WILLIAM, a merchant in Glasgow, testaments, 1728/1731, Comm. Glasgow. [NRS]

PORTER, WILLIAM, son of William Porter, a pickpocket in Glasgow, transported to the colonies, 1766. [NRS.JC27]

PORTERFIELD, ALEXANDER, a surgeon in Glasgow, 1725; testament, 1747, Comm. Glasgow. [NRS] [ERG.V.245]

PORTERFIELD, GEORGE, an advocate in Glasgow, testament, 1754, Comm. Glasgow. [NRS]

PROVAN, MATHEW, a merchant in Glasgow, 1775. [ERG.VII.448]

PROVAN, MOSES, a baxter, former apprentice to John Paterson, was admitted to the Baxter Incorporation, also . a burgess and guilds-brother of Glasgow in1754. [IBG#133][GBR]; a baxter in Glasgow, testament, 1762, Comm. Glasgow. [NRS]

PURDIE, HUGH, from Glasgow, in Boston, 1750. [SCS]

PURDIE, WILLIAM, a merchant in Glasgow, testament, 1743, Comm. Glasgow. [NRS]

RAE, ALEXANDER, a watchmaker, younger son of Peter Rae a minister, . a burgess and guilds-brother of Glasgow in 1765, [GBR]; a hammerman in Glasgow,testament, 1770, Comm. Glasgow. [NRS]

RAE, ANN, in Glasgow, 1753. [NRS.E326.1.172]

RAE, JAMES, a merchant in Glasgow, testaments, 1740/1741/1743, Comm. Glasgow. [NRS]

RAE, JAMES, born 1723, son of Robert Rae and his wife Elizabeth Dunlop, a merchant from Glasgow, educated at Glasgow University 1736, died in Virginia 1763. [SM.26.290][MAGU.17]

RAE, JEAN, in Glasgow, testament, 1735, Comm. Glasgow. [NRS]

RAE, JEAN, spouse of Robert Colquhoun a merchant in Glasgow, and daughter of the late John Rae of Little Govan a merchant in Glasgow, and cousin-german of the deceased John Rae of Tunnochside, testament, 1755, Comm. Glasgow. [NRS]

RAE, JOHN, surgeon, son of the deceased John Rae a merchant in Glasgow, testament, 1725, Comm. Glasgow. [NRS]

RAE, JOHN, a hammerman, 1728. [HHG.293]

RAE, JOHN, from Glasgow, in Boston, 1747. [SCS]

RAE, MARY and ELIZABETH, daughters of the deceased George Rae a merchant in Glasgow, testament, 1766, Comm. Glasgow. [NRS]

RAE, ROBERT, born 1723, son of Robert Rae and his wife Elizabeth Dunlop, a merchant in Glasgow, died 1753 in Virginia. [Bruton, Virginia, MI]

RAE, WILLIAM, a baxter, son in law of Walter Lochhead a baxter, was admitted to the Baxter Incorporation, also . a burgess and guilds-brother of Glasgow in 1768. [IBG#135][GBR]

RAE, Mrs, in Glasgow, 1753. [NRS.E326.1.172]

RALSTON, DAVID, a merchant from Glasgow, to America in 1762, settled at Cabin Point, Virginia. [GA]

RAMAGE, RICHARD, a surgeon in Glasgow, testament, 1763, Comm. Glasgow. [NRS]

RAMSAY, ANDREW, a merchant in Glasgow, 1753. [NRS.E326.1.172]; eldest son of the late Andrew Rae merchant and provost, . a burgess and guilds-brother of Glasgow in 1757, [GBR], also . a burgess of Irvine, 1759. [AA]

RAMSAY, ANDREW, a merchant and late Provost of Glasgow, testament, 1763, Comm. Glasgow. [NRS]

RAMSAY, JAMES, chaplain to the Royal Regiment of North British Dragoons, late a resident of Glasgow, and James Ramsay a student at the University of Glasgow, testament, 1738, Comm. Glasgow. [NRS]

RAMSAY, JOHN, a merchant in Glasgow, 1726. [NRS.HH11.15]

The People of Glasgow, 1725-1775

RAMSAY, PATRICK, born 1736, younger son of Andrew Ramsay and his spouse Janet Houstoun in Glasgow, settled in Bristol parish, Virginia, before 1760. [GA]; . a burgess and guilds-brother of Glasgow in 1776. [GBR]

RANIE, ALEXANDER, in Glasgow, 1753. [NRS.E326.1.172]

RANKIN, JOHN, a merchant, 1727. [Ramshorn MI, Glasgow]

RANKINE, JOHN, . a hammerman, 1731. [HHG.294]

RATTRAY, ALEXANDER, eldest son of John Rattray, . a freeman maltman, 1754. [MCG.131]

RATTRAY, JOHN, son of Thomas Rattray and his wife Janet Marshall, a merchant from Glasgow, to Jamaica, 1763. [NRS.B10.15.7056]

REID, ALEXANDER, a workman in Glasgow, testament, 1749, Comm. Glasgow. [NRS]

REID, JOHN, visitor of the maltmen in Glasgow, 1725; testament, 1764, Comm. Glasgow. [NRS] [ERG.V.243]

REID, JOHN, a shipmaster in Glasgow, testament, 1739, Comm. Glasgow. [NRS]

REID, JOHN, born 1749, a cooper from Glasgow, to New York, 1774. [NA.T47.12]

REID, ROBERT, a wright in Glasgow, 1725. [ERG.V.206]

REID, ROBERT, former apprentice to Peter Whyte, was admitted to the Baxter Incorporation, 1749. [IBG#135]

REID, ROBERT, a robber from Glasgow, was transported to the colonies, 1765. [AJ.925]

REID, ROBERT, a baxter, eldest son of Robert Reid a baxter, was admitted to the Baxter Incorporation, also as a burgess and guilds-brother of Glasgow in 1772. [IBG#135][GBR]

REID, THOMAS, a weaver and a burgh officer of Glasgow, testament, 1763, Comm. Glasgow. [NRS]

REID, WILLIAM, in Glasgow, 1753. [NRS.E326.1.172]

REID, WILLIAM, late Deacon of the Wrights in Glasgow, testaments, 1767, Comm. Glasgow. [NRS]

REID, WILLIAM, a merchant and tobacco factor from Glasgow, settled in Fredericksburg, Virginia, before 1775. [GA.T79.1][NA.AO12.56.292]

RENTA, JAMES, born 1747, a laborer from Glasgow, to New York, 1774. [NA.T47.12]

RESTON, THOMAS, a cloth-lapper in Glasgow, testament, 1774, Comm. Glasgow. [NRS]

RESTON, WILLIAM, in Glasgow, 1753. [NRS.E326.1.172]

RICHARDSON, JAMES, former apprentice to John Brown maltman, . a freeman maltman, 1763. [MCG.137]

RICHARDSON, JAMES, younger son of James Richardson a maltman, . a freeman maltman, 1771. [MCG.137]

RICHMOND, JAMES, a cattle thief from Glasgow, transported to the colonies in 1772. [NRS.RH2.4.255]

RIDDELL, ANDREW, a merchant in Glasgow, testament, 1747, Comm. Glasgow. [NRS]

RIDDELL, HENRY, a merchant from Glasgow, settled in Maryland before 1776; husband of Ann Glasford, a burgess and guilds-brother of Glasgow in 1781. [NA.AO12.80.17][NRS.CS16.1.179][GBR]

RIDDELL, JOHN, senior, a merchant in Glasgow, 1728, testament, 1750, Comm. Glasgow. [NRS.AC7.34.697]

RIDDELL, JOHN, a baxter, former apprentice to Thomas Scott, was admitted to the Baxter Incorporation, 1747. [IBG#135]

RIDDELL, JOHN, a merchant in Glasgow, testament, 1767, Comm. Glasgow. [NRS]

RIDDELL, JOHN, a merchant from Glasgow, settled in Dumfries, Prince William County, Virginia, before 1769. [GA]

RIDDELL, WILLIAM, a mason and wright in Caltoun of Glasgow, testament, 1738, Comm. Glasgow. [NRS]

RISH, JOHN, born 1736, a gardener from Glasgow, to Philadelphia in 1774. [NA.T47.9-11]

RISK, WILLIAM, in Glasgow, 1753. [NRS.E326.1.172]; former apprentice to Hugh Dick a merchant, a burgess and guilds-brother of Glasgow in 1770, [GBR]; a merchant in Glasgow, 1775. [Ramshorn MI, Glasgow]

RITCHIE, GAVIN, a merchant in Glasgow, testaments, 1744/1768, Comm. Glasgow. [NRS]

RITCHIE, ISOBEL, spouse to James Bryce a workman in Glasgow, testament, 1749, Comm. Glasgow. [NRS]

RITCHIE, JAMES, a merchant, eldest son of the late Gavin Ritchie a merchant, . a burgess and guilds-brother of Glasgow in 1762, a merchant in Glasgow 1769. [NRS.CS16.1.134][NA.AO12.109.256][GBR]

RITCHIE, JANET, in Glasgow, relict of John Stewart minister at Eaglesham, testament, 1729, Comm. Glasgow. [NRS]

RITCHIE, JOHN, from Glasgow, in Boston, 1732. [SCS]

RITCHIE, JOHN, a merchant in Glasgow, a bond, 1748, [NRS.RD2.167.404]; testament, 1758, Comm. Glasgow. [NRS]

RITCHIE, KATHERINE, relict of John How a writer in Glasgow, testament, 1729, Comm. Glasgow. [NRS]

RITCHIE, ROBERT, from Glasgow, in Boston, 1758. [SCS]

RITCHIE, WILLIAM, a member of the Incorporation of Weavers, 1725. [OGW#108]

ROBB, DAVID, a wright in Glasgow, testaments, 1743/1754, Comm. Glasgow. [NRS]

ROBB, DAVID, in Glasgow, son of the deceased David Robb a gardener in Glasgow, sometime servant to James Anderson the younger of Stobcross, testament, 1747, Comm. Glasgow. [NRS]

ROBB, HUGH, born 1735, a tailor from Glasgow, to New York, 1774. [NA.T47.12]

ROBB, JAMES, son of William Robb a merchant in Glasgow, settled in Port Royal, Virginia, as factor for Patrick Mitchell, before 1753. [GA.T.MJ]

ROBB, JOHN, quarter-master in Glasgow, 1759. [ERG.VI.554]

ROBB, JOHN, a book-seller in Glasgow, 1773. [Ramshorn MI, Glasgow]

ROBB, JOHN, a bookseller, eldest son of the late John Robb a bookseller, . a burgess and guilds-brother of Glasgow in 1776. [GBR]

ROBERTON, CHARLES, a merchant in Glasgow, youngest son of the late Archibald Roberton of Bedlay, testament, 1729, Comm. Glasgow. [NRS]

ROBERTON, JOHN, a merchant in Glasgow, testament, 1765, Comm. Glasgow. [NRS]

ROBERTON, JOHN, late a merchant in Glasgow, thereafter in Kirkintilloch, testament, 1766, Comm. Glasgow. [NRS]

ROBERTS, MARGARET, born 1749, from Glasgow, to New York, 1774. [NA.T47.12]

ROBERTSON, ANDREW, in Glasgow, 1753. [NRS.E326.1.172] ; a vintner in Glasgow, testament, 1772, Comm. Glasgow. [NRS]

ROBERTSON, ARTHUR, a merchant in Glasgow, 1742, a deed, 1750. [NRS.CS16.1.70; RD3.210.380]

ROBERTSON, ARTHUR, chamberlain of Glasgow, 1759. [ERG.VI.540]

ROBERTSON, DANIEL, a hosier in Glasgow, testament, 1771, Comm. Glasgow. [NRS]

ROBERTSON, EDWARD, a writer in Glasgow, testament, 1732, Comm. Glasgow. [NRS]

ROBERTSON, EDWARD, a hammerman, second son of John Robertson a merchant, was admitted to the Skinners Craft, also . a burgess and guilds-brother of Glasgow in 1753. [SFG.267][GBR]

ROBERTSON, JAMES, a merchant in Glasgow, 1730. [NRS.AC9.6414/1131]

ROBERTSON, JAMES, senior, a merchant in Glasgow, testament, 1734, Comm. Glasgow. [NRS]

ROBERTSON, JAMES, a schoolmaster in Glasgow, testament, 1747, Comm. Glasgow. [NRS]

ROBERTSON, JOHN, master weaver of the Incorporation of Weavers, 1725. [OGW#108]

ROBERTSON, JOHN, junior, a merchant in Glasgow, testament, 1733, Comm. Glasgow. [NRS]

ROBERTSON, JOHN, a carter in Glasgow, testament, 1737, Comm. Glasgow. [NRS]

ROBERTSON, JOHN, a land-laborer at Caltoun of Glasgow, testament, 1746, Comm. Glasgow. [NRS]

ROBERTSON, JOHN, a book-binder in Glasgow, a bond, 1747. [NRS.RD4.176/1.416]

ROBERTSON, JOHN, late Deacon of the Barbers in Glasgow, testament, 1747, Comm. Glasgow. [NRS]

ROBERTSON, JOHN, senior, a merchant in Glasgow, testament, 1749, Comm. Glasgow. [NRS]

ROBERTSON, JOHN, a merchant from Glasgow, settled in Virginia by 1754. [NRS.CS16.1.95]

ROBERTSON, MARGARET, in Glasgow, testament, 1729, Comm. Glasgow. [NRS]

ROBERTSON, MARGARET, wife of William Finlay a wright in Glasgow, heir to her father John Robertson a farmer in Caldtoun, also to her grandfather Andrew Robertson a weaver there. [NRS.SH.1759]

ROBERTSON, MARGARET, in Glasgow, relict of Robert Wright minister at Newburgh, testament, 1774/1775, Comm. Glasgow. [NRS]

ROBERTSON, MARY, relict of Peter Ballinie a fencing-master, sometime in Edinburgh, thereafter in Glasgow, testament, 1766, Comm. Glasgow. [NRS]

ROBERTSON, PATRICK, a merchant in Glasgow, testament, 1775, Comm. Glasgow. [NRS]

ROBERTSON, ROBERT, a merchant in Glasgow, 1725. [NRS.AC8.310]

ROBERTSON, ROBERT, a maltman and bailie of Glasgow, testament, 1735, Comm. Glasgow. [NRS]

ROBERTSON, ROBERT and JAMES, merchants in Glasgow, testament, 1745, Comm. Glasgow. [NRS]

ROBERTSON, ROBERT, born 1744, a weaver from Glasgow, to New York, 1774. [NA.T47.12]

ROBERTSON, WALTER, a merchant from Glasgow, to America before 1765, settled in Petersburg, Virginia. [NRS.CS16.1.173][GA.T.MJ]

ROBIN, JEAN, spouse to Robert Nivieson a weaver in Glasgow, testament, 1758, Comm. Glasgow. [NRS]

ROBINSON, JAMES, a merchant from Glasgow, settled in Falmouth, Virginia, in 1767. [GA]

ROBINSON, JOSEPH, in Glasgow, 1753. [NRS.E326.1.172]

ROCHFORD, BENJAMIN, a porter seller in Glasgow, testament, 1768, Comm. Glasgow. [NRS]

RODBURN, RODGER, the younger, a musician in Glasgow, testament, 1757, Comm. Glasgow. [NRS]

RODBURN, RODGER, a musician in Glasgow, testament, 1765, Comm. Glasgow. [NRS]

RODGER, JOHN, a distiller in Glasgow, testament, 1738, Comm. Glasgow. [NRS]

RODGER, ROBERT, a brewer and change-keeper in Glasgow, testament, 1753, Comm. Glasgow. [NRS]

RODGER, WILLIAM, in Glasgow, 1753. [NRS.E326.1.172]

RONALD, GEORGE, a merchant from Glasgow, settled on Cape Fear, Brunswick County, North Carolina, in 1738, in Bladen County by 1757, testament, Comm. Edinburgh. [NRS] [Bladen County Deed Book #23]

RONALD, GEORGE, in Glasgow, 1753. [NRS.E326.1.172]; a merchant in Glasgow, testament, 1759, Comm. Glasgow. [NRS]

RONALD, WILLIAM, in Glasgow, 1753. [NRS.E326.1.172]

ROSE, DUNCAN, a merchant from Glasgow, settled in Virginia by 1764. [NRS.B10.15.6969; CS16.1.154]

ROSS, ANDREW, son of Professor Andrew Ross, educated at Glasgow University, a merchant, died in Virginia, 1752. [SM.14.365][MAGU.3]

ROSS, BETTY, daughter of the deceased Andrew Ross the Professor of Humanity in the University of Glasgow, testament, 1773, Comm. Glasgow. [NRS]

ROSS, GEORGE, Professor of Humanity in the University of Glasgow, testament, 1755, Comm. Glasgow. [NRS]

ROSS, JAMES, son of Andrew Ross the Professor of Humanity in the University of Glasgow, testament, 1758, Comm. Glasgow. [NRS]

ROUAN, ALEXANDER, from Glasgow, to Jamaica, 1763. [NRS.SC36.637.405]

ROWAN, JAMES, a merchant and calendar master in Glasgow, testament, 1756, Comm. Glasgow. [NRS]

ROWAN, JOHN, a tanner and merchant in Glasgow, deeds, 1744, 1750, [NRS.RD2.167.130; RD3.210.393]; 1753. [NRS.E326.1.172; AC7.46.185/212; CS16.1.98]

ROWAN, JOHN, a thief in Glasgow, transported to the colonies, 1753. [SM.15.468]

ROWAN, STEPHEN, son of Stephen Rowan, was admitted to the Baxter Incorporation, 1738. [IBG#133]

ROWAND, JOHN, junior, a merchant in Glasgow, 1754. [NRS.AC7.46.185-233]

ROWAND, JOHN, jailor and keeper of the Tolbooth of Glasgow, 1763. [ERG.VII.116]

ROY, DONALD, born 1750, a tailor from Glasgow, to New York, 1775. [NA.T47.12]

RUSSELL, JOHN, from Glasgow, in Boston, 1755, [SCS]; in Boston, testament, 1777, Comm. Edinburgh. [NRS]

RUSSELL, WILLIAM, . a hammerman, 1727. [HHG.293]

The People of Glasgow, 1725-1775

RUTHVEN, JOHN, a music master, . a burgess and guildsbrother of Glasgow, having married ...... Peadie daughter of the late James Peadie a merchant burgess and guildsbrother thereof, 1725. [ERG.V.237]

SANDERS, AGNES, widow of James Bogle a merchant in Glasgow, testament, 1744, Comm. Glasgow. [NRS]

SANDERS, JOHN, born in Glasgow 1772, a merchant, naturalised in Charleston, South Carolina, 1805. [USNA.M1183/1]

SANGSTER, GEORGE, a tobacconist in Glasgow, testaments, 1774/1775, Comm. Glasgow. [NRS]

SAWERS, MARTHA, in Glasgow, 1753. [NRS.E326.1.172]

SAWERS, WILLIAM, a shipmaster in Glasgow, testament, 1730, Comm. Glasgow. [NRS]

SAWERS, WILLIAM, . a hammerman, 1733. [HHG.294]

SCALES, HUGH, an apprentice writer in Glasgow, 1772. [LC#3233]

SCOTT, ALEXANDER, a merchant from Glasgow, settled in Norfolk, Virginia, by 1755. [GA]

SCOTT, ALEXANDER, master of the Red Dye Society of Glasgow, 1759. [ERG.VI.547]

SCOTT, ANDREW, son of Andrew Scott, a merchant in Glasgow, a nephew of George Henderson in Bertie County, North Carolina, 1736. [Probate, 27.11.1736, Bertie County]

SCOTT, ANDREW, son of Andrew Scott, was admitted to the Baxter Incorporation, 1744. [IBG#136]

SCOTT, ANDREW, a merchant in Glasgow, testament, 1771, Comm. Glasgow. [NRS]

SCOTT, ANDREW, a baxter, eldest son of John Scott a baxter, was admitted to the Baxter Incorporation, also as a burgess and guilds-brother in 1775. [IBG#137][GBR]

SCOTT, ARCHIBALD, Deacon of the Cordiners in Glasgow, testament, 1756, Comm. Glasgow. [NRS]

SCOTT, ARCHIBALD, born 1748, a tailor from Glasgow, to New York, 1774. [NA.T47.12]

SCOTT, DAVID, a merchant in Glasgow, testament, 1733, Comm. Glasgow. [NRS]

SCOTT, GAVIN, born in Glasgow 1766, a hairdresser in Chatham County, Georgia, died 1812, probate 1812, Chatham County. [Colonial Cemetery, Savannah, MI]

SCOTT, GEORGE, son of Andrew Scott, a merchant in Glasgow, a nephew of George Henderson in Bertie County, North Carolina, 1736. [Probate, 27.11.1736, Bertie County]

SCOTT, HENDRY, son of John Scott, was admitted to the Baxter Incorporation, 1748. [IBG#136]

SCOTT, HUGH, from Glasgow, in Boston, 1731. [SCS]

SCOTT, HUGH, a merchant in North Carolina, son of Andrew Scott, a merchant in Glasgow, a nephew of George Henderson in Bertie County, North Carolina, 1736. [Probate, 27.11.1736, Bertie County]

SCOTT, JAMES, . a hammerman, 1730. [HHG.294]

SCOTT, JAMES, baxter, son of the late John Scott a baxter, and former apprentice to Thomas Scott a baxter, was admitted to the Baxter Incorporation, also as a burgess and guilds-brother in 1754. [IBG#136][GBR]

SCOTT, JAMES, junior, from Glasgow, in Boston, 1758. [SCS]

SCOTT, JOHN, a hammerman in Glasgow, testaments, 1726/1727, Comm. Glasgow. [NRS]

SCOTT, JOHN, a miln-wright in Glasgow, testament, 1728, Comm. Glasgow. [NRS]

SCOTT, JOHN, a baxter in Glasgow, testament, 1740/1741, Comm. Glasgow. [NRS]

SCOTT, JOHN, a minister in Glasgow, testament, 1742, Comm. Glasgow. [NRS]

SCOTT, JOHN, a merchant in Glasgow, testament, 1765, Comm. Glasgow. [NRS]

SCOTT, JOHN, in Glasgow, a bond, 1775. [NRS.RD2.217/1.604]

SCOTT, LAWRENCE, in Glasgow, 1753. [NRS.E326.1.172]; a merchant in Glasgow, testament, 1766, Comm. Glasgow. [NRS]

SCOTT, MARGARET, relict of John Esson a merchant in Glasgow, testament, 1737, Comm. Glasgow. [NRS]

SCOTT, MARK, a freeman maltman, also a burgess and guilds-brother of Glasgow in 1768, [MCG.133][GBR]; in Glasgow, a deed, 1773. [NRS.RD4.218.788]

SCOTT, MATHEW, from Glasgow, in Boston, 1756. [SCS]

SCOTT, ROBERT, master of works in Glasgow, 1725. [ERG.V.220/243]

The People of Glasgow, 1725-1775

SCOTT, ROBERT, a tailor in Glasgow, testament, 1738, Comm. Glasgow. [NRS]

SCOTT. ROBERT, a baxter, former apprentice to John Auchencloss, was admitted to the Baxter Incorporation, 1773. [IBG#137]

SCOTT, ROBERT, partner and manager of the Glasgow Glasshouse Company, 1775. [ERG.VII.441]

SCOTT, THOMAS, a baxter, son of Andrew Scott, was admitted to the Baxter Incorporation, 1726. [IBG#136]

SCOTT, THOMAS, a cordiner in Glasgow, testament, 1740, Comm. Glasgow. [NRS]

SCOTT, THOMAS, a baxter, eldest son of Thomas Scott a baxter, was admitted to the Baxter Incorporation, also as a burgess and guilds-brother of Glasgow in 1754. [IBG#136][GBR]; a baxter in Glasgow, 1759. [ERG.VI.549]

SCOTT, THOMAS, jailer of Glasgow Tolbooth, 1759. [ERG.VI.549]

SCOTT, THOMAS, a merchant from Glasgow, settled in Blandford, Virginia, 1771, a Loyalist in 1776. [NA.AO13.4.195; 13.31.303]

SCOTT, WALTER, a merchant from Glasgow, probate 1752, Maryland

SCOTT, WILLIAM, from Glasgow, in Boston, 1757. [SCS]

SCRUTTON, JAMES, a writing master in Glasgow, . a burgess and guilds-brother of Glasgow in 1759. [ERG.VI.546][GBR]

SELKRIG, AGNES, relict of Thomas Harvie a merchant in Glasgow, testament, 1727, Comm. Glasgow. [NRS]

SELLARS, AGNES, relict of James Taylor a stabler and change-keeper in Bridgegate, Glasgow, testament, 1775, Comm. Glasgow. [NRS]

SELLARS, JANET, in Glasgow, daughter of James Sellars, a weaver in Glasgow, and his wife Jean Crookshanks, testament, 1773, Comm. Glasgow. [NRS]

SEMPLE, JAMES, in Glasgow, 1753. [NRS.E326.1.172]

SEMPLE, JOHN, a merchant from Glasgow, settled in Virginia and Maryland before 1760, later in New York. [NRS.B10.15.7082; CS230.19/21; CS16.1.122; B10.15.7082; NRAS.396/18][PCCol.5.543]

SEMPLE, JOHN, formerly a merchant in Worcester, thereafter in Glasgow, testament, 1773, Comm. Glasgow. [NRS]

SEMPLE, THOMAS, former apprentice to James Gray, was admitted to the Baxter Incorporation in 1748. [IBG#136]

SHADDON, ROBERT, of Woodside, late a merchant in Glasgow, testament, 1774, Comm. Glasgow. [NRS]

The People of Glasgow, 1725-1775

SHANKS, JAMES, a tobacco spinner in Glasgow, testament, 1737, Comm. Glasgow. [NRS]

SHARP, ALEXANDER, a merchant in Glasgow, 1750s. [NRS.NRAS.1647]

SHAW, ISOBEL, born in Glasgow around 1715, an indentured servant in Charleston, South Carolina, who absconded in 1734. [SCGaz:16.2.1734]

SHAW, JOHN, a cabinet-maker from Glasgow, settled in Annapolis, Maryland, 1775. [GA]

SHAW, JOHN, a merchant, former apprentice to John Marshall a merchant, a burgess and guilds-brother of Glasgow in 1753, [GBR], testament, 1775, Comm. Glasgow. [NRS]

SHAW, WILLIAM, a mason, younger son of James Shaw a land laborer, a burgess and guilds-brother of Glasgow, in 1765, [GBR]; a mason in Glasgow in 1775. [ERG.VII.451]

SHEARER, ELIZABETH, relict of Robert Marshall, the elder, a dyer in Glasgow, testament, 1750, Comm. Glasgow. [NRS]

SHEARER, JOHN, eldest son of John Shearer, was admitted to the Skinners Craft, 1765, and as a burgess and guilds-brother of Glasgow in 1767. [SFG.268][GBR]

SHEARER, ROBERT, a skinner in Glasgow, testament, 1746, Comm. Glasgow. [NRS]

SHEARER, ROBERT, a skinner, eldest son of Robert Shearer a skinner, was admitted to the Skinners Craft in 1765, [GBR], also as a burgess and guilds-brother of Glasgow in 1767. [SFG.268]

SHEDDAN, JOHN, a merchant, younger son of Robert Sheddan a merchant, . a burgess and guilds-brother of Glasgow in 1770, [GBR], tacks, 1774. [NRS.RD2.217/1.1003; RD2.218.1294]

SHEID, WILLIAM, a vintner in Glasgow, testament, 1763, Comm. Glasgow. [NRS]

SHIELS, BARBARA, born 1755, a spinner from Glasgow, to Philadelphia, 1774. [NA.T47.12]

SHIRMLAW, WILLIAM, born 1761, from Glasgow, to Philadelphia, 1775. [NA.T47.12]

SHORT, GEORGE, a cordiner, a burgess and guilds-brother of Glasgow in 1759, [GBR]; a forger and a cordiner from Glasgow, who was transported to the colonies in 1766. [NRS.HCR.I.98]

SHORTRIGE, JOHN, in Glasgow, 1753. [NRS.E326.1.172]
SIMPSON, ARCHIBALD, a hammerman, 1725. [HHG.293]
SIMPSON, JAMES, a merchant from Glasgow, settled in St Kitts 1765, moved to Grenada, dead by 1779. [NRS.CS16.1.120/177][NLS.Acc.8793/13]
SIMPSON, JANET, relict of Walter Buchanan, the elder, a maltman in Glasgow, testament, 1725, Comm. Glasgow. [NRS]
SIMPSON, JANET, relict of Richard Cowlie a tailor in Glasgow, testament, 1750, Comm. Glasgow. [NRS]
SIMPSON, JEAN, daughter of the deceased Mathew Simpson a merchant in Glasgow, testament, 1773, Comm. Glasgow. [NRS]
SIMPSON, JOHN, Professor of Divinity in the College of Glasgow, testament, 1740, Comm. Glasgow. [NRS]
SIMPSON, JOHN, of Kirktounhall, a merchant in Glasgow, testament, 1744, Comm. Glasgow. [NRS]
SIMPSON, JOHN, the elder, a hammerman, 1731. [HHG.294]; an armorer in Glasgow, testament, 1749, Comm. Glasgow. [NRS]
SIMPSON, JOHN, born 1728, son of Mathew Simpson of Milncroft and his wife Marion Prentice, a merchant from Glasgow, settled in St Vincent before 1750. [NRS.RS42.17.16]
SIMPSON, MARGARET, a shopkeeper in Glasgow, testament, 1731, Comm. Glasgow. [NRS]
SIMPSON, MARGARET, in Glasgow, 1753. [NRS.E326.1.172]
SIMPSON, MATHEW, a merchant in Glasgow, testament, 1770, Comm. Glasgow. [NRS]
SIMPSON, MATHEW, a cordiner in Glasgow, testament, 1770, Comm. Glasgow. [NRS]
SIMPSON, Dr ROBERT, Emeritus Professor of Mathematics at Glasgow University, testament, 1769, Comm. Glasgow. [NRS]
SIMPSON, WILLIAM, a mariner in Glasgow, testament, 1773, Comm. Glasgow. [NRS]
SIMPSON, Mrs, in Glasgow, 1753. [NRS.E326.1.172]
SIMSON, JOHN, of Moyret, a merchant in Glasgow, later in New London, Connecticut, 1769-1772. [NRS.CS16.1.134/151]
SINCLAIR, JOHN, a hammerman, a burgess and guilds-brother of Glasgow in 1770, [GBR], a jeweller in Glasgow, testament, 1775, Comm. Glasgow. [NRS]

SINCLAIR, MARGARET, relict of George Danziell a merchant in Glasgow, testaments, 1755/1756, Comm. Glasgow. [NRS]

SKIRVAN, CHRISTIAN, relict of Thomas Hanna a merchant in Glasgow, and thereafter spouse and relict of Adam Kirkwood a tanner in Glasgow, testament, 1742, Comm. Glasgow. [NRS]

SLATER, JAMES, born 1734, a chapman from Glasgow, to New York, 1774. [NA.T47.12]

SLOSS, JOHN, in Glasgow, sometime a Lieutenant in Colonel Middleton's Regiment of Foot, testament, 1743, Comm. Glasgow. [NRS]

SMALL, THOMAS, born 1743, a smith from Glasgow, to New York, 1775. [NA.T47.12]

SMELLIE, JAMES, a merchant in Glasgow, testament, 1752, Comm. Glasgow. [NRS]

SMELLIE, JOHN, son of John Smellie, a merchant from Glasgow, settled in Kingston, Jamaica, before 1729. [NRS.SH.1729]

SMELLIE, JOHN, a merchant in Glasgow, testament, 1740, Comm. Glasgow. [NRS]

SMITH, DAVID, a baxter, son in law of James Purdon a baxter, was admitted to the Baxter Incorporation, also as a burgess and guilds-brother of Glasgow in 1763. [IBG#136][GBR]

SMITH, HENRY, a merchant and bailie of Glasgow, testament, 1730, Comm. Glasgow. [NRS]

SMITH, JAMES, a baxter, former apprentice to Andrew Duncan a baxter, was admitted to the Baxter Incorporation, and as a burgess and guilds-brother of Glasgow in 1753. [IBG#136][GBR]; in Glasgow, 1753. [NRS.E326.1.172]

SMITH, JAMES, son in law of Hugh Tennant a maltman, a freeman maltman, 1756. [MCG.132]

SMITH, JAMES, a baxter, younger son of James Smith a baxter, was admitted to the Baxter Incorporation, also as a burgess and guilds-brother of Glasgow in 1775. [IBG#137][GBR]

SMITH, JANET, relict of James Dowglas a currier in Glasgow, testament, 1754, Comm. Glasgow. [NRS]

SMITH, JOHN, the elder, a hammerman in Glasgow, testament, 1760, Comm. Glasgow. [NRS]

The People of Glasgow, 1725-1775

SMITH, LANDGRAVE THOMAS, of South Carolina, a burgess and guilds-brother of Glasgow, 1724. [GBR]

SMITH, MARGARET, relict of James Smith a hammerman in Glasgow, testament, 1740, Comm. Glasgow. [NRS]

SMITH, MARGARET, widow of Andrew Riddle a merchant in Glasgow, testament, 1766, Comm. Glasgow. [NRS]

SMITH, PATRICK, a slater in Glasgow, 1725. [ERG.V.220]

SMITH, PATRICK, born 1747, son of Patrick Smith and his wife Janet Maxwell, a merchant from Glasgow, to Jamaica, 1763. [NRS.B10.15.7085]

SMITH, ROBERT, a merchant in Glasgow, testament, 1743, Comm. Glasgow. [NRS]

SMITH, ROBERT, a merchant in Glasgow, testament, 1753, Comm. Glasgow. [NRS]

SMITH, ROBERT, a wright, eldest son of the late William Smith a wright, a burgess and guilds-brother of Glasgow in 1754, [GBR], testament, 1762, Comm. Glasgow. [NRS]

SMITH, THOMAS, a skinner, husband of Margaret Barclay, was admitted to the Skinners Craft, 1762, and as a burgess and guilds-brother of Glasgow in 1764. [GBR] [SFG.268]

SMITH, THOMAS, born 1757, a weaver from Glasgow, to New York, 1774. [NA.T47.12]

SMITH, WILLIAM, senior, a merchant in Glasgow, testament, 1755, Comm. Glasgow. [NRS]

SMITH, WILLIAM, a wright, a burgess and guilds-brother of Glasgow in 1769, [GBR], testament, 1773, Comm. Glasgow. [NRS]

SMITH, WILLIAM, a printer, former apprentice to Alexander Miller and Robert Urie printers, a burgess and guildsbrother of Glasgow in 1775. [ERG.VII.445][GBR]

SNODGRASS, JOHN, a factor from Glasgow, settled in Goochland, Virginia, 1776. [NRS.B10.12.4]

SNODGRASS, WILLIAM, a factor from Glasgow, to Virginia, 1766, later in Richmond. [NRS.B10.15.8269; AC7.58]

SOMERVELL, JAMES, son of David Somervell, formerly in Glasgow then in Jamaica, matriculated at Glasgow University, 1745. [MAGU]

SOMERVILLE, JOHN, from Glasgow, in Boston, 1743. [SCS]

SOMMERWELL, WILLIAM, in Glasgow, 1753. [NRS.E326.1.172]

SPEIR, ALEXANDER, born 1755, a clerk from Glasgow, to Wilmington, North Carolina, 1774. [NA.T47.12]

SPEIR, JAMES, a merchant in Glasgow, testament, 1741, Comm. Glasgow. [NRS]

SPEIRS, JAMES, a merchant and planter from Glasgow, settled in Virginia before 1754. [NRS.B10.15.6653]

SPITTELL, WILLIAM, a weaver in Glasgow, husband of Mary Ure, a burgess and guilds-brother of Glasgow in 1763, [GBR],testament, 1773, Comm. Glasgow. [NRS]

SPRATT, JOHN, a baxter, former apprentice to John Auchencloss a baxter, was admitted to the Baxter Incorporation, also as a burgess and guilds-brother of Glasgow in 1767. [IBG#137][GBR]

SPREULL, AGNES, widow of James Calder, the elder, a surgeon in Glasgow, testaments, 1760/1761, Comm. Glasgow. [NRS]

SPREULL, DAVID, a shipmaster in Glasgow, testament, 1731, Comm. Glasgow. [NRS]

SPREULL, JAMES, a merchant and former bailie of Glasgow, testament, 1769, Comm. Glasgow. [NRS]

SPREULL, JEAN, a daughter of the deceased John Spreull a tailor in Glasgow, testament, 1755, Comm. Glasgow. [NRS]

SPREULL, JOHN, a merchant in Glasgow, testament, 1725, Comm. Glasgow. [NRS]

SPREULL, JOHN, of Milntown, second son of the late John Spreull of Milntoun a writer, a burgess and guilds-brother of Glasgow in 1758, [GBR], testament, 1771, Comm. Glasgow. [NRS]

SPREULL, MARGARET, sister german of the late James Spreull a merchant in Glasgow, 1769. [ERG.VII.309]

SPREULL, ROBERT, a writer in Glasgow, testament, 1755, Comm. Glasgow. [NRS]

STALKER, ANDREW, in Glasgow, 1753. [NRS.E326.1.172]; a bookseller in Glasgow, testament, 1771, Comm. Glasgow. [NRS]

STARK, DAVID, a candle-maker in Glasgow, testament, 1725, Comm. Glasgow. [NRS]

STARK, ELIZABETH, in Glasgow, 1753. [NRS.E326.1.172]

The People of Glasgow, 1725-1775

STARK, JEAN, relict of John Allan a tailor in Glasgow, testament, 1726, Comm. Glasgow. [NRS]

STARK, JOHN, Dean of Guild in Glasgow, 1725; a merchant in Glasgow, 1730s, and late Provost of Glasgow, testaments, 1737/1738/1747, Comm. Glasgow. [NRS.AC7.35.1065] [ERG.V.236]

STEEDMAN, JAMES, in Glasgow, 1753. [NRS.E326.1.172]

STEEL, ALEXANDER, born 1748, a laborer from Glasgow, to New York, 1775. [NA.T47.12]

STEEL, WILLIAM, a maltman, burgess and guilds-brother of Glasgow in 1755, and a freeman maltman in 1758. [MCG.135][GBR]

STEEL, WILLIAM, born 1744, a laborer from Glasgow, to New York, 1775. [NA.T47.12]

STEEL, WILLIAM, a baxter, was admitted to the Baxter Incorporation, and as a burgess and guilds-brother of Glasgow in 17 73. [IBG#137][GBR]

STEPHENSON, ALLEN, from Glasgow, in Boston, 1758. [SCS]

STEPHENSON, JAMES, from Glasgow, in Boston, 1733. [SCS]

STEVEN, CHRISTIAN, only child of the deceased James Steven a tailor in Glasgow, testament, 1754, Comm. Glasgow. [NRS]

STEVEN, JAMES, a tailor in Glasgow, testament, 1742, Comm. Glasgow. [NRS]

STEVEN, JOHN, a baxter in Glasgow, testament, 1730, Comm. Glasgow. [NRS]

STEVEN, JOHN, a merchant and tobacconist in Glasgow, testament, 1750, Comm. Glasgow. [NRS]

STEVEN, PATRICK, a maltman in Glasgow, testament, 1741, Comm. Glasgow. [NRS]

STEVENSON, ADAM, a maltman in Glasgow, testament, 1727, Comm. Glasgow. [NRS]

STEVENSON, ALLAN, coppersmith in Glasgow, 1729. [GA.D-TC13/603S]

STEVENSON, ALLAN, a coppersmith and late Deacon of the Hammermen of Glasgow, testament, 1766, Comm. Glasgow. [NRS]

STEVENSON, ALEXANDER, in Glasgow, 1753. [NRS.E326.1.172]

STEVENSON, DAVID, a wright in Glasgow, testament, 1740, Comm. Glasgow. [NRS]

STEVENSON, DAVID, a baxter, former apprentice to James Morrison a baxter, eldest son of Gilbert Stevenson a cordiner, was admitted to the Baxter

Incorporation, and as a burgess and guilds-brother of Glasgow in 1753. [IBG#136][GBR]

STEVENSON, FRANCIS, wright, 1725; late Deacon of the Wrights in Glasgow, testament, 1737, Comm. Glasgow. [NRS][ERG.V.205

STEVENSON, JAMES, born 1767 in Glasgow, eldest son of Nathaniel Stevenson a merchant, educated at Glasgow University 1779, died in Jamaica. [MAGU][Caribbeana.4.15]

STEVENSON, JANET, daughter of John Stevenson late visitor of the maltmen of Glasgow, and Robert Maxwell a maltman in Pailsey, a marriage contract, 1727. [NRS.NRAS.195/23]

STEVENSON, JOHN, late Deacon of the Cordiners in Glasgow, testament, 1727, Comm. Glasgow. [NRS]

STEVENSON, JOHN, a maltman in Glasgow, testament, 1733, Comm. Glasgow. [NRS]

STEVENSON, JOHN, a merchant from Glasgow, a land grant in Georgia, 1751. [NA.CO5.669]

STEVENSON, JOHN, a weaver in Glasgow, testament, 1768, Comm. Glasgow. [NRS]

STEVENSON, JOHN, a maltman in Glasgow, testament, 1772, Comm. Glasgow. [NRS]

STEVENSON, ROBERT, a glazier in Glasgow, and his spouse Margaret Mack, testament, 1730, Comm. Glasgow. [NRS]

STEVENSON, ROBERT, a maltman in Glasgow, testament, 1735, Comm. Glasgow. [NRS]

STEVENSON, ROBERT, a maltman in Glasgow, testament, 1765, Comm. Glasgow. [NRS]

STEVENSON, WILLIAM, a maltman in Glasgow, testament, 1738, Comm. Glasgow. [NRS]

STEVENSON, WILLIAM, from Glasgow, in Boston, 1747. [SCS]

STEWART, AGNES, daughter of the late James Stewart a sawyer in Glasgow, 1725. [ERG.V.232]

STEWART, Sir ARCHIBALD, of Blachall, in Glasgow, testament, 1754, Comm. Glasgow. [NRS]

STEWART, CUTHBERT, a writer in Glasgow, testament, 1729, Comm. Glasgow. [NRS]

The People of Glasgow, 1725-1775

STEWART, ELIZABETH, relict of John Stirling the Principal of the University of Glasgow, testament, 1739, Comm. Glasgow. [NRS]

STEWART, FRANCIS, born 1750, a gentleman from Glasgow, to Antigua, 1775. [NA.T47.12]

STEWART, HELEN, relict of James Muirhead of Bredisholm, a resident of Glasgow, testament, 1735, Comm. Glasgow. [NRS]

STEWART, HUGH, a merchant in Glasgow, 1751,1753. [NRS.CS16.1.185; E326.1.172], testament, 1770, Comm. Glasgow. [NRS]

STEWART, JAMES, a merchant in the Trongate of Glasgow, testament, 1729, Comm. Glasgow. [NRS]

STEWART, JOHN, an innkeeper and horse-setter in Glasgow, testament, 1759, Comm. Glasgow. [NRS]

STEWART, MARGARET, in Glasgow, 1753. [NRS.E326.1.172]

STEWART, ROBERT, born 1756, a smith from Glasgow, to Philadelphia, 1774. [NA.T47.12]

STEWART, SAMUEL, in Glasgow, a bond, 1772. [NRS.RD4.218.618]

STEWART, WILLIAM, a merchant in Glasgow, testaments, 1740/1742/1743/1746, Comm. Glasgow. [NRS]

STEWART, WILLIAM, a merchant in Glasgow, testament, 1750, Comm. Glasgow. [NRS]

STEWART, WILLIAM, a stocking weaver in Glasgow, testament, 1754, Comm. Glasgow. [NRS]

STEWART, WILLIAM, senior, a gardener in Glasgow, testament, 1771, Comm. Glasgow. [NRS]

STEWART, WILLIAM, in Glasgow, a bond, 1773. [NRS.RD3.234.91]

STEWART, Mrs, born 1736, from Glasgow, to New York, 1775. [NA.T47.12]

STIRLING, ALEXANDER, a shipmaster in Glasgow, 1740. [NRS.S/H]

STIRLING, ALEXANDER, of Deanfield, a merchant in Glasgow, 1759. [ERG.VI.541]

STIRLING, HUGH, a merchant from Glasgow, to Georgia in 1734, settled in Ogychee. [NA.CO5.670.45/127]

STIRLING, JAMES, minister of the barony parish of Glasgow from 1699 until his death in 1736, testament, 1741, Comm. Glasgow. [NRS][F.3.393]

STIRLING, JAMES, in Glasgow, 1753. [NRS.E326.1.172]

STIRLING, JANET, in Glasgow, 1753. [NRS.E326.1.172]

STIRLING, JEAN, in Glasgow, daughter of the deceased William Stirling of Mulleken, and his deceased spouse Grissall Fleming, testament, 1735, Comm. Glasgow. [NRS]

STIRLING, JOHN, Principal of the University of Glasgow, testament, 1727, Comm. Glasgow. [NRS]

STIRLING, JOHN, late Provost of Glasgow, testaments, 1738/1754, Comm. Glasgow. [NRS]

STIRLING, JOHN, from Glasgow, in Boston, 1756. [SCS]

STIRLING, JOHN, a skinner, eldest son of the late William Stirling a skinner, was admitted to the Skinners Craft, also as a burgess and guilds-brother of Glasgow in 1760. [SFG.267][GBR]

STIRLING, WALTER, a merchant and late bailie of Glasgow, testament, 1743, Comm. Glasgow. [NRS]

STIRLING, WILLIAM, a surgeon in Glasgow, 1725. [ERG.V.245]

STIRLING, WILLIAM, a merchant from Glasgow, to Georgia in 1734, settled at Ogychee. [NA.CO5.670.128]

STIRLING, WILLIAM, a merchant, a burgess and guilds-brother of Glasgow in 1769, in Glasgow 1753, 1772. [GBR][NRS.E326.1.172; CS16.1.151]

STIRLING, WILLIAM, born 1746, a weaver from Glasgow, to New York, 1774. [NA.T47.12]

STIRLING, Mrs, in Glasgow, 1753. [NRS.E326.1.172]

STOBO, ROBERT, born 1726, son of William Stobo, a merchant and soldier in Glasgow, educated at Glasgow University, emigrated in 1742, settled in Williamsburg, Virginia, died 1770 in Chatham, England. [NRS.SC36.63.2][DCB]

STOBO, WILLIAM, a merchant in Glasgow, testament, 1754, Comm. Glasgow. [NRS]

STOBO, WILLIAM, a merchant, eldest son of the late Moses Stobo a land laborer in a Colston, the younger son of the deceased David Stobo in Colston, . a burgess and guilds-brother of Glasgow in 1757. [GBR]

STOCKDALE, CHARLES, H.M. Excise Supervisor in Glasgow, testament, 1736, Comm. Glasgow. [NRS]

STRANG, JAMES, a wright in Middle Quarter of Shettlestoun, barony parish of Glasgow, testament, 1725, Comm. Glasgow. [NRS]

STRANG, JOHN, a hammerman, 1726. [HHG.293]

STRANG, JOHN, a horse-setter in Glasgow, testament, 1771, Comm. Glasgow. [NRS]

STRANG, ROBERT, a merchant, eldest son of the late James Strang a merchant, was admitted to the Skinners Craft, also as a burgess and guilds-brother of Glasgow in 1753. [SFG.267][GBR]

STRUTHERS, JOHN, a maltman, husband of Hanna Steven, a burgess and guilds-brother of Glasgow in 1763. [GBR]

STRUTHERS, JOHN, born in Glasgow 1764, son of John Struthers a maltman burgess and his wife Hannah Stiven, a brewer, died in Savannah, Georgia, 1790. [Colonial Cemetery, Savannah, MI]

STRUTHERS, ROBERT, a maltman in Glasgow, testament, 1756, Comm. Glasgow. [NRS]

SUMMER, JOHN, from Glasgow, in Boston, 1731. [SCS]

SUMMERVELL, DAVID, a hammerman, 1731. [HHG.294]

SURGENER, JOHN, a stabler in Glasgow, testament, 1767, Comm. Glasgow. [NRS]

SUTHERLAND, CHRISTIAN, from Glasgow, an indentured servant in Philadelphia, 1772. [Records of Indentures in Philadelphia]

SWORD, JAMES, a merchant in Glasgow, 1763. [ERG.VII.116]

SWORD, JOHN, a merchant in Glasgow, testaments, 1744/1747, Comm. Glasgow. [NRS]

SYM, ANDREW, from Glasgow, in Boston, 1741. [SCS][NA.AO13.83.684]

SYM, JOHN, the elder, a writer in Glasgow, testaments, 1744/1745/1750, Comm. Glasgow. [NRS]

SYM, MATHEW, a merchant in Glasgow, testament, 1745, Comm. Glasgow. [NRS]

SYM, THOMAS, a hatter in Glasgow, testament, 1752, Comm. Glasgow. [NRS]

SYM, WILLIAM, a distiller in Glasgow, testament, 1768, Comm. Glasgow. [NRS]

SYME, ANDREW, a merchant in Glasgow, 1766. [NAS.CS16.1.126]

SYME, JANET, in Glasgow, 1753. [NRS.E326.1.172]

SYME, Captain WILLIAM, in Glasgow, 1753. [NRS.E326.1.172]

TAIT, JAMES, in Glasgow, 1753. [NRS.E326.1.172]

TAIT, WILLIAM, a merchant in Glasgow, 1753; 1759. [NRS.E326.1.172] [ERG.VI.546]

TANNYHILL, JOHN, born 1755, a farmer from Glasgow, to New York, 1774. [NA.T47.12]

TANNYHILL, ROBERT, born 1749, a farmer from Glasgow, to New York, 1774. [NA.T47.12]

TARBET, HUGH, from Glasgow, in Boston, 1756, [SCS]; a merchant in Boston, 1769. [NRS.CS16.1.134/294]

TASSIE, GEORGE, youngest son of the late James Tassie, was admitted to the Skinners Craft, 1762. [SFG.267]

TASSIE, GEORGE, a skinner, eldest son of the late George Tassie a skinner, a burgess and guilds-brother of Glasgow in 1773. [GBR]

TASSIE, WILLIAM, a skinner, son of Archibald Tassie a skinner, was admitted to the Skinners Craft, also as a burgess and guilds-brother of Glasgow in 1760. [SFG.267][GBR]

TASSIE, WILLIAM, a skinner, son of George Tassie, was admitted to the Skinners Craft, 1762. [SFG.268]

TASSIE, WILLIAM, born 1748, a smith from Glasgow, to Salem, New England, 1775. [NA.T47.12]

TAYLOR, ARCHIBALD, son of James Taylor and his wife Janet Marr, from Glasgow, settled in Tobago, testament, 1775, Comm. Edinburgh. [NRS]

TAYLOR, JAMES, a merchant in Glasgow, testament, 1772, Comm. Glasgow. [NRS]

TAYLOR, JAMES, an innkeeper in Glasgow, testament, 1773, Comm. Glasgow. [NRS]

TAYLOR, WALTER, a founder in Glasgow, testament, 1755/1759, Comm. Glasgow. [NRS]

TELFER, JOHN, a hammerman, 1726. [HHG.294]; a watchmaker in Glasgow, testament, 1753, Comm. Glasgow. [NRS]

TELFER, PETER, a hammerman, 1733. [HHG.294]

TELFER, ROBERT, a hammerman in Glasgow, testament, 1750, Comm. Glasgow. [NRS]

TELFER, SAMUEL, a goldsmith in Glasgow, 1775. [ERG.VII.448]

TELFER, WILLIAM, a hammerman, with a sawmill on Skinners Green, Glasgow, 1725. [ERG.V.221]

TENNENT, ADAM, in Glasgow, 1753. [NRS.E326.1.172]; a tobacconist in Glasgow, testament, 1763, Comm. Glasgow. [NRS]

The People of Glasgow, 1725-1775

TENNANT, HUGH, third son of Patrick Tennant, a freeman maltman, 1727. [MCG.131]

TENNENT, JAMES, a merchant, eldest son of Adam Tennant a merchant, a burgess and guilds-brother of Glasgow in 1752. [GBR], testament, 1763, Comm. Glasgow. [NRS]

TENNENT, JOHN, a merchant in Glasgow, testament, 1762, Comm. Glasgow. [NRS]

TENNANT, JOHN, a gardener, younger son of Hugh Tennant a gardener, a burgess and guilds-brother of Glasgow in 1768, [GBR], later as a maltman, a freeman maltman, and re-admitted as a burgess and guilds-brother of Glasgow in 1774. [MCG.134][GBR]

TENNENT, ROBERT, a maltman in Glasgow, and his only child Robert Tennant, testament, 1748, Comm. Glasgow. [NRS]

TENNANT, ROBERT, a mason in Glasgow, 1753; 1759. [NRS.E326.1.172] [ERG.VI.542]

TENNANT, ROBERT, younger son of Hugh Tennant, a freeman maltman, 1769, [MCG.131]; visitor of the maltmen in Glasgow, 1775. [ERG.VII.455]

TENNANT, WILLIAM, a cordiner, eldest son of John Tennant a cordiner, was admitted to the Skinners Craft, also as a burgess and guilds-brother of Glasgow in 1753. [SFG.267][GBR]

THERMS, JOHN, a carter and land-laborer in Glasgow, testament, 1726, Comm. Glasgow. [NRS]

THOMSON, ABIGAIL, relict of John Millar a merchant in Glasgow, testaments, 1773/1775, Comm. Glasgow. [NRS]

THOMSON, ALEXANDER, the elder, a tailor in Glasgow, and his spouse Margaret Dobbie, testament, 1729, Comm. Glasgow. [NRS]

THOMSON, ALEXANDER, a maltman in Glasgow, testaments, 1741/1745, Comm. Glasgow. [NRS]

THOMSON, ANDREW, in Glasgow, 1753. [NRS.E326.1.172]

THOMSON, DUNCAN, a hammerman in Glasgow, testament, 1754, Comm. Glasgow. [NRS]

THOMSON, GEORGE, a merchant in Glasgow, testament, 1734/1742, Comm. Glasgow. [NRS]

THOMSON, Dr GEORGE, a physician in Glasgow, 1725; testament, 1745, Comm. Glasgow. [NRS] [ERG.V.245]

THOMSON, HELEN, relict of Thomas Baird of Hole a merchant in Glasgow, and thereafter relict of Robert Warnock a merchant there, testament, 1759, Comm. Glasgow. [NRS]

THOMSON, JAMES, son of the deceased James Thomson a maltman in Glasgow, testament, 1746, Comm. Glasgow. [NRS]

THOMSON, JAMES, an Excise officer in Glasgow, testament, 1756, Comm. Glasgow. [NRS]

THOMSON, JAMES, born 1733, a coal-hewer from Glasgow, to Salem, New England, 1775. [NA.T47.12]

THOMSON, Mrs R. JANE, in Glasgow, 1753. [NRS.E326.1.172]

THOMSON, JANET, in Glasgow, 1753. [NRS.E326.1.172]

THOMSON, JANET, relict of James Buchanan a weaver in Glasgow, testament, 1774, Comm. Glasgow. [NRS]

THOMSON, JANET, relict of Adam Kirkwood a merchant in Glasgow, testament, 1730/1731, Comm. Glasgow. [NRS]

THOMSON, JOHN, a merchant in Glasgow, 1730. [NRS.AC9.6414&1131]

THOMSON, MARY, relict of Hew Warden a merchant in Glasgow, testaments, 1730/1736, Comm. Glasgow. [NRS]

THOMSON, PETER, a baxter, eldest son of William Thomson a baxter, was admitted to the Baxter Incorporation, and as a burgess and guilds-brother of Glasgow in 1772. [IBG#140][GBR]

THOMSON, ROBERT, a baxter, former apprentice to James Hoods a baxter, was admitted to the Baxter Incorporation, 1736. [IBG#139]

THOMSON, ROBERT, an indweller of Glasgow and a servant to John Crawford of Milntoun, testament, 1754, Comm. Glasgow. [NRS]

THOMSON, WILLIAM, a baxter, son in law of John Gardner, was admitted to the Baxter Incorporation, 1740. [IBG#139]

THOMSON, WILLIAM, born 1730, a tailor from Glasgow, a Jacobite transported in 1747, landed at Port North Potomac, Maryland. [NA.T1.328][P.3.372]

THORNSON, ANDREW, born 1754, a merchant from Glasgow, to Charleston, South Carolina, 1774. [NA.T47.12]

TODD, JAMES, a merchant in Glasgow, pre 1776. [NA.AO12.109.192]

TOD, JOHN, a merchant in Glasgow, testament, 1730, Comm. Glasgow. [NRS]

TRAN, ALEXANDER, from Glasgow, in Boston, 1735. [SCS]

The People of Glasgow, 1725-1775

TRAN, ARTHUR, a merchant in Glasgow, 1725, [NRS.AC8.310]; and late Dean of Guild of Glasgow, testaments, 1738/1753, Comm. Glasgow. [NRS] [ERG.V.243]

TRAN, HUGH, born 1730, son of Arthur Tran and his wife Elizabeth Warden, a merchant from Glasgow, settled in St Kitts before 1768. [NRS.B10.15.7141; SH. 1768; CS17.1.1/2/282; RD2.224/2.650]

TURNBULL, ANDREW, son in law of William Thomson, was admitted to the Baxter Incorporation, 1772. [IBG#140]

TURNBULL, CHARLES, son of George Turnbull and his wife Elizabeth ....., a merchant from Glasgow, married Rachel Robinson in Charles parish, York County, Virginia, 1759, settled in Dinwiddie County, Virginia, before 1777. [NRS.CS16.1.170; B10.15.5943][WMQ.2.16.93]

TURNBULL, DAVID, born 1757, a surveyor from Glasgow, to Jamaica, 1775. [NA.T47.12]

TURNBULL, JAMES, born 1755, a laborer from Glasgow, to Philadelphia, 1774. [NA.T47.12]

TURNBULL, ROBERT, son of George Turnbull and his wife Elizabeth ....., a merchant from Glasgow, settled in Dinwiddie County, Virginia, before 1775. [NRS.CS16.1.165]

TURNER, HUGH, in Glasgow, 1753. [NRS.E326.1.172]

TURNER, JOHN, a chapman in Glasgow, testament, 1736, Comm. Glasgow. [NRS]

TURNER, JOHN, a thief in Glasgow, transported to the colonies, 1752. [AJ.248]

TWINDALE, DAVID, a schoolmaster in Glasgow, testament, 1755, Comm. Glasgow. [NRS]

URE, ALEXANDER, a baxter, former apprentice to Andrew Scott a baxter, was admitted to the Baxter Incorporation, 1732. [IBG#141]

URE, GEORGE, a baxter, son in law of William Weir, was admitted to the Baxter Incorporation, 1750. [IBG#141]

URE, JAMES, a baxter, eldest son of the late George Ure a baxter, was admitted to the Baxter Incorporation, also as a burgess and guilds-brother in 1763. [IBG#141][GBR]

URE, JOHN, a baxter, eldest son of Alexander Ure a baxter, was admitted to the Baxter Incorporation, also as a burgess and guilds-brother of Glasgow in 1754. [IBG#141][GBR]

URE, JOHN, a baxter, son of John Ure, was admitted to the Baxter Incorporation, 1775. [IBG#141]

URIE, JAMES, a surgeon in Glasgow, son of the deceased John Urie of Holmhead, testament, 1749, Comm. Glasgow. [NRS]

URIE, JOHN, a member of the Incorporation of Weavers, 1725. [OGW#108]

URIE, MARGARET, relict of John Gillespie a merchant in Glasgow, testament, 1746, Comm. Glasgow. [NRS]

URIE, MARY, sometime spouse of James Young a merchant in Glasgow, testament, 1762, Comm. Glasgow. [NRS]

URIE, ROBERT, a printer in Glasgow, testament, 1771, Comm. Glasgow. [NRS]

VOY, ALEXANDER, a gardener, husband of Janet McArthur, a burgess and guilds-brother of Glasgow in 1741. [GBR]

WADDELL, WILLIAM, a cordiner in Glasgow, testament, 1743, Comm. Glasgow. [NRS]

WADDELL, WILLIAM, a cordiner in Glasgow, testament, 1764, Comm. Glasgow. [NRS]

WALKER, ALEXANDER, a merchant from Glasgow, a land grant in Georgia, 1751. [NA.CO5.669]

WALKER, ANN, in Glasgow, 1753. [NRS.E326.1.172]

WALKER, GEORGE, late Deacon of the Tailors in Glasgow, testament, 1764, Comm. Glasgow. [NRS]

WALKER, JAMES, a land grant in Georgia, 1751. [NA.CO5.669]

WALKER, JAMES, a baxter, son in law of John McKinlay a baxter, was admitted to the Baxter Incorporation, also as a burgess and guilds-brother of Glasgow in 1769. [IBG#142]

WALKER, JOHN, from Glasgow, in Boston, 1755. [SCS]

WALKER, JOHN, a merchant from Glasgow, settled in Norfolk, Virginia, by 1776, later in Nassau, the Bahamas, died 1784, probate Williamsburg, Virginia. [NA.AO13.32.643]

WALKER, JOHN, born 1753, a weaver from Glasgow, to New York, 1774. [NA.T47.12]

WALKER, JOHN, a skinner, youngest son of the late Peter Walker a maltman, was admitted to the Skinners Craft in 1760, and as a burgess and guilds-brother of Glasgow in 1761. [SFG.267][GBR]

WALKINGSHAW, WILLIAM, from Glasgow, in Boston, 1731. [SCS]

The People of Glasgow, 1725-1775

WALLACE, ELIZABETH, relict of William Struthers a merchant in Glasgow, testament, 1747, Comm. Glasgow. [NRS]

WALLACE, GRISSALL, relict of Walter Buchanan a baxter in Glasgow, testament, 1738, Comm. Glasgow. [NRS]

WALLACE, JOHN, the younger, a merchant 'above the Cross' in Glasgow, testament, 1726, Comm. Glasgow. [NRS]

WALLACE, JOHN, of Elderslie, a merchant in Glasgow, testament, 1728/1732, Comm. Glasgow. [NRS]

WALLACE, JOHN, only son of the deceased John Wallace a tailor in Glasgow, testament, 1729, Comm. Glasgow. [NRS]

WALLACE, JOHN, a merchant in Glasgow, testament, 1733, Comm. Glasgow. [NRS]

WALLACE, MATHEW, son of James Wallace a merchant in Glasgow, 1725. [ERG.V.221]

WALLACE, MICHAEL, treasurer of Glasgow, 1725; a merchant in Glasgow, testament, 1736, Comm. Glasgow. [NRS] [ERG.V.243]

WALLACE, ROBERT, in Glasgow, 1753. [NRS.E326.1.172]

WALLACE, THOMAS, a merchant from Glasgow, in Jamaica before 1730. [NRS.AC7.35.485]

WALLACE, THOMAS, of Cairnhill, a merchant in Glasgow, testament, 1749, Comm. Glasgow. [NRS]

WALLACE, THOMAS, in Glasgow, a deed, 1775. [NRS.RD2.217/1.742]

WALLACE, WILLIAM, in Glasgow, 1753. [NRS.E326.1.172] a merchant in Glasgow, testament, 1770, Comm. Glasgow. [NRS]

WARDEN, DAVID, son in law of Robert Whyte a maltman, a freeman maltman, 1737. [MCG.135]

WARDEN, HEW, junior, a merchant in Glasgow, testament, 1730, Comm. Glasgow. [NRS]

WARDEN, ISOBEL, relict of David Dalrymple a baxter in Glasgow, testaments, 1737/1763, Comm. Glasgow. [NRS]

WARDEN, JOHN, a member of the Incorporation of Weavers, 1725. [OGW#108]

WARDROBE, JOHN, born 1744, a tailor from Glasgow, to New York, 1774. [NA.T47.12]

WARDROP, DAVID, a mason in Glasgow, 1775. [ERG.VII.450]

WARDROP, GEORGE, in Glasgow, 1753. [NRS.E326.1.172]; a merchant in Glasgow, testament, 1759, Comm. Glasgow. [NRS]

WARDROP, JAMES, in Glasgow, 1753. [NRS.E326.1.172]

WARDROP, JOHN, a writer in Glasgow, a hammerman, 1732. [HHG.294]

WARDROP, JOHN, in Glasgow, 1753. [NRS.E326.1.172]; a cordiner in Glasgow, testament, 1757, Comm. Glasgow. [NRS]

WARDROP, JOHN, a mason, burgess and guilds-brother of Glasgow in 1762, [GBR]; testaments, 1767/1768, Comm. Glasgow. [NRS]

WARDROP, JOHN, of Auldhouse, a writer in Glasgow, testament, 1772, Comm. Glasgow. [NRS]

WARDROP, THOMAS, a maltman in Glasgow, 1725. [ERG.V.222]

WARK, JOHN, a maltman in Glasgow, testament, 1732, Comm. Glasgow. [NRS]

WARNER, MARGARET, in Glasgow, 1753. [NRS.E326.1.172]

WARNOCK, ANDREW, a baxter, former apprentice to George Graham a baxter, was admitted to the Baxter Incorporation in 1759, and as a burgess and guilds-brother of Glasgow in 1762. [IBG#142][GBR]

WARNOCK, ROBERT, a merchant in Glasgow, testament, 1752/1753, Comm. Glasgow. [NRS]

WARRAND, JOHN, a merchant in Glasgow, 1772. [NRS.CS16.1.151]

WATERSTON, MARGARET, daughter of the deceased James Waterston a hammerman in Glasgow, testament, 1752, Comm. Glasgow. [NRS]

WATSON, ALEXANDER, a merchant in Glasgow, testament, 1747, Comm. Glasgow. [NRS]

WATSON, ANDREW, a flesher in Glasgow, testaments, 1754, Comm. Glasgow. [NRS]

WATSON, ANDREW, son in law of Alexander Thomas a maltman, a freeman maltman, 1762. [MCG.134]

WATSON, DAVID, a carter and land laborer in Glasgow, testament, 1748, Comm. Glasgow. [NRS]

WATSON, DAVID, banker in Glasgow, 1773. [Ramshorn MI, Glasgow]

WATSON, ELIZABETH, daughter of the deceased William Watson, a flesher in Glasgow, and his spouse Elizabeth Glen, testament, 1770, Comm. Glasgow. [NRS]

WATSON, GABRIEL, a baxter, former apprentice to George Blair, and only son of the late Gabriel Watson a weaver, was admitted to the Baxter

Incorporation, and as a burgess and guilds-brother of Glasgow in 1772. [IBG#142][GBR]

WATSON, JAMES, a merchant in Glasgow, testaments, 1755/1757/1758, Comm. Glasgow. [NRS]

WATSON, JOHN, former apprentice to John Scott, was admitted to the Baxter Incorporation, 1734. [IBG#141]

WATSON, JOHN, son of John Watson, was admitted to the Baxter Incorporation, 1757. [IBG#142]

WATSON, JOHN, a merchant in Glasgow, testament, 1764, Comm. Glasgow. [NRS]

WATSON, JOHN, born 1755, a cooper from Glasgow, to Salem, New England, 1775. [NA.T47.12]

WATSON, MARGARET, relict of John Hamilton a wright in Glasgow, testament, 1761, Comm. Glasgow. [NRS]

WATSON, MATHEW, a grocer in Glasgow, testament, 1768, Comm. Glasgow. [NRS]

WATSON, MATHEW, a baxter, son of Mathew Watson, was admitted to the Baxter Incorporation, and as a burgess and guilds-brother of Glasgow in 1775. [IBG#142][GBR]

WATSON, THOMAS, was admitted to the Skinners Craft, 1760, and admitted as a burgess and guilds-brother of Glasgow in 1764. [SFG.268][GBR]

WATSON, WILLIAM, master weaver of the Incorporation of Weavers, 1725. [OGW#108]

WATSON, WILLIAM, the elder, a member of the Incorporation of Weavers, 1725. [OGW#108]

WATSON, WILLIAM, from Glasgow, in Boston, 1735. [SCS]

WATT, JAMES, a baxter, former apprentice to Thomas Yuill a baxter, was admitted to the Baxter Incorporation, 1725. [IBG#141]

WATT, JOHN, a mathematics teacher in Glasgow, testament, 1737, Comm. Glasgow. [NRS]

WEIR, JAMES, from Glasgow, in Boston, 1747. [SCS]

WEIR, JOHN, a baxter, son of William Weir, was admitted to the Baxter Incorporation, 1744. [IBG#141]

WEIR, WILLIAM, in Glasgow, 1753. [NRS.E326.1.172]; Principal Commissary of Hamilton and Campsie and a writer in Glasgow, testament, 1775, Comm. Glasgow. [NRS] [ERG.VII.443]

WHITE, ALEXANDER, a change-keeper in Glasgow, testament, 1738, Comm. Glasgow. [NRS]

WHITE, ARCHIBALD, a merchant in Norfolk, Virginia, died in Glasgow, testament, 1772, Comm. Glasgow. [NRS]

WHITE, HUGH, a merchant from Glasgow, in Boston, 1766. [NRS.CS16.1.126/130/171]

WHITE, PATRICK, a baxter, former apprentice to Thomas Yuill a baxter, was admitted to the Baxter Incorporation, 1732. [IBG#141]

WHITE, ROBERT, born 1718, son of James White and his wife Jane Selkrig, a painter in Glasgow, a Jacobite, transported to the colonies, 1747. [P.3.400]

WHITE, ROBERT, born 1758, a weaver from Glasgow, to New York, 1774. [NA.T47.12]

WHITE, SAMUEL, from Glasgow, in Boston, 1759. [SCS]

WHITEHILL, JANET, relict of John Spreull a tailor in Glasgow, testament, 1757, Comm. Glasgow. [NRS]

WHITEHILL, JOHN, collector of the kirkyard in Glasgow, 1725. [ERG.V.244]

WHITEHILL, THOMAS, a skinner and hatter in Glasgow, testament, 1773, Comm. Glasgow. [NRS]

WHITELAW, JAMES, a hammerman, 1726. [HHG.293]; in Glasgow, 1753. [NRS.E326.1.172]

WHITELAW, JAMES, born 1749, a farmer from Glasgow, to New York, 1774. [NA.T47.12]

WHYTE, ALEXANDER, a baxter, former apprentice to William Hanna a baxter, was admitted to the Baxter Incorporation, 1738. [IBG#141]

WHYTE, ALEXANDER, a baxter, eldest son of Alexander Whyte a baxter, was admitted to the Baxter Incorporation, also as a burgess and guilds-brother of Glasgow in1775. [IBG#142][GBR]

WHYTE, ANDREW, a baxter, son in law of James Glen a baxter, was admitted to the Baxter Incorporation, also as a burgess and guilds-brother of Glasgow in 1759. [IBG#142][GBR]

WHYTE, WILLIAM, a baxter, son in law of Patrick Whyte a baxter, was admitted to the Baxter Incorporation, also as a burgess and guilds-brother of Glasgow in 1765. [IBG#142][GBR]

WILL, THOMAS, a baxter, second son of the late Alexander Will a baxter, was admitted to the Baxter Incorporation, also as a burgess and guilds-brother of Glasgow in 1753. [IBG#142][GBR]

WILLIAMSON, JOHN, in Glasgow, 1753. [NRS.E326.1.172]

WILLISON, HUGH, a baxter, son in law of Walter Lochhead a baxter, was admitted to the Baxter Incorporation, also as a burgess and guilds-brother of Glasgow in 1756. [IBG#142][GBR]

WILLISON, JOHN, in Glasgow, 1753; a merchant, eldest son of James Willison a merchant, a burgess and guilds-brother of Glasgow in 1760. [NRS.E326.1.172] [GBR]

WILSON, ALEXANDER, a stocking-weaver in Glasgow, testament, 1755, Comm. Glasgow. [NRS]

WILSON, ALEXANDER, a type-maker, a burgess and guilds-brother of Glasgow in 1758. [GBR]

WILSON, ALEXANDER, of Glanderston, a merchant in Glasgow, testament, 1773, Comm. Glasgow. [NRS]

WILSON, ELIZABETH, relict of John Blair a cordiner in Glasgow, testament, 1745, Comm. Glasgow. [NRS]

WILSON, ISABEL, resident in Glasgow, relict of John Buntein of Geilstoun, testament, 1752, Comm. Glasgow. [NRS]

WILSON, JAMES, a maltman in Glasgow, testament, 1727, Comm. Glasgow. [NRS]

WILSON, JAMES, a merchant in Glasgow, testament, 1750, Comm. Glasgow. [NRS][NRS.AC9.1697-8]

WILSON, JAMES, youngest son of the late John Wilson, was admitted to the Skinners Craft, 1754. [SFG.267]

WILSON, JAMES, a skinner, second son of the late John Wilson a skinner, was admitted to the Skinners Craft, and as a burgess and guilds-brother of Glasgow in 1753. [SFG.267][GBR]

WILSON, JAMES, a writer in Glasgow, testament, 1770, Comm. Glasgow. [NRS]

WILSON, JOHN, . a hammerman, 1725. [HHG.293]

The People of Glasgow, 1725-1775

WILSON, JOHN, a writer in Glasgow, testaments, 1729/1731, Comm. Glasgow. [NRS]

WILSON, JOHN, a maltman, 'without the West Port of Glasgow', testament, 1741, Comm. Glasgow. [NRS]

WILSON, JOHN, in Glasgow, 1753. [NRS.E326.1.172]

WILSON, JOHN, of Shielhall, a merchant in Glasgow, testament, 1768, Comm. Glasgow. [NRS]

WILSON, JOHN, late Deacon of the Skinners in Glasgow, testament, 1773, Comm. Glasgow. [NRS]

WILSON, JOHN, a smith in Glasgow, 1775. [ERG.VII.441]

WILSON, JOSEPH, a fruiterer from Glasgow, to New York, 1774. [NA.T47.12]

WILSON, or MCDONALD, MARGARET, a vagrant in Glasgow, who was transported to the colonies in 1754. [SM.16.450]

WILSON, MARGARET, born 1751, from Glasgow, to Salem, New England, 1775. [NA.T47.12]

WILSON, NATHAN, a clerk in Glasgow, 1769. [GA.B10.15.7233]

WILSON, ROBERT, a hammerman, 1728. [HHG.293]

WILSON, ROBERT, a maltman in Glasgow, testament, 1745, Comm. Glasgow. [NRS]

WILSON, ROBERT, a merchant in Glasgow, testament, 1747, Comm. Glasgow. [NRS]

WILSON, WILLIAM, a horse-thief in Glasgow, transported to the West Indies in 1775. [SM.37.523]

WILSON, WILLIAM, jr., a merchant in Glasgow, in Virginia 1768-1776. [NRS.CS17.1.5/351][NA.AO12.109.312]

WINGATE, AGNES, spouse to the deceased Robert Pollock a merchant in Glasgow, testament, 1735, Comm. Glasgow. [NRS]

WITHERFORD, JAMES, in Glasgow, 1753. [NRS.E326.1.172]

WITHERSPOND, JAMES, . a hammerman, 1729. [HHG.293]

WODDROP, THOMAS, son of Thomas Woddrop, a shipmaster from Glasgow, settled in Virginia 1765. [NRS.CS16.1.122]

WODDROPE, HENRY, a writer in Glasgow, testament, 1727/1748, Comm. Glasgow. [NRS]

WODDROPE, THOMAS, a maltman in Glasgow, testaments, 1753/1754, Comm. Glasgow. [NRS]

The People of Glasgow, 1725-1775

WOOD, AGNES, spouse to the late Archibald Gray a merchant in Glasgow, testament, 1736, Comm. Glasgow. [NRS]

WOOD, JAMES, a baxter, son of William Wood, was admitted to the Baxter Incorporation, 1753. [IBG#142]

WOOD, JOHN, a merchant from Glasgow, in Virginia by 1760. [NRS.AC7.50]

WOOD, NICOLL, a baxter, third son of John Wood a barber, was admitted to the Baxter Incorporation, also as a burgess and guilds-brother of Glasgow in 1752. [IBG#141][GBR]

WOOD, ROBERT, a member of the Incorporation of Weavers, 1725. [OGW#108]

WOOD, ROBERT, son of John Wood, was admitted to the Baxter Incorporation, 1748. [IBG#141]

WOOD, ROBERT, a bricklayer in Glasgow, 1763. [ERG.VII.115]

WOODROP, ALEXANDER, from Glasgow, in Boston, 1739. [SCS]

WOODROP, WILLIAM, a factor from Glasgow, settled in Essex County, Virginia, before 1770. [GA]

WOODROW, AGNES, relict of John Auchinloss late Deacon of the Baxters in Glasgow, testament, 1752, Comm. Glasgow. [NRS]

WOODROW, ANDREW, a planter from Glasgow, emigrated to Virginia in 1768. [SNQ.10.140]

WOODROW, JAMES, late Deacon of the Wrights in Glasgow, testament, 1762, Comm. Glasgow. [NRS]

WOODROW, Dr JOHN, a physician in Glasgow, 1753. [NRS.E326.1.172]; testament, 1770, Comm. Glasgow. [NRS]

WOODROW, Mrs, in Glasgow, 1753. [NRS.E326.1.172]

WOODRUP, ALEXANDER, from Glasgow, in Boston, 1739. [SCS]

WOTHERFORD, JAMES, a founder and bailie of Glasgow, testament, 1775, Comm. Glasgow. [NRS]

WOTHERSPOON, ALEXANDER, a maltman in Glasgow, testament, 1748, Comm. Glasgow. [NRS]

WOTHERSPOON, CHRISTIAN, spouse to John Miller a tailor in Glasgow, thereafter wife of Peter or Patrick Ferguson a workman there, testament, 1761, Comm. Glasgow. [NRS]

WOTHERSPOON, JAMES, a skinner, former apprentice of James Barclay, was admitted to the Skinners Craft in 1765, and as a burgess and guilds-brother of Glasgow in 1768. [SFG.268][GBR]

WOTHERSPOON, ROBERT, a master cordiner in Glasgow, 1725. [ERG.V.237]

WRIGHT, DANIEL, a merchant in Glasgow, testament, 1752, Comm. Glasgow. [NRS]

WRIGHT, GEORGE, a baxter, son of John Wright a baxter, was admitted to the Baxter Incorporation, 1748. [IBG#141]

WRIGHT, GEORGE, a baxter, son of John Wright a baxter, was admitted to the Baxter Incorporation, 1763. [IBG#142]

WRIGHT, JAMES, a baxter, second son of John Wright a baxter, was admitted to the Baxter Incorporation, also as a burgess and guilds-brother of Glasgow in 1756. [IBG#142][GBR]

WRIGHT, JAMES, was admitted to the Skinners Craft, 1760. [SFG.268]

WRIGHT, JAMES, a tailor in Glasgow, testament, 1773, Comm. Glasgow. [NRS]

WRIGHT, JOHN, a merchant in Glasgow, 1727.[GA.D-TC13/603s]

WRIGHT, JOHN, a baxter, son of John Wright a baxter, was admitted to the Baxter Incorporation, 1732. [IBG#141]

WRIGHT, JOHN, a baxter in Glasgow, testament, 1740, Comm. Glasgow. [NRS]

WRIGHT, JOHN, a merchant in Glasgow, testament, 1755, Comm. Glasgow. [NRS]

WRIGHT, JOHN, a baxter, son of John Wright a baxter, a burgess and guilds-brother of Glasgow in 1756, [GBR], also to the Baxter Incorporation, 1759. [IBG#142]

WRIGHT, JOHN, a surgeon, lately on board the Indiaman *Lord Mansfield*, thereafter resident in Glasgow, testament, 1764, Comm. Glasgow. [NRS]

WRIGHT, MALCOLM, a weaver in Glasgow, testament, 1751, Comm. Glasgow. [NRS]

WRIGHT, WILLIAM, born 1707, a postillion from Glasgow, emigrated via London to Virginia in 1725. [CLRO.AIA]

WYLLIE, HUGH, son in law of James Dunlop of Garnkirk a merchant, a burgess and guilds-brother of Glasgow in 1762, [GBR], a merchant in Glasgow and in Virginia, 1765, died 1782 in Glasgow. [NRS.CS16.1.122]

The People of Glasgow, 1725-1775

WYLLIE, MATHEW, a baxter, son in law of Walter Lochhead a baxter, was admitted to the Baxter Incorporation, also as a burgess and guilds-brother of Glasgow in 1751. [IBG#141][GBR]

YETTS, JAMES, sometime in Langshaw, thereafter an indweller in Glasgow, testament, 1741, Comm. Glasgow. [NRS]

YOOLL, JAMES, a baxter, son of James Yooll, was admitted to the Baxter Incorporation, 1770. [IBG#147]

YOOLL, THOMAS, a baxter, eldest son of James Yooll a baxter, was admitted to the Baxter Incorporation, also as a burgess and guilds-brother of Glasgow in 1767. [IBG#145][GBR]

YOUNG, ALEXANDER, born 1749, a wright from Glasgow, to New York, 1774. [NA.T47.12]

YOUNG, ALEXANDER, born 1755, a tailor from Glasgow, to New York, 1774. [NA.T47.12]

YOUNG, ELIZABETH, a sewster in Glasgow, testament, 1754, Comm. Glasgow. [NRS]

YOUNG, HUMPHREY, a baxter, former apprentice to James Morrison a baxter, was admitted to the Baxter Incorporation, also as a burgess and guilds-brother of Glasgow in 1757. [IBG#145][GBR]

YOUNG, JAMES, a merchant in Glasgow, testament, 1733, Comm. Glasgow. [NRS]

YOUNG, JAMES, a merchant from Glasgow, settled in Albemarle County, Virginia, by 1745. [GA][VMHB.1/2]

YOUNG, JAMES, eldest son of Thomas Young, was admitted to the Skinners Craft, also as a burgess and guilds-brother of Glasgow in 1760. [SFG.267][GBR]

YOUNG, JAMES, a skinner, eldest son of the late Robert Young, was admitted to the Skinners Craft, also as a burgess and guilds-brother of Glasgow in 1760. [SFG.267][GBR]

YOUNG, JAMES, born 1751, a laborer from Glasgow, to New York, 1774. [NA.T47.12]

YOUNG, JOHN, born 1732 in Glasgow, son of John Young and his wife Marion Anderson, a saddler who emigrated to Philadelphia in 1762, settled in New York, died there 1798. [ANY.I.193]

YOUNG, JOHN, a baxter, son in law of John Lang a baxter, was admitted to the Baxter Incorporation, also as a burgess and guilds-brother of Glasgow in 1774. [IBG#147][GBR]

YOUNG, MATHEW, from Glasgow, in Boston, 1732. [SCS]

YOUNG, PETER, a skinner, youngest and third son of Patrick Young a skinner, was admitted to the Skinners Craft, also as a burgess and guilds-brother of Glasgow in 1753. [SFG.267][GBR]

YOUNG, ROBERT, a merchant in Glasgow, testament, 1762, Comm. Glasgow. [NRS]

YOUNG, THOMAS, a skinner, second son of the late James Young a glover, was admitted to the Skinners Craft, also as a burgess and guilds-brother of Glasgow in 1754. [SFG.267][GBR]

YOUNG, THOMAS, born 1753, a surgeon from Glasgow, to Wilmington, North Carolina, 1774. [NA.T47.12]

YOUNG, WILLIAM, son of William Young in Glasgow, settled in Northampton County, Virginia, before 1749. [NRS.S/H]

YOUNG, WILLIAM, a glover, youngest and fourth son of the late Patrick Young a glover, was admitted to the Skinners Craft, also as a burgess and guilds-brother of Glasgow in 1756. [SFG.267][GBR]

YOUNGER, JANET, in Glasgow, 1753. [NRS.E326.1.172]

YOUNGER, THOMAS, born 1747, son of Andrew Younger and his wife Helen House, in Glasgow, later in Wilmington, North Carolina, died in Lucie, Jamaica, 1795. [GM.65.794]

YUILE, GEORGE, from Glasgow, in Boston, 1746. [SCS]

YUILE, JOHN, from Glasgow, in Boston, 1759. [SCS]

YUILL, ARCHIBALD, from Glasgow, in Boston, 1750. [SCS]

YUILL, JAMES, a baxter, son of Thomas Yuill, was admitted to the Baxter Incorporation, 1733. [IBG#145]

YUILL, JAMES, from Glasgow, in Boston, 1753, [SCS]; later in Truro, Nova Scotia, 1761. [NRS.RS42.15.96; CS16.1.115]

YUILL, JOHN, a merchant in Glasgow, testaments, 1739/1740, Comm. Glasgow. [NRS]

YUILLE, THOMAS, a merchant in Glasgow, 1728. [NRS.AC7.34.708]

www.ingramcontent.com/pod-product-compliance
Lightning Source LLC
Chambersburg PA
CBHW051107160426
43193CB00010B/1355